Contents

D0792497

CYBERNETICS & HUMAN KNOWING
A Journal of Second-Order Cybernetics, Autopoiesis & Cyber-Semiotics

Cybernetics and Human Knowing is a quarterly international multi- and transdisciplinary journal focusing on second-order cybernetics and cybersemiotic approaches.

The journal is devoted to the new understandings of the self-organizing processes of information in human knowing that have arisen through the cybernetics of cybernetics, or second order cybernetics its relation and relevance to other interdisciplinary approaches such as C.S. Peirce's semiotics. This new development within the area of knowledge-directed processes is a non-disciplinary approach. Through the concept of self-reference it explores: cognition, communication and languaging in all of its manifestations; our understanding of organization and information in human, artificial and natural systems; and our understanding of understanding within the natural and social sciences, humanities, information and library science, and in social practices like design, education, organization, teaching, therapy, art, management and politics.

Because of the interdisciplinary character articles are written in such a way that people from other domains can understand them. Articles from practitioners will be accepted in a special section. All articles are peer-reviewed.

Subscription Information

Price: Individual $63 / £40.50. Institutional: $121 / £78 50% discount on complete runs of back volumes. For subscription send a check in $US (drawn on US bank) or £UK (drawn on UK bank or Eurocheque), made payable to Imprint Academic to PO Box 1, Thorverton, EX5 5YX, UK, or credit card details (Visa/Mastercard/Amex), including card expiry date. Contact sandra@imprint.co.uk

Editor in Chief: Søren Brier, Copenhagen Business School, department of Management, Politics and Philosophy, Blågårdsgade 23 B, room 326. DK-2200 Copenhagen N sbr.lpf@cbs.dk

Associate editor: Jeanette Bopry, Instructional Sciences, National Institute of Education, 1 Nanyang Walk, Singapore 637616. bopry@nie.edu.sg

Managing editor: Darek Eriksson, Mid Sweden School of Informatics, Ostersund. darek_eriksson@hotmail.com

Joint art editor: Bruno Kjær, Royal School of Library and Information Science, Aalborg Branch. bk@db.dk

Joint art editor and ASC-column editor: Pille Bunnell pille@interchange.ubc.ca

Journal homepage: www.imprint-academic.com/C&HK
Full text: www.ingenta.com/journals/browse/imp

Copyright: It is a condition of acceptance by the editor of a typescript for publication that the publisher automatically acquires the English language copyright of the typescript throughout the world, and that translations explicitly mention *Cybernetics & Human Knowing* as original source.

Book Reviews: Publishers are invited to submit books for review to the Editor.

Instructions to Authors: To facilitate editorial work and to enhance the uniformity of presentation, authors are requested to send a file of the paper to the Editor on e-mail. If the paper is accepted after refereeing then to prepare the contribution in accordance with the stylesheet information on the preceding two pages. Manuscripts will not be returned except for editorial reasons. The language of publication is English. The following information should be provided on the first page: the title, the author's name and full address, a title not exceeding 40 characters including spaces and a summary/ abstract in English not exceeding 200 words. Please use italics for emphasis, quotations, etc. Email to: sbr@kvl.dk

Drawings. Drawings, graphs, figures and tables must be reproducible originals. They should be presented on separate sheets. Authors will be charged if illustrations have to be re-drawn.

Style. CHK has selected the style of the APA (*Publication Manual of the American Psychological Association*, 5th edition) because this style is commonly used by social scientists, cognitive scientists, and educators. The APA website contains information about the correct citation of electronic sources. The APA Publication Manual is available from booksellers. The Editors reserve the right to correct, or to have corrected, non-native English prose, but the authors should not expect this service. The journal has adopted U.S.English usage as its norm (this does not apply to other native users of English).

Accepted WP systems:
MS Word and rtf.

the music soars
a dynamic tapestry of sound
both weaving and already woven
in an eternal present
each moment shaped by
the form of its history,
each moment of sound enriched
being layered on the memory
of its arising

awareness floating on the music
my gaze wanders
and without remarking
i see:
high cathedral arches
tall stained glass windows
a deep altar alcove
carven images in niches
and gilded iconic paintings

a thought arises:
the music will be over
like the meal enjoyed,
and my reading of the book -
I may not see this cathedral again

so it is with any work of art:
brief appreciation
long creation

we all accept that
as "the cost"
or simply
as "the way it is"

Cybernetics And Human Knowing. Vol. 12, nos. 1-2, pp. 5-10

Patterns That Connect Patterns That Connect:
A Thematic Foreword

Frederick Steier and Jane Jorgenson[1]

In the film *Mindwalk*, Sonja Hoffman, a physicist played by Liv Ullmann, is asked by a politician (played by Sam Waterston) to name those thinkers whose work embodies this "new systems thinking" Hoffman is speaking so highly of. Three names come to her—with the connector among them being Gregory Bateson. Such is Bateson's legacy that this film, made over a decade after his death, sees fit to put his name out there as a systems thinker that the world of film viewers ought to become familiar with. *Mindwalk* is an extended peripatetic conversation between a physicist, a politician and a poet, set in the inspiring natural and designed space of Mont St. Michel, with the haunting minimalist music of Philip Glass. It is fitting that Bateson's name should be invoked, certainly as a systems thinker whose work we need to know, but also as someone whose passions connect those with such diverse backgrounds and ways of seeing, as a physicist, politician and poet.

This special double issue of *Cybernetics and Human Knowing* is dedicated to the work of Gregory Bateson on the occasion of his centennial celebration. How do we connect Bateson, the cybernetic epistemologist with Bateson, the poet concerned with metaphoric process? How do we connect Bateson the scientist interested in human and animal communication and behavior with Bateson the learning theorist? How do we connect Bateson interested in the ecology of cities, with Bateson interested in an ecology of mind? And how might we, following Bateson, make these connections while examining our own assumptions, including the relational contexts within which we make them. And how might we explore our assumptions in ways that allow us challenge deeply held obsolescent traditions—including diverse dualisms that have rendered such connections, such "in-betweenesses" as blindnesses in our ways of understanding.

The authors in this volume in many ways parallel the range of interests and areas of concern to Bateson. Included here are family therapists, communication scholars, anthropologists, psychologists, musicians, education theorists, as well as those whose work simply is self-described as cybernetics and systems practice. Yet, such traditional classificatory schema obscure the ways that each of them as individuals move fluidly across traditional disciplinary boundaries, and they also prevent our noticing the connections among all of them as a system of inquirers whose diverse interests are

---

1. Both from the Department of Communication, University of South Florida. Contact Fred Steier at
    Email: fsteier@shell.cas.usf.edu

connected by the threads of systems thinking and cybernetics. Awareness of these connections creates the potential for a network of conversations among the authors, from which multiple perspectives and new knowledge can emerge.

Bateson consistently invites us to look to patterns that connect. "Break the pattern which connects the items of learning and you necessarily destroy all quality," he tells his fellow regents at the University of California. "What pattern connects the crab to the lobster and the orchid to the primrose and all four of them to me? And me to you?" he asks us to consider at the outset in *Mind and Nature* (p. 8). His focus on both the content and relationship aspects of all messages invites us to think about pattern also in human relationships and how we create patterns that we live and that define us. And Bateson's ideas of the relationship of content and process invite us to carefully consider patterns across time, and perhaps time as patterned occasion.

So in this introduction we bring together these essays not only as separate works, but as an interconnected web—or the beginning of a web, at least to the extent that a book whose pages unfold in numerical sequence might allow. We will introduce the essays individually, but also highlight some manner of connection of each with the succeeding piece.

Thus we try here to create a way of introducing the volume whose process itself mirrors Bateson's very ideas that have meant so much to us.

In Julio Cortazar's *Hopscotch*, the reader is offered, in addition to the regular ordered sequence of chapters, an alternative suggested sequence. This alternative sequence allows new ideas and images to unfold with different readings. We invite the reader to try this with this volume as well. We realize that the features unconcealed by the connections we make are just some of many, and we hope that creating patterns between essays allows new features emerge in the relationship, in the in-between.

These authors, clearly, share a passion for Bateson's vision, and his concern for the relationship between our ways of knowing and our experienced worlds. They write from their personal engagement with his ideas and their awareness of how those ideas have informed their work. At the same time we see how their thinking, having been enriched by Bateson's ideas, can, in turn, inform and extend Bateson's work.

The kinds of connections discernible across essays are diverse. They include domains of content, cybernetic principles—even the manner in which the writers weave their own patterns that connect. What, then, are patterns that connect our patterns that connect?

Mary Catherine Bateson recasts the theory of the double bind in the context of Bateson's ecological and environmental concerns. Her essay invites us to consider various forms of double bind inherent in the human situation. Rather than seeking to eliminate dissonances between logical levels, she invites us to think about preparing future generations to embrace them, and links this awareness to the design of educational systems.

Together, Mary Catherine Bateson and Will McWhinney encourage us to explore movement across different levels of learning, and to think about ways of linking that movement process to possibilities for transforming our learning institutions.

Will McWhinney draws on recent developments in neurophysiology to reconsider and extend the distinctions and relationships among Bateson's levels of learning. McWhinney uses a Chinese parable, "The White Horse," as a vehicle for rethinking third order learning, Learning III, as a "spiraling path of action, withdrawal and return, of increasing creativity, humility, and good will," a meta-praxis.

Will McWhinney and Frederick Steier together encourage us to explore the linkage between communication and learning at multiple levels while considering what this linkage might mean in "designing for engagement."

Frederick Steier explores the interplay between Bateson's ideas of "frame" and "flexibility" through the lens of understanding activities at a science center. In making these connections, he raises questions about frames for learning and play, while developing the importance of creating contexts for "exercising frame flexibility" in social systems.

Frederick Steier and Thomas Hylland Eriksen invite us to extend Bateson's ideas about flexibility and its entailments to scenes of everyday life, giving particular attention to the patterns connecting different social systems we engage in.

Thomas Hylland Eriksen focuses on Bateson's idea of flexibility as uncommitted potential for change. He raises questions about relationships between flexibilities across the domains of time and space and explores the consequences for "new work" in the knowledge-based economy. His investigation into emergent social forms with new information and communication technologies in turn allows for adding to what he feels is the untapped potential in the concept of flexibility itself.

Thomas Hylland Eriksen and Peter Harries-Jones invite us to take Bateson's ideas seriously in our understanding of and enactment of "natural" and designed environments.

Peter Harries-Jones develops an ecological aesthetics building on Bateson's epistemology of recursive systems. Drawing upon the fundamental recognition of our participation in our environment, Harries-Jones has us consider consequences of an ecological aesthetics for significant environmental issues, for our own ecological understanding, and for our conceptualization of the sacred and the beautiful.

Peter Harries-Jones and Bradford Keeney invite us to consider questions of recursion and circular processes for how we develop and sustain an ecosystemic understanding in diverse domains and in different cultural settings.

In "Circular Epistemology and the Bushman Shamans" Bradford Keeney draws on more than a decade of fieldwork among the Kalahari Bushman. He finds the embodiment of Bateson's ecological understanding in the Shamans' performance of sacred dances, which manifest the recursive relationship between stability and change and their sense of being in the world. This in turn offers new insight, realized through an imaginary dialogue between Bateson and a Bushman shaman, into the dynamic circularities at the heart of human encounters.

Bradford Keeney and Douglas Flemons invite us into a world organized around the relationship between cybernetic thought and therapeutic transformation in diverse forms. The Kalahari Bushman shaman meets Obi-wan Kenobi. What do we learn?

Anticipating Star Wars III, Douglas Flemons juxtaposes his engagement with Bateson's ideas with the practices of Jedi Master Obi-wan Kenobi. Flemons links his experiences in family therapy, hypnosis and the teaching of composition together with the circularities of making and completing distinctions. For Flemons, these connections afford insights into the importance of relationship as an organizing principle while also encouraging us to think about how to balance integrity with invention.

Douglas Flemons and Malloy, Bostic St. Clair, and Grinder encourage us to think seriously about the construction of cybernetic formalisms involving the circular processes of making and completing distinctions, and issues of emergence.

Extending Warren McCulloch's famous essay, "What is a Number that a Man May Know it and a Man that He May Know a Number," Thomas Malloy, Carmen Bostic St. Clair, and John Grinder set out to extend this mutual approach to "number" to the world of formalisms. They do this by exploring emergence as a formalism while embedding our knowing of emergence in discrete dynamic systems. This allows insight into human judgement of perceptual similarity.

Malloy, Bostic St. Clair, and Grinder, and Kenneth Cissna and Rob Anderson create opportunities for us to make connections between formalisms of processes of emergence, and the emergence of new ideas in dialogic moments, allowing us to rethink "emergence" in general.

Kenneth Cissna and Rob Anderson bring their interest in dialogic processes to a particular occasion—a conversation that took place between Bateson and Carl Rogers, in 1975. Although Bateson and Rogers themselves dismissed the meeting as a failure at the time, Cissna and Anderson's sensitive reading from a dialogic perspective allows us to see how significant new ideas did in fact emerge from the meeting, including Bateson's conceptualization of context.

Together, Kenneth Cissna and Rob Anderson, and Wendy Leeds-Hurwitz afford opportunities to explore processes of social interaction, whether in the moment or sustained over time.

Wendy Leeds-Hurwitz explores the legacy of Bateson's methodological commitments to a "natural history" approach to understanding human communication. She describes how she and others have taken up Bateson's ideas of pattern, structure and process in detailed empirical studies of interaction. Such work demonstrates the formation of an "invisible college" grounded in the principles of a natural history approach.

Wendy Leeds-Hurwitz and Alfonso Montuori invite us to consider the relationship between networks of conversation and issues of social creativity.

In "Gregory Bateson and the Promise of Transdisciplinarity" Alfonso Montuori connects Bateson's ideas to his own experiences in transdisciplinary inquiry. Combining his own work as a professor and a musician, Montuori creates possibilities for an ecology of creativity. Such an understanding of creativity is itself used to inform a transdisciplinary approach rooted in the interplay between Bateson's rigor and imagination, which allows for a significant reconnection of a knower to knowing contexts.

Alfonso Montuori and Mary Catherine Bateson invite us to take seriously what it means to see in new ways, and to invite others into those new ways of seeing - but also to link this very question to our learning institutions.

And so on…

In addition to the essays, there are the regular featured columns and book review. In his column, Virtual Logic—The One and the Many, Louis Kauffman develops a sustained inquiry into the couplet, "how can multiplicity arise from a unity" and "how can a unity arise from a multiplicity" and in so doing allows for a recasting of ideas of emergence.

Peter Harries-Jones contributes this issue's ASC column in the spirit of the special issue. In "Gregory Bateson, Heterarchies and the Topology of Recursion," he elegantly complexifies our understanding of Bateson's appreciation of recursive logics. Harries-Jones connects Bateson's own logics of the "in-between" with Warren McCulloch's notion of heterarchical orderings in ways that afford recommendations for meaning emergent in the model of the topological form of a torus.

Ranulph Glanville offers this issue's book review, of *The International Encyclopaedia of Systems and Cybernetics, second edition*, which is edited by Charles Francois.

Photos and poems throughout the issue are contributed by Pille Bunnell.

The authors in this volume, then, celebrate the Bateson Centennial, with contributions rooted in Bateson's ideas and ideals. These essays, through offering personal stories of Bateson's influence, while at the same time demonstrating opportunities for its extension, can be read as a gift to a creative spirit on his 100th birthday.

Cybernetics And Human Knowing. Vol. 12, nos. 1-2, pp. 11-21

The Double Bind:
Pathology and Creativity

Mary Catherine Bateson[1]

The double bind is a recurrent characteristic of life, not limited to the context of psychopathology, where the concept was first developed within the narrowed focus of Bateson's work during his period in Palo Alto. Bateson pointed out that it is not appropriate or possible to count double binds: it is also not appropriate or possible to prevent their occurrence. Instead, we should ask why some individuals are particularly vulnerable and how education can strengthen individuals to deal with multiple logical levels.

From time to time I have puzzled about a comment that my father Gregory Bateson made to me as we walked in the woods between sessions of the Conference on Conscious Purpose and Human Adaptation at Burg Wartenstein, the castle owned by the Wenner-Gren Foundation, in Gloggnitz, Austria (M. C. Bateson, 1972/2004a). It was a comment that I found rather shocking. "Nature," he said, "is a dirty, double binding bitch." What I will try to do here is to contextualize that comment in relation to the different periods of Gregory's life and work, and by doing so to suggest a different way of looking at the double bind that is not limited to pathology.

Double bind theory was developed in that period of Gregory's life when he was most involved with psychiatry, psychotherapy, and the study of schizophrenia. The Wenner-Gren conference where Gregory made that comment, however, took place long after he had withdrawn from the group of colleagues with whom he studied schizophrenia and developed the double bind concept. During the interval he had spent time in the Virgin Islands and in Hawaii studying dolphins and had become deeply concerned about environmental issues. When Gregory was working on the double bind, I was still a teenager, but I remember him talking about it and explaining that the class of all pens is not a pen and you cannot write with it to illustrate the theory of logical types and how they relate to the double bind. I remember sitting behind a one-way mirror watching him working with a family in which there was a diagnosed schizophrenic member.

By the time of the Conference on Conscious Purpose and Human Adaptation, however, a decade later, I was collaborating with him as an adult. Practically speaking, I relearned his thinking backwards. By that time, still writing metalogues of fictionalized father-daughter conversation, he was using information theory and cybernetics to understand the maladaptative behavior of humans in the biosphere. We were gathered at Burg Wartenstein to talk about the abuse of natural systems, not

---

1.   President, Institute for Intercultural Studies, New York City; and Professor Emerita George Mason University, Fairfax, Virginia. Email: mcatb@attglobal.net. URL: www.marycatherinebateson.com.

about psychotherapy, but there he was, pulling me back to the early work with this rather shocking comment that suggested that the dysfunctions in the human household might be part of a larger pattern.

First a little bit of history. Gregory did not have a particularly "good" war. He had come to America with my mother in the 1930s and was still a British subject, so when World War II broke out in Europe, he returned to his country as quickly as possible, asking how he could serve. He was told they didn't have any use for an anthropologist, so he sailed back to the United States and spent the war in the Pacific working for the OSS, the parent organization of what is now the CIA, where he was involved in psychological warfare and disinformation.

In effect, he was contributing to the war effort by using his understanding of culture and the nature of communication to create confusion in the enemy. I don't think he was very good at it. None of his stories sound very convincing. He deeply believed in the importance of defeating the Axis powers, as did most intellectuals at that time, but the act of disrupting or distorting communication was, I believe, something he found very painful. For a period after the war, Gregory was in an extended depression. He went into analysis with a Jungian, Elizabeth Hellersberg, separated from my mother, and moved to California. A lot of people were pulling strings to find a job for him, and it turned out that there was a category, "ethnologist," in the Veterans Administration system that he could be described as uniquely qualified for in spite of being a non-citizen, so he got a job working with psychiatric patients at the Veterans Administration Hospital in Palo Alto.

There he started working with alcoholics, one of whom was also a diagnosed schizophrenic. (It is useful to bear in mind that diagnostic categories have shifted since that time.) I can remember listening with Gregory to tapes of schizophrenic "word salad" as he commented that there was a structure to this seemingly chaotic rant. Not to put too fine a point on it, he said, "there's method in his madness." Gregory came to the conclusion that at the root of schizophrenia there was a logical incongruence, a disruption in thought and communication, that could be seen as either caused or exacerbated by patterns of relationship in the families of schizophrenics. These patterns were referred to as the double bind.

The biggest problem in understanding and making sense of double bind theory is the tendency to think that double binds are things that can be counted. The double bind was actually an abstract pattern of relationships that might show up in particular exchanges, but these always depended on the broader context. Let me give you the well known example of a young man who had been in hospital and was somewhat recovered from an acute schizophrenic episode when he was visited by his mother. Gregory's account of the event: "He was glad to see her and impulsively put his arm around her shoulders, whereupon she stiffened. He withdrew his arm and she asked, 'Don't you love me any more?' He then blushed, and she said, 'Dear, you must not be so easily embarrassed and afraid of your feelings.' The patient was able to stay with her only a few minutes more, and following her departure he assaulted an aide and was put in the tubs" (G. Bateson 1956/2000c, p. 217).

In this sequence, the young man makes a gesture of affection and the mother's stiffening conveys a rejection of that affection on her part—she forbids his expression of affection. But she then interprets his reaction as meaning that he doesn't love her—he is punished for his response—and is forbidden to notice her rejection. She continues to express affection verbally and to blame the failure of the interaction on him. Her next comment is that he mustn't be afraid to express his feelings. It's a nasty story, and clearly it is painful and disruptive for the patient and pushes him back into violent behavior.

The double bind is created in interaction between two or more parties or entities (I'm deliberately avoiding saying 'persons' here, which is the usual phrasing—really we are dealing with parts of some larger whole) in a significant non-transient relationship that continues over an extended period, with the same pattern repeated again and again. In this pattern there is a contradiction between messages at different logical levels: a primary injunction and a second conflicting injunction at another level affecting the interpretation of the first. There is some real emotional danger or threat in this situation, no possibility of withdrawing from it, and no possibility of naming the problem.

So there Gregory was, studying mental patients, setting the stage for the familiar process whereby insights into human psychology and human biology have arisen from the effort to address pathology. Historically, we have had to go backward from Freud's efforts to understand the psychopathology of his patients in order to progress toward a theory of health, against which those problems can be compared and perhaps treated. We learn about the immune system as a system that maintains health in the human body by studying the points where it fails. This sequence happens all the time in biomedical research, except that often the final step—the study of the functioning system and its healthy development—is omitted.

Over time, as Gregory and the other members of his group focused on schizophrenia as a research topic, it was not only because they found these patients so interesting, but also because that was where the funding was (not, for instance, in the analysis of humor, which interested them during the same period and has certain similarities). Schizophrenia was a problem and there was money available for research that might lead to a solution to that problem. In the same way, biologists at present are diligently writing grant applications to demonstrate that the basic science they are interested in doing on, let us say, the immune system or the brain or what have you, will contribute to the search for a cure for HIV-AIDS, because at the moment in the United States that is where the research money is. Except for a series of accidents—the war work, the VA job, the availability of support for research on schizophrenia—I don't believe that Gregory would have focused on pathology as a starting point. Ironically, he became best known (outside anthropology, which has largely focused on his pre-war work) for identifying the double bind as a pathology in communication within families which, it was hypothesized, would either cause or exacerbate schizophrenia. This meant that he was focusing on exactly the thing that shadowed his efforts during the war, the disruption of communication. I don't think you can make sense of Gregory's work unless you look at him as someone with a primary interest in understanding wholeness, rather than someone with a primary interest in pathology.

The question that Gregory was posing at Burg Wartenstein concerned the failure of human beings to understand the systemic character of the natural world, of which we are a part. This was posed in terms of the failures of conscious purpose in leading to actions taken to achieve specific goals or solve specific problems. And of course that's how most medical and psychiatric research is structured, largely oriented toward problem solving rather than toward understanding. Gregory was pointing out that this approach itself is often destructive in the long term. When you have something that seems to be a solution, you say "fine, that's all I need." In our day, it's probably a psychoactive drug. We have found that when you dose various kinds of mental patients, they are no longer such a problem, and so you cease asking the broader question of what is wrong with the entire system in which the pathology develops and you frequently ignore side effects until it is too late. Today there is also a preference for blaming problems on genetics in order to avoid thinking more broadly about human experience.

At Burg Wartenstein, Gregory was arguing that attending only to small portions of larger systems and seeking to achieve narrow purposes was the source of human destructiveness in the biosphere: he had identified a problem. But he was adamant about rejecting the search for a solution (a "quick fix"): "the temptation in our position at the present time, vis-à-vis this enormously complex set of problems, is to grab quick, quick, but *quick* at anything that will obscure the darkness of the subject and, above all, give us something to do, preferably with our larger muscles. There's a very high probability that we will walk precisely into just those operations that fall into place as part of this whole system and increase by a negligible fraction the rate at which the world is approaching hell." (M. C. Bateson, 1972/2004a, p. 302)

Instead, Gregory directed the conference to ways of thinking about wholeness in the arts and religion and through primary process. If you go back to a paper that he wrote in 1949, called "Bali: The Value System of a Steady State" (G. Bateson, 1949/ 2000b), what you find is a set of ideas about the aesthetic perception of wholeness and about the characteristics of a system in balance that is not inclined to go into runaway. Bali represented for him a possibility that I think underlies much that he said at later times in talking about wisdom and about the sacred. At Burg Wartenstein, Gregory tried to give a definition of "the ugly." His example of ugliness was what is called Still's lesion, which he described as the "central myth of osteopathy" (M. C. Bateson, 1972/2004a, pp. 294-95). This is a maladjustment, an irregularity in the rhythmic progression of the spine, which is to say a disruption of pattern, that then becomes the origin of a wide range of other disorders. That lesion, that break in pattern, was for him emblematic of ugliness. The double bind is like that.

When Gregory said "nature is a dirty double binding bitch," one might wonder whether he was speaking about his own mother, and the answer is that he probably was, and perhaps other women in his life as well; it was surely no accident that the project focused primarily on the schizophrenogenic mother. But blaming the mother was not the central issue in double bind theory. I think the central issue was the nature of distortion in the patterns of communication and thought and the circumstances under which such distortion becomes intolerable. Even the double bind, I believe, should not be looked at simplistically as a problem to be fixed. The fact is, although you do see rather horrifying examples in the families of patients, there are double binds throughout experience that do not necessarily lead to mental illness and may even lead to creativity, and the question is why some individuals find them so devastating (Kafka, 1971).

The double bind is all around us. There is no escape. Just pick up the newspaper. I was interested, in rereading Gregory's early papers recently, to see that in 1941 Gregory was writing about what a mistake it would be after the war to enforce democracy (G. Bateson, 1942/2000a). Where have we heard that idea lately? He wrote about the danger of setting up what he called "demo-Quislings" in the former Axis powers. This parallels one of the classic double binds, which is to say to a child or to a patient, "You must be free, you must make your own choices." There's the contradiction: If you must be free, then you are not free.

In fact, there are two logical levels of freedom at issue, just as there are two logical levels in the Epimenides paradox, "I am lying," that create an oscillation: If I'm lying, then I'm telling the truth, but…et cetera. We might say that right now one of the causes of the insanity in Iraq is the conflict between the primary injunction, you must be democratic and free to choose your own form of government, and the secondary injunction to accept the fact that foreign soldiers will stay there and be the judges of what counts as democracy. You are not free to withdraw or to comment on the limitation placed on your freedom lest you be thought disloyal or ungrateful. This is a double bind, and a lethal one, which the Iraqis can neither articulate nor escape.

As human beings, however, we are all subject to multiple double binds that develop through recurrent patterns in contexts of learning. The double bind is not only a clue to understanding schizophrenia and a wide range of other learned or acquired psychopathologies (Sluzki & Veron, 1976, p. 261), but part of the fabric of ordinary life. As with all theories that see the etiology of psychopathology in childhood learning, the more interesting question is why some people survive apparently undamaged—or whether perhaps all human beings or all those raised in particular cultures are damaged in the same way, accepted as normal.

Perhaps the most basic double bind affecting all human beings is that we can know at one level that we have evolved to fight for individual survival, and at another level, that as a species with bisexual reproduction, we depend on death. We are all caught, as they say, between a rock and a hard place, knowing at one level, a rational level perhaps, the necessity of death, and at another level, deeply programmed to struggle against death. Much of religion appears to be an effort to escape this double bind apparently inflicted by a loving and just deity. Somehow rationality is insufficient. Even for people who have a very clear idea that they are indeed dying and struggle to accept death as appropriate, as consciousness is reduced, the deeply rooted habit of trying to stay alive stubbornly asserts itself and they become unable to deal with the contradiction, which also asserts itself in the conflicted emotional responses of their friends and relations.

Living in an individualistic Western society, we are double bound by being told we are free and by being subject to a large number of social controls that make us unfree (Sluzki & Veron, 1976, p. 252). In the same volume, a 1965 paper by Ronald Laing (Laing, 1965/1976) identifies the same kind of paradox in the Marxist concept of mystification, where at one level people know they are being exploited and at another level are told they should be grateful, and Wilden and Wilson (1976, pp. 263-286) point out that our entire economic system depends on continuing growth in a context where unlimited growth must lead to self destruction. By the time we met at Burg Wartenstein, Gregory had begun to speak of economic growth as an addictive process, and the ideas for his 1971 paper on alcoholism were developed in the following weeks (G. Bateson, 1971/2000e).

Earlier, I defined the double bind as two contradictory injunctions at different levels of communication, involving two parties or entities, where it is not possible either to name the contradiction or to escape it. Whatever the terminology, it is important to notice that a double bind need not involve two *persons*. The confusion of logical levels that creates the double bind would seem to occur most easily where one system is embedded in another. Thus, the double binding interaction in the example reported earlier is not an event between mother and son but between the son and the dyad or family of which he is a part. It can also occur within the person or organism, or between the individual and the social unit, and, most significantly, between an organism or a species and its environment.

From Gregory's point of view, the unit of survival *is* the organism in its environment. We try to solve immediate problems like insect pests with DDT, but in order to do so we refuse to acknowledge the systemic character of the world we are part of. We block this reality from perception just as the schizophrenogenic mother forbids the child to articulate the contradiction, the double bind, in which he or she is trapped. To do so would be to say something bad about the mother and perhaps to lose her. Similarly, we are unwilling to analyze the contradiction between our purposes and our survival (as individuals or as a species) or the contradiction between being organisms that necessarily must die and being convinced of the need to stay alive. Much of the paranoia produced by such contradictions is simply taken for granted.

Gregory equated "system" in the systems theory or cybernetic sense with "mind," showing that a system can learn, can respond, can interpret events, can self-correct in various ways (G. Bateson, 1979/2003, pp. 91-128). And he pointed out that if you accept this definition, a mind is not necessarily something contained in an envelope of skin. A mind could be two persons in interaction, or a woodsman and an axe and a tree. It could be an entire ecosystem with some capacity to respond and adjust to changes. From that point of view, the mother and the son in the story quoted earlier, although we can see that they are two people and have two brains, are caught in a single maladaptive system, a self maintaining circuit, and they are functioning as one faulty mind. Double bind is not only something that happens to a mind but something that happens in a mind.

Our species is part of a system, a larger mind, in Bateson's sense. We are part of the natural world but behaving as if we were outside of it, generating contradictions and inconsistencies and ugliness. We happen to be the "conscious" piece of the larger system but on this matter the nature of the interaction is kept out of awareness. We are in any case only conscious of a tiny part of what goes on inside ourselves, and this is necessarily the case. We can only say that we have an awareness of part of the mind that we are. It would be impossible to be totally self conscious, creating an infinite regress of awareness of awareness of awareness. So we are capable of internal contradictions (like autoimmune disorders), and we are capable of being part of larger interactions in which there are lethal pathogenic contradictions in which we blindly play a destructive role.

One of my favorite remarks of Gregory's was a definition of love in cybernetic terms that I enjoy repeating to students because it seems to them so unromantic. (One of my students once asked me, after reading *With a Daughter's Eye* (M. C. Bateson, 1984/2001), "Didn't you and your parents ever have normal conversations?") Gregory said, "You could say that love is a rather difficult-to-define concept, related to things we have been discussing—systems. At least a part of what we mean by the word could be covered by saying that 'I love X' could be spelled out as 'I regard myself as a system, whatever that might mean, and I accept with positive valuation the fact that I am one, preferring to be one rather than fall to pieces and die; and I regard the person whom I love as systemic…'" There you've got a rephrasing of the golden rule, right? Aha. But Gregory took it another step forward, which is very important, because he went on to say, "'and I regard my system and his or her system as together constituting a larger system with some degree of conformability within itself.'" (M. C. Bateson, 1972/2004a, pp. 279-80). That's not in the golden rule. That's the piece of Gregory's thinking that you come up against when you speak the language of individualism, because Gregory looked at human individuals not only as systems, but as components in larger systems which themselves have intrinsic value. So a community has a value. A family has a value. What the students are failing to recognize in this phrasing is a translation of the profoundly romantic declaration of lovers, we are one person.

Where does this take us? What do we do about this rather horrifying tendency to produce ugliness, about the unacknowledged contradictions we keep getting into, perhaps most easily in Western industrialized societies? The consequences are especially grave because we in the West have the power to inflict those contradictions more widely and more disastrously on the planet than ever before. I would argue that since we are unable to avoid double binds we should learn to recognize and work with them under comparatively secure circumstances.

Some of the psychotherapists who were part of the Bateson group became interested in the use of paradoxical interventions in psychotherapy. They observed Frieda Fromm-Reichmann at work, and Milton Erickson, one of the great hypnotherapists. In both cases, the therapists deliberately created contradictions.

Double binds do create psychopathologies but they can also be used to provoke resolution or to stimulate creativity. There is an illuminating story that Gregory told of a dolphin used to demonstrate reinforcement learning in an aquarium show. In order to provide new examples in each show, the trainer rejects the performance that was rewarded the previous day, which frustrates and distresses the dolphin. Eventually, the dolphin transcends the process by a step to a higher logical type (G. Bateson, 1969/ 2000d, pp. 276-278). Suddenly, with great excitement, the dolphin produces a long series of previously unobserved behaviors, having grasped the abstract notion that what is rewarded is novelty, a *class* of behaviors rather than any particular behavior.

In this sense, the double bind raises questions for education. All children have the experience of being rewarded for behaviors which are then taken for granted—most adults do not get praised for their success in tying their shoes or using the potty! Yet novelty is not always rewarded either. Artists must learn that their creative work is only valued if it is recognizably the same as previous work (but different) and children quickly recognize that they are graded not on either learning or creativity but for correct answers.

If double binds are inherent in the human situation, we need to think about how children can learn to observe and diagnose logical inconsistency and to move up the ladder of logical types to resolve paradox. Paradox can be a powerful teacher, as it is in Zen training, as well as a source of psychopathology. We have to root out the dysfunctional double binds that are built into educational processes in schools but we also have to ask whether there are ways to build into the process of schooling the capacity to function consciously at multiple levels.

The human capacity to learn and to pass on learning is a wonderful thing, but it is important to recognize that with every new increment of learning, dissonances are created which have to be somehow resolved, both within and between individuals. Let's say I learned something yesterday, which means that today I know something you don't, that we may need to sort out to maintain the conformability between our understandings of the world. We live in a chronic situation of adapting to unfamiliar ideas and new learning which creates constant dissonance with old ideas, often through the disparity between learning at home and in school. Most schooling imposes these contradictions without being mindful that the costs involved for children are high even though the emotional stakes in school are not as high as they are at home. To succeed in school, first of all, you have to define yourself as ignorant, and second, if you're an immigrant or come from a minority group, you are probably put in the position of learning a piece of the majority culture that makes you a betrayer of your family. Furthermore, the system proclaims the legitimacy of questioning—but only up to a point and then punishes it.

New learning may also threaten valuable learned premises about the learning process, undermining future learning. I grew up being told that if I burned myself I should put butter on the burn. Then at a certain point they told me, no, don't do that, put the burn under running water or even better put ice on it. Not only had I learned one version of how to deal with a burn, but in the process of learning that, I had also been learning about who to believe, about the nature of validity and authority. If you come and tell me, "that's wrong, that's a superstition," the danger is that you are disrupting a more abstract pattern that may be essential for my future learning. This has been pointed out about African American children who speak a perfectly regular, predictable dialect of English that happens not to be standard. And they're told they are speaking wrongly as if they were just making random mistakes. They're not. They are speaking grammatically, but it's a different grammar, but because their usage is not random, the corrections violate their sense of pattern. The risk in school is that in introducing new material, we are also disrupting what Gregory wrote about as deutero-learned premises of how to learn, how to deal with context and pattern, who to believe, what relationships are teaching relationships.

You can go two ways. You can say that putting butter on a burn is false and superstitious and old-fashioned and you shouldn't believe the people who tell you to do that, or you can say that the point of putting butter on a burn is to cut off contact with oxygen to prevent the oxidation from continuing. There are several ways to stop that process of burning: You can deprive it of oxygen or you can lower the temperature, and with water or ice you do both. So basically, whoever told me to put butter on a burn was telling me something that made sense and I was right to listen to them, but the new approach is a more efficient way to achieve what they were teaching me. That kind of correction is not disruptive of future learning (M. C. Bateson, 2001/2004c).

To say that something previously learned is an error is disruptive, so it only makes sense to do so when that disruption is desired. To say that the Biblical version of creation is a superstition or a lie is far more disruptive than saying it is a metaphorical or poetic version of a truth. The ideal is to make the student able to think at multiple levels, to understand the relationship between alternative grammars where one is socially preferred, the different kinds of efficiency of different procedures, the possibility of different truths that are not contradictory because they are "true" in different ways. Perhaps the current global epidemic of fundamentalism is a side effect of massive exposure to new ideas and information in ways that threaten the entire willingness to learn.

The double bind is endemic in human life. The Bateson group found the shifts in logical type that create double binds in humor and religion, in metaphor and poetry and throughout the arts, and they observed creative ways of dealing with them. You cannot eliminate the dissonances between logical levels. What we need to do is to find a way of preparing children to live at multiple levels by embedding an awareness of multiple levels in our education systems. This is why the budget cuts going into effect all over the United States to eliminate the arts from education and to focus everything on correct answers on exams are so dangerous and destructive.

With two parents who were both anthropologists, I grew up in a household in which participant observation was the norm, a technique that involves experience at multiple levels: participating and observing oneself and the other at the same time. In our house that was how you looked at your breakfast. I find that many people, however, if I tell them that my parents kept notes on me and took hundreds of photographs, are shocked because they find the notion of scientific observation, intellectual looking, alienating (M. C. Bateson, 2001/2004b, pp. 331-332). People tend to feel that the role of observer is a distancing role and incompatible with love, with participation in a loving interaction. Having literally been trained in participant observation from a very young age, I am convinced that that was for me a primary way of learning to function at multiple levels: to be in engagement, interacting, participating, and at the same time observing and analyzing and learning (M. C. Bateson, 1991/2004c). Critical to this is the element of self-observation that today is called reflexivity: being aware of one's own responses within that context. Clinicians also sometimes use the related term disciplined subjectivity, which means to be engaged and attentive and observant, self-observant and also willing to act. The same layering of experience is involved in action research, and indeed we need to demand of all those who act on the lives of others—parents, teachers, reformers—that they express respect and love by bringing their highest intelligence to bear and that they cultivate multiple layers of awareness, always struggling with the paradoxes created by necessary uncertainty.

Gregory hesitated to act. He hesitated to act for many levels of reasons—all these things have multiple layers of causation—but at least part of his hesitation, I think, was his war time experience, the unwillingness to use insight as a tool for problem solving that might become destructive manipulation. Still, in the last decade and a half of his life he was saying that we must arrive at a new consciousness and a new level of grace in the way we interact with the natural world, of which we must know ourselves as a part. There was both anger and grief in that half-joking comment he made to me that day, that "nature is a double-binding bitch," but it was said of a relationship with nature that we cannot leave and cannot do without, a relationship which must finally be one of love.

REFERENCES

Bateson, M. C. (2001), *With a daughter's eye: A memoir of Margaret Mead and Gregory Bateson.* New York: HarperCollins. (Originally published in 1984 by William Morrow & Company, New York)

Bateson, M. C. (2004a). *Our own metaphor: A personal account of a conference on conscious purpose and human adaptation.* Cresskill, NJ: Hampton Press. (Originally published in 1972 by Alfred A. Knopf, New York)

Bateson, M. C. (2004b). Multiple kinds of knowledge: Societal decision making. In M. C. Bateson, *Willing to learn: Passages of personal discovery* (pp. 320-338). Hanover, NH: Steerforth Press. (Originally published in M. J. McGee (Ed.), *Diversity and design: Studying culture and the individual. Proceedings of the 4th Annual Qualitative Research in Education Conference.* Athens, GA: Center for Continuing Education, 1991)

Bateson, M. C. (2004c). Learning in layers. In M. C. Bateson, *Willing to learn: Passages of personal discovery* (pp. 250-262). (Originally published in R. Soder et al. (Eds.), *Developing democratic character in the young,* pp. 114-125, by Jossey-Bass, 2001)

Bateson, G. (2000a). Social planning and the concept of deutero-learning. In G. Bateson, *Steps to an ecology of mind* (pp. 159-176). Chicago: University of Chicago Press. (Book originally published in 1972 by Chandler Publishing company, San Francisco. Paper originally published in L. Finklestein (Ed.), *Science, philosophy and religion: Second symposium* by the Conference on Science, Philosophy and Religion in Their Relation to the Democratic Way of Life, Inc, New York, 1942. Date of symposium: 8-11 Sept., 1941)

Bateson, G. (2000b). Bali: The value system of a steady state. In G. Bateson, *Steps to an ecology of mind* (pp. 107-127). Chicago: University of Chicago Press. (Book originally published in 1972 by Chandler Publishing company, San Francisco. Paper originally published in 1949 in M. Fortes (Ed.) *Social structure: Studies presented to A. R. Radcliffe-Brown,* published by Clarendon Press, Oxford.)

Bateson, G. (2000c). Toward a theory of schizophrenia. In G. Bateson, *Steps to an ecology of mind* (pp. 201-227). Chicago: University of Chicago Press. (Book originally published in 1972 by Chandler Publishing company, San Francisco. Paper originally published in 1956 in the journal *Behavioral Science, 1*(4).)

Bateson, G. (2000d). Double bind, 1969. In G. Bateson, *Steps to an ecology of mind* (pp. 271-278). Chicago: University of Chicago Press. (Book originally published in 1972 by Chandler Publishing company, San Francisco. Paper dated 1969).

Bateson, G. (2000e). The cybernetics of "Self": A theory of alcoholism. In G. Bateson, *Steps to an ecology of mind* (pp. 309-337). Chicago: University of Chicago Press. (Book originally published in 1972 by Chandler Publishing company, San Francisco. Paper originally published in 1971 in *Psychiatry, 34* (1), 1-18).

Bateson, G. (2003). *Mind and nature: A necessary unity.* Cresskill, NJ: Hampton Press. (Book originally published in 1979 by E. P. Dutton, New York)

Kafka, J. S. (1971). Ambiguity for individuation: A critique and reformulation of the double bind theory. *Arch.Gen.Psychiatry 25*, 232-239.

Laing, R. (1976). Mystification, confusion, and conflict. In C. E. Sluzki & D. C. Ransom (Eds.), *Double bind: The foundation of the communicational approach to the family* (pp. 199-218). New York: Grune & Stratton. (Paper dated 1965).

Sluzki, C. E., & Veron, E. (1976). The double bind as a universal pathogenic situation. In C. E.Sluzki & D. C. Ransom (Eds.), *Double bind: The foundation of the communicational approach to the family* (pp. 251-262). New York: Grune & Stratton. (Paper dated 1971).

Wilden, A. & Wilson, T. (1976).The double bind: Logic, magic, and economics. In C. E.Sluzki & D. C. Ransom (Eds.), *Double bind: The foundation of the communicational approach to the family* (pp. 263-286). New York: Grune & Stratton.

Treats

I do not consume treats
I taste them
as I would smell a rose
one or two breaths
the aroma suffuses me
and I am satisfied

Cybernetics And Human Knowing. Vol. 12, nos. 1-2, pp. 22-35

The White Horse:
A Reformulation of Bateson's Typology of Learning

Will McWhinney[1]

Bateson, anthropologist, queried the forms of learning and introduced us to deutero-learning. Bateson, system logician, constructed a logic-based typology of learning/change processes. Bateson, psychologist, suggested the power and the danger of third order learning. I argue that his typology, while immensely evocative, added to the confusion in the learning theories he aimed at resolving. I argue that learning LII and LIII are not distinct types only of use: LII changes and stabilizes; LIII is a path of continuous change. These re-characterizations elucidate the divergent paths of LIII, one following a hierarchical logic, the other a transformation of the psyche.

> In a remote village in China lived an old farmer, Cho Tan, his wife and grown son, poor like their neighbors. One day a great white stallion trotted into his barnyard. Clearly he wanted to stay. The neighbors came around, expressing amazement at Tan's good fortune. He simply acknowledged their envious congratulations and went back to work.
>
> A few days later, the horse disappeared. Neighbors again came by to commiserate with Tan; He simple raised his hand to say, "We'll see." A few days later the stallion reappeared with half a dozen mares. The neighbors gathered expressing amazement of his good fortune. As the wild mares came into the barnyard his son jumped upon one; he was thrown and broke his leg. And crowd's expressions turned to consolation. Again the old man raised his hand to indicate, "Wait."
>
> Shortly thereafter army's conscriptors came and drafted all the young men to war. But the farmer's son was left in his bed. "Your are so lucky." He responded with a soft smile and turned back to his field. His wife was there; she had broken through the ground into a hole, sorely wrenching her back. "Oh, how unfortunate you are."
>
> "So…," he walked back to the house carrying his wife.

Does the old farmer in the ancient parable demonstrate the kind of response to changing affairs that Gregory Bateson evoked with his image of *Third Order Learning (LIII)*? It is important to know what it would be like appreciating the continual change that is posited as the highest form of learning available to humans. What would it be like to reflect on the principles, presumptions, and paradoxes of every construct that one faces? It could be a world of unending turmoil, of swirling disconnected data; or like that of the Chinese farmer, staying cool while experiencing radical changes in his fortunes.

I am not clear what his answer would be for Bateson's own discussion of the diverse types of learning includes diverse answers. He began his quest in an attempt to go beyond the paradoxical outcomes of various learning experiments, presenting his explanatory model in "Social planning and the concept of deutero-learning" (1964). He approached the task by evoking the Theory of Logical Types, developed by Bertrand Russell (1913). He presented a parallel between learning types and a

---

1. Institute for the Study of Transformative Education. Email: Will@isote.org

classical logic model to specify five learning types designated Learning Zero through LIV.

In brief, the model describes a first order of learning (LI) that is available for all living entities: only humans and most mammals have access to the second and third orders. Bateson indicates LIII is seldom achieved; it requires a psychological transformation achieved rarely and then mostly by the likes of Zen Buddhists, Indian gurus and western mystics. I hazard to guess that the old Chinese farmer with the white horse would be such a rare human. Bateson also presents LIII as a logical class of behaviors building new learnings on "contents within contents" in a hierarchy of types. Bateson's followers have taken both paths: Argyris and Schön (1978), and many others followed on the programmatic definition more; Morris Berman (1981) followed the mystical and psychoanalytic path and Lars Qvortrup (2004) focuses on reflection as used in both paths.

While the model has been widely adopted I believe it is time to reconsider it both for its logic and in the light of new neurophysiology that gives us a broader setting within which to understand Bateson's typology, particularly the role of *reflection* as a precursor to learning.

I review the theory in terms Bateson introduces, first using his own ideas about feedback, cybernetics, and dynamics of the psyche, then introduce a neuro-physiological model developed by Rodney Cotterill (2001) to suggest a new construction of the difference between types LI and the higher forms: LII and LIII. And following this review I look at the events and tools that lead to the unrelenting search that LIII requires.

Appreciation of Difference

I begin with Bateson's famous phrase: "*A difference which makes a difference*" — quoted from a 1970 address titled, "Form, Substance, and Difference" to establish an epistemology implied in Bateson's cybernetic arguments. He defines a difference as the perception of the unit of information—sometimes as simple as a hummingbird noticing the color of a flower or as completed as a novel by Dostoyevsky. Its title points to an immense set of qualities and relationships. The difference is recognized as a change remembered from what the world was like at one moment as compared to how it appears in the next. A critical ability for noting and reflecting on a difference is *time-binding*, the process of connecting (remembering) over time, space or other dimensions.[2] Time-binding allows us to know that an observation made at one moment is differentiable from the quality or qualities observed at the next moment, therefore, to notice differences and respond to them. This capacity to remember over some interval is a defining quality of living organisms that we can represent with a feedback circuit. Memory is an ability of devices provided with three elements

---

2. Alfred Korzybski (1933) introduced the term *time-binding* as essential in the development of language.

connected in a feedback loop as illustrated in Figure 1. It is a cybernet implied by Bateson's description of learning. (1972, p.293)

Figure 1: A Basic Cybernet for LI

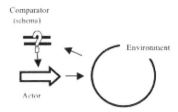

This representation is a version of the common cybernet: The actor stimulates the environment, the comparator notices changes in the environment including the actor's impact and the state of the environment, and feeds back a corrective message to redirect the actor's next act. This fundamental system model is included in Bateson's discussion of learning and in the consciousness models of Libet (1985) and Cotterill (2001). All these models ignore the motivational aspects that are embedded in the interaction between the comparator and the actor.

In this model a difference is defined functionally as that which the comparator notices as a change in the environment due to the actor's behavior. What the comparator notices is that which has been valued, positively or negatively, in the organism's prior events. The comparator holds the memory for the cybernet and with that memory it establishes a pattern of response. By noting the difference it directs (corrects) the actor's behavior.

The cybernet is a defining feature of all living organisms. It is present in the simplest single cell organisms and everywhere in multi-cell organizations. The interest here is in the behaviors that are enabled by relations of cybernets intertwined in the central nervous system of more complex animals and of the societies they form. Bateson's adoption of the theory of logical types was an effort to explain the paradoxical behavior of these complexes. There is no question that his work helped free up learning theorists to go beyond the stimulus-response models of the early years of the 20th century. The cybernetics model inverted the passive S-R image of learning, replacing it with the image of living organisms probing the environment and receiving responses to their impact on the external or internal environment, e.g., reaching out to get nutrients. Bateson's modeling brought his earlier conceptualization of deutero-learning into a general model of learning and organizes all types of learning and change models applicable across the evolutionary spectrum. His construction of third order learning expanded the role of reflection and thus reframes change phenomena. It also added an evocative diffuseness that I hope to resolve in new model based on neurological and consciousness research.

A NEURO-PHYSIOLOGICAL MODEL

In the years since Bateson evolved the ideas of deutero-learning and the type theory there have been immense advances in the understanding of how the mind works. In part, this work supports the typological analogy, providing a neurological explanation of the difference between LI and the models of LII and LIII. It does not support a typological difference between LII and LIII.

Rodney Cotterill (2001) presented an important integration of the research on the brain structure. His neuro-physiological work radically undermines any support remaining for the stimulus-response schema, replacing it with motor-environment-mind schemata of complex feedback loops. The complex of feedback loops enables one to "know what one knows." Cotterill goes beyond this, writing:

> The ability to know that one knows is referred to by psychologists as first-order embedding. Higher embedding, such as that exemplified by knowing that one knows that one knows, merely depends on the ability to hold things in separate patches of neuronal activity in working memory. This manifests itself in the creature's intelligence, which also dictates its ability to consolidate existing schemata into new schema. (2001, p. 28)

This ability, labeled intelligence, is a unique feature of mammalian brains. Intelligence and reflection are explained as due to functioning of the web of feedback loops, both internal and external, that evolved in higher animals. The internal loops involve the motor cortex, amgydala, sensory cortex and other neural and motor elements, coupling memories, emotions, and schemata embedded in diverse feedback loops, enabling reflections and reflections-on-reflections, and through comparisons (e.g., noting differences), establishing awareness and focus. These skills in turn support the evolution of the web of reflections and schemata construction. The structure of schemata varies with its use; some parts of the network have more focusing power, others more reflective capacity. They vary in their resistance to modification. Generally, a person operates with a web of cybernets with different characteristics such as time delays, memory durations, and diverse coupling with neural elements. A person can use focus to build a hierarchical net of cybernetic learning units, which express such rules as those of arithmetic and grammar. More commonly the rules are more chaotic, collecting items into classes as George Lakoff characterized in the title of his classic study of types, *Women, Fire and Dangerous Things: What Categories Reveal About the Mind.* (1987)

The significance of the Cotterill model for a theory of types arises from two properties of the mammalian neurophysiology:

- The division between the simple cybernets and the reflective networks that exist only in the neuro-physiology of mammals.
- The structures that the motor-environment-mind feedback loops form are modifiable, inter-coupled networks. With use they take on fixed patterns we call habitual actions, learnings, and characteristic behaviors. With focus and strong

training they can embed ascending abstractions like a *Russian doll*, but such orderly hierarchies are rare in human brains, most likely in mathematicians' minds.

I assert that this model of the functioning of the mind indicates that Bateson' typology is specific to linear embedding in the organized mind. The linear typology is an exception embedded within a context of network types. It is mostly found in minds of the yet-to-be-educated infant and, as will see, the rare LIII mind.

Before developing this assertion I introduce a description of Bateson work, in part expressed as a system theoretic feedback model.

Orders of Learning and Change

Bateson was a master at creating analogies between formal and quantitative models and the phenomena he observed. His ingenuity led to deep insights—if not explanations—of social and psychological behaviors. Early on he used: Richardson's warfare model to understand ethos in the Balinese culture; Cannon's feedback models and von Neumann's theory of games to simulate schismogenesis; Ashby's models for understanding social system stabilities, Shannon's communication theory, and a variety of other system theory elements for learning behaviors. To unravel the prevailing paradoxes in experimental data of Pavlov, Maier, Hull and others, he mapped their observations, in information theory terms against the theory of logic types developed by Bertrand Russell (published in Russell and Whitehead's *Principia Mathematica*, 1913). He used Russell's theory to differentiate the logic types of learning (LI) and change (LII and LIII). Most visibly he used the central proposition of Russell's argument that the name of a class cannot be a member of that class; so the learning events of LII is the name of a set of alternatives for LI, similarly those of LIII name a schema for generating LII outcomes. This analogy has proved to be wonderfully evocative for a whole approach to learning and change theories, even though it appears that a hierarchical classification model, which Bateson describes (1972, p.287), appears to be too rigid both on logical and neurological grounds to explain the phenomena of change.

I begin the discussion of each of the four orders of learning quoting Bateson's definitions as reprinted in *Steps to an Ecology of Mind* (1972, p. 293) from a speech he delivered in 1964. He couched the learning in information theoretic terms correlating the experimental data with the model formulated according to the theory of types.

Zero Order

Learning Zero is *"specificity of response,* which—right or wrong—is not subject to correction." Its forms are mathematical and logical, as used in theoretical fields such as astrophysics and, ideally, in administrative law. Zero order programs are static, unerringly carrying out the specified deductive operations; they display no learning. In a paradox of logic and evolution, the zero order presents the most formal and sophisticated construction of the first four orders. Bateson writing as a system theorist defines a zero order system as one that has settled into equilibrium. Had he been an economist, he might have seen zero order knowledge as an input-output matrix that lacks any corrective features. Had he framed this model somewhat later than the 1964 paper on deutero-learning, he might have exemplified the zero order as computer programs.

First Order (LI)

LI is *"change in specificity of response* by correction of error of choices within a set of alternatives." The first order can provide a "revision of choice within an unchanged set of alternatives." That which is learned is how to select the most rewarding alternatives from an available set. Bateson typified LI as trial-and-error learning, habituation and conditioning following experimental work of Pavlov, Hull, and others. Morris Berman (1981), in his extensive comment on Bateson's model introduces a common language definition: "the simple solution to a specific problem."[3] This is the learning all living things acquired from experience; humans also get it indirectly from cognitized sources such as textbooks.

There are three important aspects that take the LI beyond the Zero level: *alternatives, temporality* and *evaluation.* They are functions of the three parts appearing in Figure 1: an actor who learns, a context that contains the correct answers, and a comparator that evaluates the degree of difference between the actor's output and the world context. The comparator, as presented in Figure 1, may be a person's own expectations, standards or some societal role like a teacher, supervisor or parent. This comparison requires the comparator to have a memory of what has happened in a prior period. The learning is achieved by noticing the differences of which Bateson writes, in a single quality in the simplest organism, a multi-quality difference in complex organizations. An actor shows LI with improved selection from a given set of alternatives, a context such as skill in welding metal as defined in manufacturing standards. His learning might come from recognizing that the color of hot metal is an indicator of its malleability. A LI may be built on an unlimited number of prior LIs, e.g., the first order learning in golf depends on a variety of an athlete's prior learning, at least starting muscle coordination, and cognitive action sequences, and evolving with trainings, conventions of the sport, social mores and many more. The many LI learnings are integrated into a composite 'golfer.' The identified learning about golf can arise in any one of the elements of a person's game. Such learning shows changes in the learner but not in the context. These learnings are permitted and organized by a variety of assumptions and propositions that are not readily accessible, yet which set the comparator's responses to events. Bateson calls these unarticulated determinants

---

3.   I quote this definitions and those of higher versions from Berman's (1981, p. 346) glossary.

"tacit," laying in what Carl Jung labels the "unconscious" and Jurgen Habermas calls the "lifeworld."

The outcomes of first order efforts are traditionally identified as *learning*, about a given context or environment. The actor has learned according to the rules of the "game" the comparator is umpiring. What we normally think of as change is achieved by changing the rules, selecting alternatives that were not in the given "deck." So, the second and higher orders of learning models are about creating new games, with new plays and objectives, inventing games of inventing games and so on. [4]

Second Order (LII)

LII is *"change in the process of Learning I, e.g.,* a corrective change in the set of alternatives from which choice is made." Morris Berman's version: "Progressive change in the rate of LI." Lars Qvortrup (2004) as well as Bateson viewed it as *reflective knowledge.* LII follows from reflecting on the self-constructed or externally given sets of alternatives. In terms of the cybernet, the selection process begins with a search among comparators (or its assumptions) and a confrontation with the paradoxes presented by the reflection on their variety. (Figure 2) The learning follows when one is able to reflect among approaches to a problem, to select among schema for resolving the situation. This ability is only present in the neural structure of mammals (and perhaps some birds) as Cotterill asserts.(1995)

LII begins with a search for assumptions of the schemata-in-use, reflecting on their appropriateness in the present situation, then identifies a new schema and selects an alternative favored by a reflective schema—in effect adopting a new cybernet where the action agent is the first cybernet.[5]It is a hierarchical arrangement, in which the reflective second cybernet redirects the first, which in turn selects the action. (Of course, if the first cybernet is also a mammal or human it may reflect on the second order's adapted criteria and *participate* in the choice of actions.

With LII a person or group reflects on the schema that it used to select alternatives in the LI schema and expanded their alternatives beyond those generated by the schema-in-use. A new schema is chosen that more adequately presents the issue. For example, on finding that a psychotherapeutic treatment was Third Order Learning (LIII) resolving a child's problems, those involved might reject the schema that the genesis was in the child's psyche. The therapist might adopt a new hypothesis that the family system is not working and thus look for new alternative schema that engage the family.

---

4. See McWhinney (2005) (in preparation) *Grammars of Engagement,* for examples of games in which the criteria are changed by the play itself.
5. More accurately, there have been innumerable learnings prior to the one identified in the LI event. Learning begins with the first difference and there are many more choices made before the organism comes to the level of articulation assumed in the logical typology.

Figure 2: A Second Order Cybernet

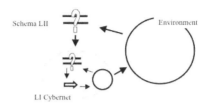

A cybernet in which the actor is also a cybernet, initially having only LI capabilities. The LII schema will utilize LI as sources of alternatives; the larger environment will include the LI cybernet and its environment (it becomes the context of the original contexts). The LII schema reflects on the LI cybernets performance and its assumptions, and modifies the basic cybernets to deal with environmental information more inclusively.

Twenty years earlier Bateson labeled the reflective approach *deutero-learning* as opposed to *proto-learning* that became LI in the typology. Argyris & Schön (1978), following Bateson, labeled a similar concept "double-loop learning": double implying two stages on the road to a choosing new schema: the first considers the schema-in-use; the second explores for a resolution in terms of a newly accepted schema. The second-order concept has become extremely popular as a formal expansion of Kurt Lewin's model (1936), which proposed the sequence of unfreezing, change, and refreezing. The second-order work revised the 'change' phase of Lewin's popular model, connecting it to other classic models of creativity, transformation and revolution.

Bateson and Berman viewed deutero-learning as a system-stabilizing phenomenon, whether for individuals or society. With persistent or dramatic reinforcement of proto-learning early in life, individuals adopt traits and characteristic behaviors. Both give as examples developing a life philosophy of instrumentality and traits such as passivity, self-aggrandizement, and a source of our beliefs about reality. (Berman, 1981, pp. 218-219). These learnings come to form a person's personality.[6] Similarly patterns of reinforcement can establish an organization and a culture's character and image. In both levels memory of the reinforcing occasions often becomes buried in the unconscious, perhaps structured into some genetic determining factors.

Not surprisingly, those who used double looping to carry out a LII program settled with the new more inclusive model, regressing to make refinements in the performance of the newly established model and propagating it. Return to LI protects themselves from the chaos of continual change. The users have opened their vision momentarily, recognized contradictions and opportunities, then reset their blinders to eliminate further cost of ambiguity and search.

---

6. I have proposed a quite different model of the way in which realities and traits are formed, but this is not the place to argue their relative usefulness. See for example, McWhinney (1995).

The distinction presented in the next section eliminates the typological difference between LII and LIII asserting that second order changes are not logically distinct from third order change processes. There are no learning processes that are unique to the second order. All reflective processes end in a changed world (LII) a stable eddy in of a stream of change (LIII) that involves further coupling among feedback loops in the immensely complicated motor, sensory, and evaluative functions of the mind/body physiology. LIII produces a continual chain of the contextual embedding, contexts within contexts within…

I begin an exposition of third-order learning and discuss how and why I refigure the learning processes into a continuum of increasing acceptance of change and of the paradoxes and enigmas that otherwise block one's understanding of and contact with the lifeworld.

Third Order (LIII)

LIII is "*A change in the process of LII*, e.g., a corrective change in the system of sets of alternatives from which a choice is made." Also, Bateson, Berman and others described it as "learning in the context of the context." Qvortrup, (2004) defines third order as knowledge about the preconditions of reflexive knowledge; he also called it an "event of knowledge."

Bateson's definition seems to be a logical extension of LII, yet he notes that

> something of this sort [LIII} does occur in psychotherapy, religious conversion, and in other sequences in which there is profound reorganization of character. Zen Buddhists, Occidental mystics, and some psychiatrists assert that these matters are entirely beyond the reach of language. (p.301)

Berman reinforces this psychological characterization: "An experience in which a person suddenly realizes the arbitrary nature of his or her own paradigm, or LII, and goes through a profound reorganization of personality as a result" and "identical to religious conversions of the archaic traditions." Schön (1987) gave a similar definition: reflection on reflection-in-action; stepping back and reflecting critically on both underlying assumptions and purposes and on the reflections themselves. Note that such a definition applies to LII but it calls for a stream of reflections on the qualities of our problem-solving efforts. Sometimes the stream flows linearly, but more commonly involuted in a web of schemata as George Lakoff has noted in several works (1987, 1999).

The idea of a third kind is widely used; some closely follow Bateson's work but many simply use the idea of a third to claim a higher level of change phenomena, thus adding diffuseness the interpretations of third order. However the diffuseness is in part due to the classification scheme that Bateson used, which I assert made a difference of type due to differences in temporality: LII lead to a stability, LIII to accepting continuous change. Every event in a world of LIII is a LII change; the person making those changes comes to know that events are but a temporary resting places.

Change and LIII

Learning and change are our daily companions, much of it characterizable as LI, but most humans are aware of the continually changing context and hypothesize models with which to adapt their reactions. Every hypothesis challenges some assumptions, and confronts one with paradoxes, often trivially, sometimes deeply. Depending on the depth of the inquiry, the challenge will deal with the given context or a more abstract consideration of the context of that context—the model of that type of models. The degree of abstraction determines the order as Bateson and others indicate. Rather, I see a continuum of inquiry and propose that is better identified in what one does after responding to the new context: with LII the actor settles into a new schema, ignoring new data and contradictions in the service of gaining stability; with LIII the actor continues to respond to awarenesses of assumptions that now renders a schema unjustified and paradoxes that interfere with resolution of issues. The continual confrontation toward core questions and assumptions forms the path of LIII.

I ground my restatement of the learning orders with a simple example, an industrial change effort I participated in many years ago. The occasion came in the work of a design team made up of industrial engineers, managers and some of the workers who would staff a new soap packaging plant.

At one session a conversation began like this:

"Why do production lines have to be straight?" a worker on the team inquired. The engineer replied, "Because the packages spill going round curves." "Have you ever tried with these packages?" "Not on this product." "Well …"

Over the next weeks the workers convinced the engineers to design a U-shaped line allowing a worker to stand in the middle and work two stages of packing the paper product. Folding the line was a small innovation, but one which turned out to be attractive to everyone's advantage.

An observer might have called this a deutero-learning, LII event, but let us look at it. Overtly or unconsciously the effort involved:

- Questions of purpose or value. The overt purpose was an economic design while achieving it; the participants gained a new sense of themselves as individuals and as a group and an awareness of some more encompassing purposes of their work.
- Exposure of assumptions. Engineers have the answers, workers do not know technical material; what is, is best—new ideas are not likely to work. These and other assumptions were clearly challenged.
- Imaging/simulation. Physical models were built to test the operations, 'going around the curves.' Workers imaged their ability to turn from a task on one side of the line to one on the other. These models were graphic metaphors.
- Contraries/contradictions. A long list of polarities: The engineers' technology versus the workers' practice; the engineers' education versus the workers' experience; the willingness of workers to do double the work without double

compensation. Facing these polar and other conditions led to a revision of everyone's long held beliefs.

- Ego withdrawal. Acceptance by the engineers that the workers had the better insight into the technology.
- Meditation. Stepping back from engagement to quiet the mind. In this phase of the effort the team did not do formal meditation. Later, the production workers started meditation as a group with the overt purpose to settle out (emotionally) as they gathered in the back room of a saloon to review their week's work.

We did not explore what it was that took place in the minds of the participants. All these methods, more or less consciously, were employed in the design of this menial task of putting soap in a box. However, there were three types of outcomes: most of the participants accepted the new design and they *refroze* it as Lewin suggested, returning to do LI learning to improve performance on the job. Some participants continued using these methods in their daily work and a very few left their employment to find situations in which to engage in perpetual exploration. How did the three groups differ?

The first group—and largest—continued on without challenging assumptions, settling into this work process that was more satisfying having made the LII change per Lewin's model of unfreeze-change-refreeze. Other occasions arose when they again challenged the status quo, but at about the same depth of risk to their jobs as well as their egos.

The second group became second-order change agents within the company or as private consultants or academics. They learned a technique for inducing LII changes. I quote a woman at a different plant who copied the methodology in her community: "They [young supervisors] are screwing up our work here, but you ought to see [how it works at] my church." where she had taken her learnings. Others went on to make this form of change their profession. Their work seldom confronted the contradictions or lifeworld assumptions of those recruited to the model of change.

A third group left on a path of search, looking for ways to deepen their inquiries into what I call LIII behavior. Those I knew found the search difficult and, in many instances socially dysfunctional, even schismogenic just as Bateson and Berman suggested. For those, the LIII path was a spiral; at moments rising with new insights giving one a sense of omnipotence; and later, slipping into the abyss of self-doubt and of the source of reality. Their practices never quite worked, their retreats to the spiritual context seldom resolved into a re-engagement with the practical world. The path to LIII seemed to them as difficult as the literature of transformation predicts, and seldom if ever was maintained.

The variety of methods used to achieve change can all be viewed as tools of creativity, all produce some degree of individual creation, some produce systemic change effecting families, organizations and communities. Some open individuals to new vistas, particularly meditations. Others challenge views of reality, time and causality. All the challenges take a person or group a step along a path to LIII. There is no set route yet many tales follow one of two common paths of transformation. Those that take the more rational interpretation of Bateson's LIII, e.g., Mason and Mitroff (1981) and Schön (1987) assume a linear path of continual exploring. The psychological interpretation describes the path as spiraling (McWhinney, 1997). Bateson indicates both routes use the same learning processes for building increasingly abstract context of contexts of contexts... However Bateson showed more concern for the psychological path leaving its definition ill-defined, even mysterious.

A common first step along the path comes with a successful change event such as illustrated above. Some begin with a change followed by another more confronting event that is overwhelming, calling for those involved to go deeper, confronting more established assumptions and more embedded paradoxes. The difficulties are received as personal failures as epic as Ulysses' or the Biblical Job's, and as challenging as that faced by Faust or that which overwhelmed Edgar Allen Poe. The disturbances can be social as in the fight against prejudices in the American South; they may also arise from issues of truth and faith as contributed to the acceptance of heliocentric theories in the 16th century.

The next stage is often into a liminal space, a retreat, a "return for a better start." This too is a stage in the classic tales of death and rebirth. There the liminal space is often in retreat from one's community: 40 days in the desert, or a stay in a sanctuary or sanitarium. Today it is more likely to be closely networked among supporters—co-students or a therapy group.

In a 1964 essay, Bateson identified a number of tools of change for the LIII path that would be employed in the retreat and in preparation for re-engagement:

- *Accepting contradictions.* In movement toward LIII an individual or a group identifies the contradictions of increasingly essential issues. Bateson quotes William Blake "Without contraries is no progression."(sic) Eventually one may deal with an issue of such as discrimination and eventually with the basic ontological polarities such as self-other, holism-atomism, and determinism-volunteerism (McWhinney, 1997), often going beyond resolving paradoxes to accept both poles as essential to articulation of an issue.
- *Learning the context of contexts of LI.* Transcending the comfort of stability—not settling on LII results. LI and LII behaviors are gradually overcome with accepting higher levels of contradiction and uncovering and challenging assumptions until one is no longer at peace with LII achievements or with the *lifeworld* of which Habermas writes. (1987, p. 298)
- *Letting go of one's* self. Becoming free of roles or the habits of personality, e.g., *dependency, judgmental* and *prideful.* For Bateson letting go frees one of personality traits, even one's concept of reality and causality.

I add to Bateson's list:

- *Imaging.* Using dreams, drawings, and autobiographic works to free individuals to engage with emotions and ideas not limited to words. And to gain awareness of constraints of language, particularly of the established grammar and vocabulary and of the rules of art, design, and style.

These are the tools of LIII but their use does not assure success. Most often one exits the liminal enclaves just to refreeze with another LII model. (McWhinney, 1997) Alternatively a person or culture stagnates, lacking commitment to engage with issues back in the "real" world. The resulting liminal wandering becomes a dismal schismogenic trap. William Blake prayed,

> May God us keep
> From Single visions & Newton's sleep.

Staying with LIII is not arriving at a place but following a path of continual questioning assumptions and values, accepting the consequences of holding polarities, and tolerating uncertainty. It is characterized as a spiraling path of action, withdrawal and return, of increasing creativity, humility, and good will. And along the way Bateson suggests one would become increasingly an outsider from normal society, at times with great clarity and other times with distraught, and schismogenic. Bateson characterizes one who operates with third order perception as able:

> "To see the world in a grain of sand" — William Blake

There is no final achievement, no stability no firm boundaries, no limits in discourse. So rather than thinking of LIII producing an increase in knowledge, I propose that the continuous expansion of learning about… and reflecting about…, be organized as meta- to learning, better as advanced levels of engagement, a *meta-praxis*. (McWhinney, 1997). *Praxis* refers to the work of LI and LII. Meta-praxis does not depend on a particular logic of inclusion or a particular concept of causality or reality but on the ability to stay present.

Summary

The major thesis of this paper is to suggest that LII and LIII are phases of a change processes; one being a stopping place, the other of fluid continuance. LII is achieved in our every day change efforts — with continuing drift among assumptions, purposes and values. LIII is not an achievement rather a transcendence of fixity of character and social norms. Bateson's modeling of LIII as type above LII is applicable to the path of hierarchical ascendance achieved by iteratively embedding contexts within contexts. It is a model of ideal behavior, however it is rarely followed. The vast majority of human choices are made in the labyrinthine structure of coupled feedback loops guided more by the events in one's life than the logician's syllogisms The neuro-physiological model, which Cotterill displays, appears to better explain most people's and cultures' paths of learning.

The Chinese farmer Tan to whom the White Horse came seems to have progressed far along a path of LIII. He demonstrated a disconnection from causality and showed no belief that events necessarily follow from those that precede; he accepts contradictions as the nature of life; and displays a freedom from ego involvement. The tale suggests he stays in this mode irrespective of events in his life. Perhaps he is able to stay engaged without being diverted from his course by results.

> With his wife and son abed, Tan returned to the field to fill in the cavity that his wife had broke open. As he probed the hole he saw that it was a tomb; he found that it held a jeweled casket and a pot of gold coins. The neighbors heard of his find and again acclaimed his good fortune. Tan waved acknowledgment and returned to hoe in his field…

References

Argyris, C. & Schön, D. (1978). *Organizational learning: A theory of action perspective*. Reading, MA: Addison-Wesley.

Bateson, G. (1972). *Steps to an ecology of mind*. New York: Ballantine Books

Berman, M. (1981). *The re-enchantment of the world*. Ithaca, NY: Cornell University Press

Cotterill, R. M. J. (1995). On the unity of conscious experience. *Journal of Consciousness Studies, 2*, 290-312

Cotterill, R. M. J. (2001). Cooperation of the basal ganglia, cerebellum, sensory cerebrum and hippocampus: Possible implications for cognition, consciousness, intelligence and creativity. *Progress in Neurobiology, 64I* (May), 1-33.

Habermas, J. (1982). *The philosophical discourse of modernity: Twelve lectures*. Cambridge, MA: The MIT Press.

Lewin K. (1936). *Principles of topological psychology*. New York: McGraw-Hill.

Lakoff, G. (1987). *Women, fire and dangerous things: What categories reveal about the mind*. Chicago: University of Chicago Press.

Lakoff, G. & Johnson, M. (1999). *Philosophy in the flesh: The embodied mind and its challenge to western thought*. New York: Basic Books.

Libet, B. (1985). Unconscious cerebral initiative and the role of conscious will in voluntary action. *Behavioral and Brain Sciences, 8*, 529-539.

Mason, R. & Mitroff, I. (1981). *Challenging strategic planning assumptions*. New York: John Wiley.

McWhinney, W. (1995). The matter of Einstein square dancing with Magritte. *Cybernetics & Human Knowing, 3* (3), 3-23

McWhinney, W. (1997). *Paths of change: Strategic choices for organizations and society*. Newbury Park, CA: Sage Publications.

Qvortrup, L., (2004). The Third space of knowledge, leadership, and creativity. Paper presented at the Conference on Leadership, and Creativity, Bramstrup, Denmark, June 2004.

Schön, D. (1987). *The reflective practitioner: How professionals think in action*. San Francisco: Jossey-Bass.

Whitehead, A. N. & Russell, B. (1913). *Principia Mathematica* (2nd ed.). Cambridge: Cambridge University Press.

Cybernetics And Human Knowing. Vol. 12, nos. 1-2, pp. 36-49

Exercising Frame Flexibility

Frederick Steier[1]

Two of Gregory Bateson's key ideas, systemic flexibility and framing, are woven together to provide a vehicle for exploring the interplay of learning and play at a science center. Questions of content and relationship aspects of frames, and the importance of mutability of frames are developed. Against a backdrop of balancing stability and change, systemic processes for exercising frame flexibility are offered. These serve to both offer implications for the importance of designing for engagement, as well as extending Bateson's ideas of frame and flexibility that served as the starting points.

In Mind and Nature, Bateson stresses the importance of what he calls "the case of binocular vision." (Bateson, 1979). What I try to do in this paper is to invite the reader to consider what happens when we take two of Bateson's most powerful ideas—those of *frame* and *flexibility* and put them together. Rather than just doing this in the abstract, I would like to do this through the lens of ongoing work at a science center that is asking questions of understanding its own activities that invite the interdependence of these two powerful ideas. In cybernetic fashion, I would also like to consider what looking at these ideas through the lens of my own engagement at the science center might itself mean for extending these ideas. So, in effect, giving something back to the ecology of ideas we might call Gregory Bateson and his legacy.

To do this, it is important to realize that the themes of this paper are both relational (including my relationship with you, the reader) as well as content orienting. And it also means that the paper unfolds as a kind of oscillation between ideas and practice, certainly no linear path. At the same time, the paper is personal, as my own assumptions are revealed and played with in the course of making this mutual connection.

Gregory Bateson reads Calvin and Hobbes

One of our favorite family games is to imagine a famous person, a friend, or a fictitious hero, reading what we are reading at that moment. What would she think? With whom would he identify? So it was when reading Bill Watterson's wonderful comic strip, Calvin and Hobbes, which we chose to look at through Gregory Bateson's eyes. Within the creative world of Calvin and Hobbes, which particular strip or sequence would Bateson enjoy the most? Calvin is a young boy and Hobbes his toy stuffed-animal tiger playmate, who comes alive for Calvin when they are alone together, but reverts to inanimate status in the presence of others. Their interaction in

---

1. Department of Communication, University of South Florida. Email: fsteier@shell.cas.usf.edu

situations that involve family, school, friendship and modern life affords reflection on many deep rooted assumptions about learning, relationship and play.

At first we thought of any of those sequences involving "Calvinball," that delightful cybernetic game that Calvin and Hobbes play, where the rules of the game keep changing, and the only "real" rule is that there are no "real" rules beyond playing in the moment. It is in a very real sense a second order game about the ways that we construct rules and games that are rule-driven. Calvinball, as practiced by Calvin and Hobbes, is a total immersion into fun and play, and invites comparison with the otters Bateson so enjoyed observing.

But then perhaps it is another strip or sequence that might be even more attractive to Bateson, one produced in Attack of the Deranged Mutant Killer Monster Snow Goons (Watterson, 1992).

Just previous to this sequence of three strips, we find Calvin seated at the dinner table with his mother and father, having a conversation about dinner conversations. Calvin wants to be excused from the table to watch television, while his parents want to retain the sacredness of the dinnertime ritual. "Calvin, dinner is the one time during the day that we set aside to be together and talk. There's more to being a family than just living in the same house. We need to interact once in a while," observes Calvin's father. Unfortunately, a phone call for Calvin's mother interrupts the conversation, and the irony is not lost on Calvin. This is followed by:

Calvin (to Hobbes, who is relaxing on the sofa): c'mon Hobbes, we have to go outside.
Hobbes: We have to?
Calvin: Yeah, dad won't let me watch tv. He says it's summer, it's light late, and I should go run around instead of sitting in front of the tube. Can you believe it? What a dictator!
Hobbes: How cruel it is to be forced to play.
Calvin: I'll show him. I refuse to have fun.

Calvin and Hobbes now crouched outside in a starting position for a race.
Calvin: OK, next we'll race to that tree over there.
Hobbes: This race will determine the championship of the universe.
Calvin: Oh…wait. How long have we been out here?
Hobbes: I dunno. An hour maybe.
Calvin: Really? Geez, where does the time go? Hang on, I'll be right back.
Calvin: (runs back to house, then, speaking to dad from outside the house through an open window): I'M NOT HAVING FUN!

Dad (walking outside): It's getting dark, Calvin. Time to come in and go to bed!
Calvin: But Hobbes and I were catching fireflies. Can't we stay out a little longer?
Dad: Ha! First you didn't want to go out, and now you don't want to come in!
Dad (continuing): See, by not watching TV, you had more fun, and now you'll have memories of something real you DID, instead of something fake you just watched.

Calvin: (later, in bed with Hobbes): Nothing spoils fun like finding out it builds character.

What does the frame, so alive in this comic strip, of "it builds character," do? Of course, we cannot isolate this question from the history of interactions of Calvin and Hobbes with Calvin's father and mother, and the contingencies of their relationship that allows repeated sequences of interaction to accrue meaning over time. In this case, "it builds character" is a repeated theme that allows for a potential reframing of often unfortunate events (such as being subjected to storms while camping out). In that sense, in Calvin's family, character building is not unrelated to learning lessons. But another lens into their world is that of the interplay of content and relationship aspects of messages, or, in Bateson's (1968) earlier terms, the report and the command aspects of messages. For Calvin, the overriding relational message here might be "Being father means I help you best by reminding you of a valuable life lesson." It is one Calvin hears as his father's attempt to legislate meaning—which is what makes Calvin's remark to his father, of "I'm NOT having fun" all the more poignant, as an expression of autonomy and self-creation of meaning in a relationship. The sequence then becomes a charming and all-too-real example of the importance of understanding the command or relationship aspect of our own messages in the eyes of others— relationship aspects we, as speakers in a relationship, are often unaware of. And beyond this, it also affords reflection about how we construct frames, for ourselves, for others, and for our relationships with others.

But enough, already—perhaps the Calvin in you, the reader, is thinking: "What is that Steier doing—he is ruining a good story by telling us what it should mean to us, creating a lesson about content and relationship, and contingencies of relationship, and by so doing destroying the fun of the Calvin and Hobbes example. He is being father to the Calvin in us, and a rather dogmatic father at that" And you, reader, could be right.

At the same time, we should consider what the message: it builds character (for you) does, its possibilities and its constraints, as it is both constraining and enabling.

This question turns out to be important to me as I engage in my role as a scientist-in-residence at the Museum of Science and Industry (MOSI), in Tampa, Florida. This role is itself interesting as the "science" that I bring to the space is that of cybernetics and systems perspectives, certainly not traditional sciences the way that most educational institutions define scientific fields. MOSI would like to be understood as a community learning institution, while at the same time, as an organization, it is interested in questions of exactly what that means—both to those who work there, as well as to those who visit. Asking about, and holding open the meaning of its own image is key since this ambiguity also has implications for how those involved think about activities that take place within—activities such as "doing" science and learning, but also exploration and play.

Yet, if we are serious about MOSI as a community learning institution, how do we design the space there for Calvin (and Hobbes)? And Calvin's family?

Designs for learning and play at a science center

As noted at the outset, this paper has a joint intent—seeing what Bateson's work might mean to design and experience at a science center, while at the same time, exploring what bringing Bateson to MOSI does for offering new possibilities for Bateson's work. In other words, can we learn more about Bateson's work by understanding how it informs (and is then informed by) its use in a place that might be at the intersection of learning and play? In this way, we can consider the science center as both a space and occasion for learning about ideas-in-use. This encourages certain systemic questions, such as:

How does an organization or an institution that is about learning, entertainment and science, but also a community center, and perhaps even a "third place"—one of those increasingly rare public places for interaction that is neither work nor home (Oldenburg, 1999), balance stability and change in a turbulent environment? How does a community institution learn about its own learning through questions posed by visitors? How does a community institution come to appreciate the frames it affords visitors to create a context for their learning (or fun)—frames that that same institution may not be aware of affording? And how might these questions be linked in an ongoing program of "design" of learning and play opportunities, or even learning conversations that would explore learning at multiple intersecting levels? And most importantly, are there tensions between possibilities for design for learning, and design for play (and if so, where and when are these tensions?).

These are questions that I, with my colleagues at MOSI, have come to explore. They have come about as embedded in a wonderfully recursive loop at a science center where playing with labyrinths of infinities, loops within loops, within loops, is not seen as a descent into hell, but as fun, and as an opportunity for learning at multiple levels. These questions can be seen as strongly connected to Bateson's work, as it, as a whole, has so radically altered how I see and understand my world of patterns. What was it exactly about Bateson's work that was feeding my questions, and those of my colleagues—as we might realize—a concept dear to Margaret Mead's heart—"the significance of the questions that we ask" (Mead, 1975). What do our questions "do" to our situations at hand? How might we be making use of Bateson's ideas—not just as a collection of separate concepts, but as a system of interrelated ideas (or was it playthings?)—an ecology of ideas (Vickers, 1968). And though we felt that we might learn a lot about how our own assumptions guide our understanding of everyday life at the science center, we also felt that we might use Bateson's ideas to enhance the programs whose practice informed our inquiry. So, perhaps our program was one of actionable knowledge generation?

Some further context setting: the Museum of Science and Industry (MOSI) and related inquiry

Readers of *Cybernetics and Human Knowing* may be familiar with MOSI. It has been described in some detail, in other work, as a springboard for exploring questions related to deeply systemic issues. For example, MOSI was at the heart of a piece written with the president of the organization, Wit Ostrenko, entitled "Taking cybernetics seriously at a science center: Reflection-in-interaction and second order organizational learning" (Steier & Ostrenko, 2000). This was in a special issue in memory of and devoted to extensions of the work of Don Schön. And it surfaced again in a special issue dedicated to the work of Heinz von Foerster, entitled "Ethics and Aesthetics of observing frames" (Steier & Jorgenson, 2003). For the reader who might be thinking "oh no, not another MOSI article," the intent is not to exploit the science center (or bore the reader with redundancies) but to build on questions that have, through our previous inquiry, become part of everyday life at MOSI through ongoing cybernetic approaches.

MOSI is one of those places that is a museum in the public sense of the word, but also trying to be a "non-museum" in the sense that the kinds of space into which visitors are invited is decidedly not one of hands-off viewing of glass-enclosed valued artifacts. Rather it is a place that invites active learning (or is it active fun?) by hands-on possibilities. (As Wit Ostrenko noted, "We call it MOSI because we are not really a museum," "We want to be more than that—it's how we change people's lives by making science "real" [Steier & Ostrenko, 2000]). An important feature of MOSI is that there are, on the floor moving from exhibit to exhibit, staff who are called interactors. The choice of the term interactors is significant insofar as at one time they were called explainers; however, to mark the shift from answering questions to creating possibilities for inquiry or even learning about the scientific learning process itself, the shift from "explainer" to "interactor" was enacted. This shift also has significance in regard to the design of exhibits at MOSI, since, to a large extent, the interactors are indeed part of the exhibits, and their behavior and interaction with guests part of the visitor experience. Thus our earlier question of "designing for Calvin and Hobbes" needs to take the interactors into account.

In "Taking cybernetics seriously" we explored how the development of an action research program rooted in second order organizational learning might unfold at a science center. This allowed for an ongoing program of (1) understanding precisely what diverse constellations of visitors (grandparents/grandchildren; friends, parents and children, school groups, individuals, etc.) did at the science center (how did visitors construct their experience?), (2) how might we translate that understanding into programs of action, allowing interactors to be more dialogic (within the frame of the interactor as "amateur"—as lover of diverse worlds), (3) to how, in general, to design for learning conversations and surprise, to (4) how to allow a science center and its community to be a forum for second order organizational learning, and, in essence, community learning. At the heart of this was a rethinking of Schön's (1983, Schön & Rein, 1994) notion of reflection-in-action to be more of a "reflection-in-interaction," where the ability to change one's action to make a difference in the situation-at-hand is done in concert with others who are simultaneously doing the "same" thing. In "Ethics and Aesthetics," we used Heinz von Foerster's elegant dual principles of his ethical and aesthetic imperatives [act so as to always increase the number of choices, and, if you want to learn how to see learn how to act] to inform ethnographic observations of family interactions at a particular exhibit—the Bernoulli blowers, a way of playing with aerodynamics. We used these imperatives to explore the multiple senses of observing frames. That is, we became concerned with what frames were made use of to allow for interpretation of observed behavior and interaction (which may have included learning, having fun, passing the time together, testing the exhibit, testing one's parents, doing "family," etc.). Yet at the same time, in deeply second order fashion, we also became concerned with the frames we created for our own observing process—frames for HOW WE do our observing—questions that invite exploration into our own relationship to the "what" we are claiming to observe.

So are we observing as caring parents looking for insights into our own family dynamics, or as supposedly detached spectators? Or from some frame that combines non-evaluative observation with integration into our own lives, but comes from questions we ask of ourselves?

Emergent themes

In the fashion of action research, and taking seriously issues of recursion, work from these earlier papers has become part of the ongoing second order learning and playing process at MOSI. What questions, as well as concern for assumptions embedded in underlying threads has this work unconcealed—not only from the theory at stake here, but also from the praxis? In other words—what issues emerged, triggered by the earlier work, that invite further cybernetic inquiry?

Certainly it was recognized that a key lies in Bateson's idea of frame itself. Understood as frames for understanding, do "education" or "learning" and "entertainment" or "play" invite different worlds? This is not just a fanciful question, as MOSI's geographical setting makes it all the more interesting. Orlando, Florida, home of Disneyland, is but one hour away, and visitors may be coming to MOSI having just visiting that scene that serves as a powerful model for the world of entertainment. At the same time, the University of South Florida is directly across the street, with a bridge being built over the eight lane highway that separates the two. So frames of entertainment and education loom large as possible contexts for visitor experience. Yet, from another perspective, we see emergent questions of adaptation and flexibility. How mutable are the frames we create, and how do we adjust them as we learn to recognize what our observing frames "do" to situations, especially where that doing involves the worlds of our others. This question also is revealed in current debates, especially prominent in the United States, of the limits and values around science and science education (including value systems embedded in questions of adaptation itself).

What if we bring together ideas of frames with ideas of flexibility—not just in the sense of reframing, but in the sense of frames themselves as part of a system of relationships, and as part of an evolutionary process. If we go back to our main question here of designing for Calvin and Hobbes, what resources do these issues bring to our inquiry?

To do this, let's play with the idea of frame through the lens of the frames introduced in both the Calvin and Hobbes, and the MOSI stories from a possible point of view.

The message: This is character building, The message: This is learning, (and frames for frames).

At first glance this seems a misreading of Bateson's seminal work on "The message: This is play" (Bateson, 1956, 1972a). And yet maybe it is not. Of course, at one level, we learn about how offering a message within the context of "play" creates a situation where the meaning of what is said or done is not that which the message would ordinarily convey. So a nip on the neck becomes an indication of a playful gesture, rather than an act of aggression. Indeed, as Bateson notes (1972a, p. 180), "this is play" becomes, "the actions in which we now engage do not denote the actions for which they stand would denote." So of course at a deep level, Bateson's theory of fantasy and play is about play itself. And for a science center interested in inviting visitors to have fun — to play with the exhibits — there is much to be learned here. And in that sense, the message: this is character building, or this is learning, would not fit as an entailment of this idea very well.

Yet, at the same time, "The message: This is play" is also about the communication processes involved in rendering the above possible in a relationship — the metacommunicative process whereby a frame gets offered and heard for sense-making of any communicative behavior. How does a sign become a signal and how might it, as signal, become an invitation to a frame? So important is this notion that, for many, "the message: this is play" becomes a metaphor for, or perhaps IS an invocation of metacommunication, and the very idea of frame. How do we jointly construct what conversation we are in? So *the message* is clearly operating at two levels simultaneously, each informing the other, each offering cues for the other, as the status of those cues as *cues* emerges in a recursive process.

It is interesting to go back to the Macy Conferences on group processes — specifically the 1955 conference (Schaffner, 1956) where Bateson presented "The Message: This is play." It is a joy to read to the conversation (or is it a dialogue?) between the participants in response to Bateson's ideas. Of course, there are many understandings possible for what is going on, but one possible reading of the process is how Bateson keeps trying to shift levels, to get his colleagues to see that he is talking about the framing process itself, not just about what constitutes play — important and as interesting as the latter topic might be. Yet, Bateson's colleagues often shift the topic back to that of how we might distinguish play (and related ideas) from non-play, for example — is a given activity play? or not? — and to the inherent and necessary ambiguities of the idea of play. Through this conversation, it is possible also to get a real sense of Bateson's struggle with how to talk about what he is trying to say, which later shows up in his choice of the concrete notion of *frame* over the related, but more abstract, and logic-based, notion of class. Frames connote something more pliant and mutable—more flexible and emergent, while *class* can imply more rigidity and structure. Yet, ironically, could it be that Bateson in interaction with his colleagues, had a hard time sustaining the conversation at the level of what *the message: this is play* stood for as a signal about joint messaging processes, rather than only about play.

The Macy Conference dialogue about play can be seen as illustrating, not unlike Calvin and Hobbes, joint improvisation about both content and relationship—how we come to appreciate when we are (and are not) in the same conversation. Was Bateson heard as "presenting a paper" with ideas well thought out in a systematic program of inquiry—or was he heard as inviting others into joint exploration into a world of ideas not necessarily fully thought through as a complete system, but in the process of forming. Have you ever tried to do the latter at an academic conference? So, it is also about how we go about sustaining that ongoing "joint conversation" at the same we realize that we may not be. But it is also about the relational valence of messages, when offerings become heard as a speech act of a command—here a command for how to make meaning of experience.

So, we wonder, what does the message *This is learning* or the message *This is character building* do for frame creation, whether in MOSI, school, home or in the playground. Can the message be offered by an institution, or an exhibit, in a way that affords learning OR character building at the same it invites very real possibilities for play. And yet, could the articulation of the message, whether uttered or implied by subtle behavioral or textual cues, embedded in a particular history of interactions, negate its own possibility, for at least some? Could this negation be so whether the message is uttered, or implied by subtle behavioral or textual cues, or as part of a designed feature of an exhibit or gallery?

Don Norman, the philosopher of design, recently gave a commencement address to students at Northwestern University (Norman, 2001), on the future of education, with particular attention to lessons learned from video games and museum exhibits. He noted how museums (and here he seems to be focusing on more interactive museums, such as MOSI) and video games make use of similar themes, with the themes being rooted in: "meaningful activities, learning that takes place invisibly, not as the objective, but naturally, effectively." "Participants don't think of themselves as interacting with technology, they think they are doing something interesting…they exploit social interaction and cooperation. The result is intense concentration, true learning, with people anxious to back back and do it again." He concludes: "people learn many things, if only they care about the topic. People are hungry for learning, as long as it isn't called education" (Norman, 2001, p. 5).

There are lessons to be learned from Norman's lessons learned, particularly about issues of framing possibilities for learning, fun, and perhaps even character building. Of course, at a content level, it is worth thinking about in terms vital to the questions we are asking with MOSI—but at the relational level, it encourages us to think about our own framing activities—and how a message heard could be one of relational control. And it would be a relational control that negates the possibilities that the desired frame might invite, while at the same time being heard as offering a rigid setting. Recognition that frames can be relational as well as content-orienting is critical. But Norman indicates a design for engagement with playthings coupled with engagement with ideas.

Consideration of the above dilemma opens up for question our very frame-creating resources. Do we insist on one frame (as a frame monopoly) for the behavior of our "others"—if this were even possible? What are our resources for enacting alternative frames—and the consequences for how we understand what others are doing, whether in designed environments, or natural environments?

It is possible to link these questions to Bateson's notions of adaptation and flexibility.

Flexibility

Interestingly, among different meanings of the word play we can also find the notion of flexibility. Then, how much "play" is there within a given frame? How much play is there between our frames? These questions are linked to the much larger issue, central to much of Bateson's work, of how to balance stability and change in systems. Here we might think about how to balance stability and change in thinking about the content and relationship aspects of offered frames.

Bateson linked questions of adaptation, not only in issues of somatic change, but also in social settings such as urban planning (Bateson, 1972b), to issues of flexibility. Consistent with holding to a focus on a whole circuit of organism plus environment, Bateson's *adaptation* can be understood as more of an adaptation WITH, as a co-evolution, rather than simply an adaptation TO. He, following Ashby (1952), recognized that for a system to adjust to new circumstances, it had to have an available store of uncommitted variation to allow for future change. Systems that might fit in one environment but were too rigid, would not be able to make any adjustment if that environment changed. Flexibility then becomes a key property for systems in order to balance change with stability.

There are several interrelated issues when thinking about flexibility, and they appear, in the larger ecological sense, as themes throughout Bateson's work.

For example, flexibility must be understood as a property of a system, and as such, is concerned with relationships. To be flexible, a system must retain (or even increase) its variety of potential responses. Yet at the same time, as Bateson noted, increasing variety in one domain can lead to decreasing variety, as a compensation, in another related domain. In short, there is an economics of flexibility (Bateson, 1972b, 1991). Within this economics of flexibility, we need consider fully what are the consequences of related increased and decreased flexibilities.

At the same time, building on an economics of flexibility, there is also the question of how we in the course of our everyday lives, need recognize the value of habit. We don't need, or even want, to repeat the same process of selection among alternatives, when that selection process itself is not needed. Of course, recognition of when habit works, and when to question it, is also a mark of successful mutual adaptation. Lest we rely on habit too strongly without question, we run the risk, as Bateson repeatedly noted of addiction to obsolescent forms. Building on this last point, merely having the options, the available variety, is not enough. We need to balance an appreciation of habit formation with an understanding that we need to exercise our flexible options, trying them out from time to time, lest we lose them as possibilities- much like exercising a muscle whose use we may need at some later point, rather than allowing it to atrophy.

What we have here is a vast network of interrelated issues connected through a systemic concern for flexibility. We need appreciate these interrelationships in order to link back to our issues of mutability of frames.

Frame Flexibility

As noted any social system needs to have a "safety net" to allow for trying (playing with) the variations, to create possibilities for learning. This safety net is not in the variations themselves, but in the larger system/environment, and is also a property of that entire system. The larger system's culture must appreciate learning by "getting it wrong" (Bamberger & Ziporyn, 1992) and even encourage possibilities in this direction, while at the same time ensuring that the safety net is there. Successful adaptation allows for a linkage of flexibility to learning.

One of the dangers that Bateson was well aware of was how we often, in the course of a supposedly successful adaptation, lose needed variety. He notes how critical it is to not lose variety when adapting to new circumstances, realizing how it is that many adaptations, especially those seen as "successful" in one domain or context, lose the variety necessary for future adaptations. Organisms or organizations thus become increasingly rigid in the face of seemingly successful change—but sooner or later find themselves in an environment where the way of being that might now be needed to allow for fit has been lost. Carried to an extreme, a system's continual eating up of variety as it adjusts can lead to, at some point, no options remaining other than to continue doing what is being done—and any future environmental change will lead to loss of survival for that system. Thus, a key issue with regard to flexibility is how to use our available variation in a way that does not lose potential for future change (here we might recall von Foerster's (1973) ethical imperative of acting so as to increase the number of choices).

Yet again, as Bateson repeatedly pointed out, and was noted above, increase of flexibility in one domain can also be linked to loss of flexibility in another. Indeed, in this volume, we see how, as Thomas Hylland Eriksen so neatly points out, new information and communication technologies afford possibilities of being at work while we are at home (an increase of flexibility of space). But at the same time, our way of adjusting to this heightened state of spatial flexibility has led to a decrease of flexibility in time (we are, alas, always at work, as Eriksen so neatly expresses in his "Tyranny of the Moment" (2001), in a plea for "slow time").

If we extend our ideas of flexibility to that of our frame enactments, we might wonder how increasing our variety of frames might show up as a loss in another domain. And this would be a good question. But, at the same time, we need to be careful about our frame for asking. Often this is done as though there were a cause and effect relationship between the increase in flexibility in one domain and a logical decrease in flexibility in another. We need be aware of how it is WE who create a compensation, in the sense of Maturana and Varela (1987), to the perturbation of that change—in a relationship. It will often, in retrospect, appear as an unintended consequence (we don't want to always be at work—at least most of us). Note that recognizing our involvement in the responsive nature of the relationship here only strengthens Eriksen's point.

Moving to thinking about the mutability of frames, we recognize the need for increasing variety in the domain of our frame enactment, which can lead to loss of variety in another domain (although not necessarily cause it). At the same time, we need recognize how ignoring the mutability of frames can allow a kind of frame dogma can creep in. We need to continue to exercise what might be called our "frame flexibility," trying out alternative frames whenever possible—but also creating systemic conditions that allow for that kind of play. Yet we also need to balance our exercise with knowing when a habitual frame will work, while at the same time not allowing that habitual frame to become dogma. Often it is not the originators of new, alternative frames, that adhere to their constructions in unbending ways, but those who see promise in their enactment, but lose the process that produced them. Tom Robbins, in *Still Life with Woodpecker*, a wonderfully systemic novel, puts it nicely:

> The problem starts at the secondary level, not with the originator or developer of the idea but with the people who are attracted by it, who adopt it, who cling to it until their last nail breaks, and who invariably lack the overview, flexibility, imagination, and, most importantly, sense of humor, to maintain it in the spirit in which it was hatched. Ideas are made by masters, dogma by disciples...

> There is a particularly unattractive and discouragingly common affliction called tunnel vision, which, for all the misery it causes, ought to top the job list at the World Health Organization. Tunnel vision is a disease in which perception is restricted by ignorance and distorted by vested interest. Tunnel vision is caused by an optic fungus that multiplies when the brain is less energetic than the ego. It is complicated by exposure to politics. When a good idea is run through the filters and compressors of ordinary tunnel vision, it not only comes out reduced in scale and value but in its new dogmatic configuration produces effects the opposite of those for which it originally was intended. (Robbins, 1980, pp. 85-86)

Of course, ideas are not necessarily frames (although they can operate in that way), but the process described is similar.

Exercising frame flexibility

In an example of how a clever adaptation has shown up as a decrease in variety, at least in the experience of some, we might consider a university situation. In the face of increased enrollments and insufficient space for large classes, universities have moved classes to spaces not designed for teaching. One solution was to realize that the theaters in the local mall were not used during the day and those movie theaters could be used as classrooms. Students could go to the theater at the mall for their classes (and even buy popcorn on the way in). It seems like a solution where both the mall owners and the universities gain. Yet in terms of issues of frames, the classroom in the mall has become a scene of performance—which in itself might not be a bad thing. Indeed, understanding teaching and learning (and studenting) as cultural performance affords many possibilities that traditional models may not allow. Yet, what seems to be happening is that the kind of performance expected, from a student, is that which invites passive spectatorship on the part of the learner who demands to be entertained. I am not reporting the result of any designed study here, but self-reports of colleagues' experiences. A question is one of the loss of the active student learner as an adaptation to the "malling" (or is it mauling?) of learning. We might look at the use of power point in a similar way—as a loss of the ability to see the *in-between*. Has our adaptation to one "successful" mode of teaching and learning found ourselves addicted to that new adaptation. Are there ways of trying different frames for learning and performing at the mall? In the classroom? In the science center? At the same time, it is important for us to think about the cues that are observed by all in a designed learning environment, cues that offer possibilities for frame-creating for learning of which we may be unaware. So here a distinction, perhaps, between frames for entertainment (passive) and frames for play (active) may be appreciated. Yet am I beginning to sound a bit like Calvin's father?

At MOSI, the tension between enacting frames of entertainment, play and learning shows up actively in the design process. It is important to understand the exhibit galleries as made up of, not only the designed spaces, but as a conversation between the interactors, the designers, the material AND the visitors, as well as the spaces in-between.

In our overall program of learning about our own learning process, and playing with our own play, how might ideas of exercising frame flexibility play out here? How might we think about this in designing for Calvin and Hobbes? Of course, at the heart of our design question is an understanding of how we observe the interactions taking place in the galleries in order to think about future design issues—including that of the frames that visitors enact.

Many visitors to MOSI appear in diverse family constellations, including grandparent/grandchildren groups. Bringing Calvin and Hobbes into MOSI has allowed for an understanding the family dynamics of learning and playing in this public space. Is the interactor offering glimpses into Florida's ecosystem "explaining," "entertaining" or possibly, without realizing it, "taking sides in a family argument"?

What manner of clinical sensitivity might be required? We have invited family therapists to work with our interactors and designers to help work with issues of (inter-generational) family conversations and to help exercise that needed flexibility of frame construction (and even whether, back to the above, whether frame is the right word here). How would we afford different frames for learning and play for Calvin's family?

Bringing the intersection of frame construction and enactment to that of flexibility through the lens of MOSI also invites other hard questions?

What if Gregory Bateson is playing the role of Calvin? Is he inviting us to focus on relational frames that will alter the content from one of listening to facts to affording joy? How do we listen for different frames at the relational level—and how does that affect our way of thinking about the entire design process. Perhaps a clue is to think about, as suggested by Don Norman's work, above, design for engagement—engagement with ideas, engagement with tools, and even engagement with frames for learning AND play (and even character building).

Of course, design for engagement could well involve creating possibilities, even encouraging possibilities for learning by getting it wrong. Suggestions of What if?—try this—oops—well try this, oops, what is going on here? that's weird—hey, this is fun! (I'm NOT having fun—well, ok). Second order learning without calling attention to it as a legislated frame.

Perhaps at the heart of a research and design program linked to exercising frame flexibility might be a rethinking of what we think of that difference that makes a difference, that we call information. Here we mean information not only of content within a frame, but information about what might be guiding the choice and enactment of a particular frame for a visitor. For example, in many science centers, there is the accompanying text, often next to the exhibit, often explaining the underlying principles. What manner of relationship does that text invite for the visitor with the exhibit as a whole? Does the text override the invitation to play to become one of learning facts, rather than learning to learn about being curious? (Steier, 2003). What are the other cues about enacted frames—whether the frames are ones of learning, play, edutainment (yes, that is a word now) that may be invisible in our own seeing, silences in our own listening? We have played with the idea of meaningful noise (Keeney (1983), Steier and Ostrenko (2000)) as a way of thinking about how we construct information -and of course this includes me thinking about my own worlds with others.

I'll try to bring Calvin, Hobbes and Gregory Bateson to my observing at MOSI.

References

Ashby, W. R. (1952). *Design for a brain*. London: Chapman and Hall.
Bamberger, J. and Ziporyn, E. (1992). Getting it wrong. *Ethnomusicology and Music Cognition, 3,* 22-56.
Bateson, G. (1956). The message "This is play." In Schaffner, B. (Ed.) *Group processes: Transactions of the second conference, October 9, 10, 11, and 12, 1955*(pp. 145-242). New York: The Josiah Macy, Jr. Foundation.

Bateson, G. (1968). Information and codification: A philosophical approach. In J. Ruesch & G. Bateson (Eds.), *Communication: The social matrix of psychiatry* (pp. 168-211). New York: W. W. Norton. (originally published in 1951)

Bateson, G. (1972a). A theory of play and fantasy. In *Steps to an ecology of mind* (pp. 177-193). New York: Ballantine Books.

Bateson, G. (1972b). Ecology and flexibility in urban civilization. In *Steps to an ecology of mind* (pp. 494-504). New York: Ballantine Books.

Bateson, G. (1979). *Mind and nature: A necessary unity.* New York: Bantam Books.

Bateson, G. (1991). The new conceptual frames for behavioral research. In R. Donaldson (Ed.), *A Sacred Unity: Further steps to an ecology of mind/ Gregory Bateson* (pp. 93-110). New York: Harper Collins.

Eriksen, T. H. (2001). *Tyranny of the moment: Fast and slow time in the information age.* London: Pluto Press.

Foerster, H. von (1973). On constructing a reality. In F. E. Preiser (Ed.), *Environmental design research, Vol.II* (pp. 35-46). Stroudberg: Dowden, Hutchison and Ross. [Also in Von Foerster, H. (1981). *Observing Systems* (pp. 287-309). Seaside, CA: Intersystems.]

Keeney, B. (1983). *Aesthetics of change.* New York: Guilford Press.

Maturana, H. R. & Varela, F. J. (1987). *The tree of knowledge: The biological roots of human understanding.* Boston: New Science Library.

Mead. M. (1975). *Male and female.* New York: William Morrow.

Norman, D. (2001). *The future of education: Lessons learned from video games and museum exhibits.* (Commencement address, Northwestern University School of Education and Social Policy, June 2001). Available from http://www.jnd.org/dn.mss/NorthwesternCommencement.html

Oldenburg, R. (1999). *The great good place.* New York: Marlowe and Company.

Robbins, T. (1980). *Still life with woodpecker.* New York: Bantam Books.

Schaffner, B. (Ed.) (1956). *Group processes: Transactions of the second conference, October 9, 10, 11, and 12, 1955.* New York: The Josiah Macy, Jr. Foundation.

Schön, D. (1983). *The reflective practitioner.* New York: Basic Books.

Schön, D. and Rein, M. (1994). *Frame reflection: Toward the resolution of intractable policy controversies.* New York: Basic Books.

Steier, F. & Jorgenson, J. (2003). Ethics and aesthetics of observing frames. *Cybernetics and Human Knowing, 10* (3-4), 124-136.

Steier, F. & Ostrenko, W. (2000). Taking cybernetics seriously at a science center: Reflection-in-interaction and second order organizational learning. *Cybernetics and Human Knowing, 7* (2-3), 47-69.

Steier, R. (2003). Playing with art, learning science. Unpublished manuscript, Stanford University, Palo Alto.

Vickers, G. (1968). *Values systems and social process.* London: Tavistock Publications.

Watterson, B. (1992). *Attack of the deranged mutant killer monster snow goons.* Kansas City, MO: Andrews and McMeel.

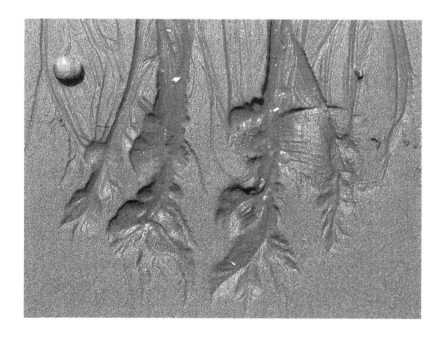

Cybernetics And Human Knowing. Vol. 12, nos. 1-2, pp. 50-60

Mind the Gap:
Flexibility, Epistemology and the Rhetoric of New Work

Thomas Hylland Eriksen[1]

This article explores Bateson's definition of flexibility as "uncommitted potential for change", relating it to contemporary issues and scientific controversies and thereby showing the huge, largely untapped potential of the concept. The main empirical example is the "new economy", where the term flexibility is used aggressively to advertise its virtues. However, it is argued, flexible work tends to render the worker more flexible in relation to space, but less flexible regarding time. This illustrates another point in Bateson's analysis of flexibility, namely that flexibility gained in one domain tends to reduce flexibility in another. The ensuing problems are familiar enough – fragmentation, alienation, stress – but poorly understood, and Bateson's flexibility concept makes it possible, in fact, to deal with the unintentional side-effects of "new work" as a kind of environmental problem.

Flexibility is to specialization as entropy is to negentropy. (*Steps to an Ecology of Mind, p. 505*)

The term flexibility has become a major catchword in the *new economy*. Flexible work and flexible organization, moreover, are marked, and marketed, as good innovations. They connote openness to change and a willingness to do things differently as opposed to the rigid formality associated with the *old economy*, and seem to entail a great degree of freedom and choice on the part of the employee. Creativity is good; routine is bad.

However, there is also another story to be told about flexibility. As has been argued by Castells (1996), Sennett (1998), Bauman (2000) and many other contemporary social theorists, the restructuring of capitalism entails a new kind of relationship between persons and their work. In many cases, the employee may no longer be expected to be on time, but s/he should at least be online. The term flexibility is often used to describe this new situation. Jobs are flexible in the sense that they are unstable and uncertain, few employees hold the same jobs for many years, the content of jobs can be changed almost overnight, and the boundaries between work and leisure are negotiable and chronically fuzzy. In his book about the psychological consequences of the new, unstable work regimes, Sennett (1998) argues, moreover, that flexible work leads to a fragmentation of the person. His informants typically complain about the lack of linear narrative in their lives; they move from task to task, from job to job and in some cases from house to house, without ever feeling that what they do has cumulative results and can be fitted into an over-arching, linear narrative about their lives.

---

1. University of Oslo/Vrije Universiteit Amsterdam. Email: g.t.h.eriksen@sai.uio.no

I propose to do two things: To present the theoretical concept of *flexibility* as it was originally sketched by Gregory Bateson and show its untapped analytic potential, and to discuss whether or not *the new flexibility* in the working place can be said to increase flexibility in a theoretical sense.

As an analytical term, flexibility is rarely used in the social sciences, and most anthropologists are, if anything at all, likely to associate it with Bateson's late work on ecology. In "Ecology and Flexibility in Urban Civilization" (Bateson, 1972a), Bateson defined flexibility as "uncommitted potential for change" (Bateson, 1972a, p.497). The context for his usage of the word was the emerging environmental degradation which first attracted widespread attention in the early 1970s. Bateson argued that increased energy use entails a loss of flexibility in the sense that it shrinks the opportunity space. In a society which is built around the daily use of the car, for example, it is difficult to revert to slower and less energy-intensive means of transportation. More fundamentally, his view was that the flexibility used (and used up) by growing populations harnessing much of the available energy for their own purposes, reduced the flexibility of the environment.

Bateson describes a healthy system, flexibility-wise, by drawing an analogy with an acrobat on a high-wire.

> To maintain the ongoing truth of his basic premise ("I am on the wire"), he must be free to move from one position of instability to another, *i.e.*, certain variables such as the position of his arms and the rate of movement of his arms must have great flexibility, which he uses to maintain the stability of other more fundamental and general characteristics. (Bateson, 1972a, p. 498)

Maintaining flexibility in the system as a whole, Bateson adds, "depends upon keeping many of its variables in the middle of their tolerable limits" (Bateson, 1972a, p. 502). In order to use the term accurately, it is thus necessary to specify the parameters limiting the upper and lower threshold values, and also to demonstrate the significance of wider systemic connectedness which affects, and is affected by, flexibility in the realm under investigation.

Although the word is used surprisingly rarely in academic work, ideas of flexibility which are compatible with, and largely true to, Bateson's concise definition are widespread and important in many areas of intellectual exploration. Let us briefly consider some examples.

Flexibility and rigidity

In cognitive theory, a major theoretical issue concerns the way in which knowledge is being selected, sifted and organized. In a book offering a critical overview of the state of the art in the field, Nørretranders, in *The User Illusion* (1999), distinguishes between information and exformation, the latter being potential information that is consciously or unconsciously selected away or filtered out. Sperber and Wilson's (1986) notion of *relevance*, largely informed by linguistics and Darwinian selectionism, is a kindred concept. While the dynamics of information exchange and knowledge development are not random, they are also far from predictable. There is much, much more potential knowledge present in our surroundings, in our brains and in our bodies than that which is being used. The "uncommitted potential for change" is very considerable.

In one of the late-20th centuries controversies about natural selection, Gould and Vrba (1981, see also Gould 2002) introduced the term *exaptation* to denote phenotypical features whose functioning had undergone change due to changes in the wider system. These structures were, in other words, flexible and responded, like the acrobat on the high-wire, to changing parameters in their surroundings.

In another debate about natural selection, Rose (1996) and others have argued that there cannot be a simple relationship between DNA and the organism, between genotype and phenotype, since there are important phenotypical effects arising from the interaction between hereditary material and its surroundings. Already at the level of cell chemistry, this kind of flexibility in hereditary material is evident. For one thing, it is well known that there are common characteristics in humans that are inborn but not genetic, which are caused partly by the mother's diet during pregnancy.

A third debate relating to neo-Darwinian theory concerns memetics, or the view that ideas spread and replicate themselves in a manner analogous to the replication of genes. In a recent edited book about memetics (Aunger 2000), several anthropologists – Sperber (2000), Bloch (2000) and Kuper (2000) – voice their objections to this, in their view, simplistic view of cultural transmission (see also Ingold 2001). Their main argument, which has also been developed at great length by Sperber elsewhere (Sperber 1996), is that contextual factors which could be described as noise, redundancy, distortion and recontextualisation tends to modify even simple, apparently straightforward concepts when they are transferred between individuals. In other words, the *memes* are malleable and flexible by virtue of their embeddedness in complex, largely unpredictable processes.

In research on identity politics, similarly, many have shown how rule-bound adherence to tightly closed bodies of cultural norms and conventions are practically incompatible with life in culturally complex societies. As Bauman once put it: "If the modern 'problem of identity' is how to construct an identity and keep it solid and stable, the postmodern 'problem of identity' is primarily how to avoid fixation and keep the options open" (Bauman 1996, p. 18).

In sociological and anthropological studies of technology and science, moreover, a main research strategy consists in looking at the unintentional side-effects of technological change – in other words, a kind of flexibility that could not conceivably have been intended by the initiators of the changes. Technologies are generally much more flexible than their inventors have imagined, simply because users are more varied and complex than the technologies themselves.

Such studies also often illustrate one of Bateson's most important points regarding flexibility, namely that there is a tendency that increased flexibility in some areas leads to reduced flexibility in others. In line with this view, it could be argued that Gutenberg's fateful invention led to enhanced flexibility in the transmission of information, but to a loss of flexibility in linguistic variation (standardization of dialects) and in locally embedded world-views (knowledge was frozen and externalized). Similarly, the car made people living in the suburbs spatially more flexible, but less flexible locally. The car pulled them out of the local milieu and deprived them of some of the moral ties that could have been drawn upon in their relationship to their neighbors. The telephone had similar effects.

At an even more general level, it is often said that even a perfect knowledge of the norms and values in a given society does not enable us to predict how people will act. This is not necessarily because the norms themselves are flexible, but because the contexts of action necessitate their interpretation; in order to be useful, of course, norms must be interpreted.

Many of the issues relating to flexibility can be translated, remaining with the Batesonian spirit, as map/territory or menu/food issues. In other words, there is a variable and indeterminate relationship between model and reality. Simplistic genetic determinism or adaptationism in biology, or structural-functional determinism in classic social anthropology, or even cultural determinism in cultural anthropology, fail to grasp the grey zones of indeterminacy and variability, and they do so in ways which are actually quite closely related. To take an example from current public debate in Europe and North America: After 11 September 2001, some well-intentioned commentators argued that in order to understand the Muslim world, one should begin by reading the Koran. Naturally, such an endeavour would teach us little that is useful about Muslims. Not only is the Koran only a map or a menu; it is also a map/menu which is known only patchily by most of its adherents, the vast majority of whom have a sketchy or non-existent knowledge of Arabic.

Of course, the fact that there is indeterminacy, improvisation and ambiguity in social life is far from unfamiliar in anthropology; it has been explicitly recognized by, among others, Gluckman (1964), Bourdieu (1977) and many others, including even the card-carrying materialist determinist Marvin Harris in a paper about the relationship between norms and behavior (1975). Earlier still, Firth (1951) introduced the concept of social organization, distinguishing it from social structure in the manner that we might distinguish *parole* from *langue* or territory from map. However, if we follow Bateson, we may – instead of throwing our hands up in despair over the loss of precision entailed by growing complexity – try to find out if it might not be possible to describe and come to terms with forms of flexibility accurately.

Some implications

Some of Bateson's original examples of flexibility lend themselves easily enough to accurate descriptions; he draws chiefly on grand cultural history of the *big ditch* kind. Essentially, he argues that simpler technology and less intensive exploitation of the natural environment entails greater flexibility since most of the potential for change has not been used up. A more recent example, too recent for Bateson to have taken into account, is the Green Revolution in India from the 1970s onwards, which entailed the introduction of new cereal strains to enhance productivity. With hindsight, it appears that the green revolution reduced flexibility in two ways: it led to a reduction of genetic variation in the cereal strains, and to a reduced flexibility regarding population size since the Indian population was stabilized at a higher level than before, making it impossible to revert to the earlier cereal strains without risking major famines. Even if the new cereals should be shown to be environmentally harmful in the longer run (which some critics have argued), the change was irreversible and led to reduced flexibility.

However, Bateson did recognize that unspecified and unacknowledged potential for change is useless, in other words that increased complexity in knowledge itself implies flexibility. There can thus be no unambiguous, objective definition of flexibility, and moreover, the parameters defining the range of options can also be changed. Just as it does not make sense to talk about evolution of a single species independently of the wider ecosystem, the term flexibility can only be meaningful on the background of a description of the context.

Narrow parameters always suggest vulnerability. In animal species, a narrow genetic range tends to be associated with vulnerability, specialization and poor adaptability to environmental changes. One current example is the cheetah population in East Africa and elsewhere. The cheetah is highly specialized and displays little internal genetic variation (O'Brien et al. 1985), and some biologists have argued that the species was on the verge of extinction around 10,000 years ago. As a result, it is adapted to a single biotope (dry savanna) and vulnerable to disease. Furthermore, criticism of current attempts at artificial selection among humans (through new reproductive technologies) point in the same direction, warning against the unintended consequences of a planned reduction in intraspecies genetic variation. Similarly, the Norwegian philosopher Peter Wessel Zapffe points out, in his lamentably untranslated, major treatise on tragedy from 1943 (Zapffe 1984 [1943]), that the human hand, with its opposable thumb, displays a remarkable lack of fixity, or flexibility as I would put it: Unlike a claw or paw, it is not obvious what it should be used for. The uncommitted potential for change is considerable.

As mentioned, Bateson suggests that growing flexibility in one field tends to lead to the loss of flexibility in another. However, the model does not necessarily result in a zero-sum game: in some cases, conditions of *matching flexibility* are achieved, that is to say complex systems where a desired level of flexibility is maintained in both, or all, of the relevant interacting systems. When there is no attention to matching flexibility, the relationship between systems, or subsystems, becomes skewed. His main example is the relationship between civilization and environment, as he puts it. Civilization becomes ever more flexible in terms of cultural production, individual choice and so forth, and as a result, the culture–environment relationship loses flexibility because of increased dependency on massive exploitation of available energy and other resources.

In order to appreciate this view of flexibility, it is necessary to think in terms of cybernetic systems with governors and threshold levels (upper and lower): under stress, the system is pressed towards one of its limits which consequently, if unchecked, leads to system collapse. Loss of flexibility may entail changes in tolerance limits (new ways of exploiting nature etc.), which could in turn deepen the more fundamental flexibility deficit. Bateson's general policy advice is Aristotelian: keep activities/systemic features within the middle range – you can always do less of it, and you can always do more of it – however, he does not even begin to indicate how to justify changes in tolerance limits which is, of course, a crucial issue in planning and politics since one man's flexibility can be another man's straitjacket.

Sometimes, deliberate reduction of flexibility in one respect stimulates flexibility in another. In the realm of word processing, it may appear that Microsoft Word, a huge, bloated package including multi-language dictionaries, a bewildering array of formatting options, graphics editors, irritating automatic functions which are almost impossible to turn off as well as numerous other features, offers an enormous extent of flexibility among the users. This is not necessarily the case in practice: flexibility gained in one area may be parasitical on flexibility in another. Many Word users have, during the last two decades, spent much of their creative energy simply trying to come to terms with the software (Eriksen 2002), thereby being effectively deflected from their work. By contrast, Unix-based word processors such as TeX (LaTex) and LyX give the user little choice in formatting. For example, they do not allow footnotes in headings, more than one space between words or more than one line between heading and text. For advanced page layout, dedicated software is recommended. As a result of the reduced flexibility in the realm of formatting, increased flexibility may well obtain with respect to the content of whatever it is that the user is writing.

In the realm of poetry, the sonnet and the haiku are arguably the most perfect forms. The former imposes a strict set of structural rules forcing the poet to exercise creativity within delineated boundaries, while the latter imposes similar constraints regarding length: If you cannot say it in seventeen syllables, don't. (It remains to be seen, but compact, accurate, haiku-like communication may be one of many unintended consequences of the constraint on length imposed by the SMS technology.)

As I write this paragraph in December 2004, I am distracted by two visual impressions: A poster depicting a solemn John Coltrane at the time of the recording of *Blue Train*, and the leaden skies outside my window. Now, Coltrane, a pioneer in jazz improvisation, was aware of the importance of constraints for the exercise of flexibility. Unlike the free improvisers who succeeded him, he kept a few sets of variables relatively constant, chiefly the rhythm and the melody line. The melody was always repeated immediately after his lenity forays into improvisation. Freedom needs a ceiling and a floor.

Why do things have outlines [in paintings], the semi-fictional seven-year old Mary Catherine Bateson asks her father in the eponymously titled metalogue (Bateson

1972b). Because, her father answers in many different ways, with and without the help of William Blake, boundaries are necessary.

The dark clouds, driven across the Atlantic by unusually strong winds and heavy with rain, are atypical of Oslo in the week before Christmas. Normal mid-December temperatures are several degrees below freezing, and strong winds are rare in this sheltered part of Scandinavia. If the mild weather continues, I'm going to have to mow my lawn in January. Global climate change is clearly occurring now, and it has in all likelihood been triggered by human activity. The increased flexibility of movement resulting from the usage of non-renewable energy sources seems to reduced the ability of the biosphere to maintain a relatively stable (or slowly changing) global climate. It has become much more flexible in a few domains and less flexible as a total system.

Flexibility and new work

It is now time to turn to my main example, discussing how Bateson's systemic view of flexibility relates to the term flexibility as it is being used in the new economy of cellphones, laptops, waiting lounges and e-mails. The term flexibility is often used to describe this new situation: Jobs are flexible in the sense that they are unstable and uncertain, few employees hold the same jobs for many years, the content of jobs can be changed, and the boundaries between work and leisure are poorly defined. Summing up the dominant, current views of these concepts, Webb explains:

> Flexibility is, at least in theory, multi-dimensional, covering employment contracts, skills, management and information systems, business strategies, and organization structures. Networks are regarded as the means of enhancing flexibility because they are seen as fluid, permeable, infinitely expandable and dynamic. (Webb, 2004, p. 721)

Bateson's pivotal ideas about flexibility that should be considered in a critical examination of the role of flexibility in new work:

(i) Flexibility is uncommitted potential or elbow room, and
(ii) flexibility gains in one area tend to imply flexibility loss in another.

As Sennett (1998) showed in his pioneering book about the human consequences of *new work*, people seem to become less flexible by becoming more flexible. Sennett begins his book like this:

> Today the phrase "flexible capitalism" describes a system which is more than a permutation on an old theme. The emphasis is on flexibility. Rigid forms of bureaucracy are under attack, as are the evils of blind routine. Workers are asked to behave nimbly, to be open to change on short notice, to take risks continually, to become ever less dependent on regulations and formal procedures. (Sennett, 1998, p. 9)

The tone suggests that flexibility is not necessarily a good thing. Sennett intimates that employees in the new economy are deprived of stability, safety, security and predictability. However, he does not say that they have become less flexible; on the contrary, he sees flexibility as the enemy. In this he draws on the emic (native) delineation of flexibility rather than using a more analytic definition of the term. Using Bateson's definition, we may ask: Where does the increased, uncommitted potential for change occur in the contemporary business usage of the word flexibility? It appears that the increase in flexibility takes place in the employee's use of space and in his short-term commitments. In the long term, flexibility evaporates altogether, since the time horizon typical of new work is extremely short. The trade-off in this kind of flexibility budget, thus, appears to consist in a swapping of the short-term with the long-term, or freedom with security, or even space with time: New work, I would like to argue, enhances flexibility regarding space but accordingly reduces it with respect to time.

Take the VCR (more recently the DVD), as an alternative to the cinema. Many would say, if asked why they prefer to watch films on television rather than in the cinema, that it makes them more flexible since it enables them to see the film whenever they want. If the parameters defining limits of flexibility pertain to space and time, this assumption must be misguided. If one fills two hours of the evening watching a film, filling a gap which may manifest itself between the children's bedtime and one's own, one effectively reduces one's "uncommitted potential for change." Instead of doing anything or nothing in this precious time of the evening, one narrows down the options to zero by filling the period with media consumption. However, the video indisputably increases spatial flexibility, since it enables us to watch films anywhere. As my colleague Tian Sørhaug once put it, in an assessment of the consequences of new work: You may no longer have to be on time, as long as you're online.

One recent innovation typically associated with flexibility is the home office. In Scandinavia (and some other prosperous, technologically optimistic regions), many companies equipped some of their employees with home computers with online access to the company network in the early 1990s, in order to enhance their flexibility. This was intended to enable employees to work from home part of the time, thereby making the era when office workers were chained to the office desk all day obsolete. In the early days, there were widespread worries among employers to the effect that a main outcome of this new flexibility would consist in a reduction of productivity. Since there was no legitimate way of checking how the staff actually spent their time out of the office, it was often suspected that they worked less from home than they were supposed to. If this were in fact the case, working from home would have led to a real increase in the flexibility of time budgeting. However, work researchers eventually came up with a different picture. By the late 1990s, hardly anybody spoke of the home office as a convenient way of escaping from work; rather, the concern among unionists as well as researchers was now that increasing numbers of employees were at pains to distinguish between working hours and leisure time, and were suffering symptoms of burnout and depression. The home office made it difficult to distinguish between contexts that were formerly mutually exclusive because of different physical locations.

The blurring of the boundary between work and leisure can be seen as a result of increased spatial flexibility for office workers. In addition to the home office, laptop computers, cellphones and – increasingly – their merger through the advent of wireless Internet access, are in some quarters hailed as liberating innovations enabling people to work any time, anywhere. Consider the following examples.

Some time ago, I urgently needed an electronic form to be filled in and submitted to the powers that be, that is, in this case, the central administration of the University of Oslo. It was well beyond the deadline, but the only person who had the correct version of the form on her computer was on sick leave. I asked other members of the administrative staff whether someone perhaps knew her password or even had a copy of the form on their own computer, but alas – only one known copy existed. Finally, one of her colleagues said, "But surely you can send her an e-mail?" I responded, sheepishly, "But she's at home with the flu, right?" He said, "Well, yes, but don't you worry, naturally she responds to e-mail!" I shouldn't have done it, but I did: I sent her an e-mail, and a couple of hours later I got the form. It saved my day, but it also made me reflect on the working conditions that impel people on legitimate leave to get out of bed, put on their dressing-gown and slippers, turn on their computer and respond to e-mail. Of course, had she not done it, the workload would have accumulated while she was away. In the era of the e-mail, it does not matter whether or not people are in their office. They can be reached anyway. In a sense, they are always in their office. The tyranny of the e-mail is an integral part of the 24-hour society and illustrates a form of spatial flexibility which makes people much less flexible regarding time.

Talking to an executive at a large communications company in Norway, I was told that at their new location, they would only have office space for 60 per cent of the employees. This would save the corporation a lot of money, but the solution was marketed internally as an exciting innovation. Nobody would have their own desk, but were free to work wherever they pleased. Working from home, from the airport train or from a cottage in the mountains, would now be unproblematic and morally perfectly justifiable, the executive proudly told me. Speaking to other employees, I got this view confirmed, but many saw problems as well. Some were concerned about the lack of privacy entailed by the new office arrangement; one could no longer make confidential phone calls from the desk, and would have to wander far away to have a meeting under four eyes. Others felt homeless in an environment where they couldn't even pin a picture of their children on the wall. One said that as a consequence of this de-territorialization of the working space, they would in practice have to be online and with their cellphones turned on most of the time. It would from now on be unthinkable, he added, to go away for the weekend without bringing the mobile and the laptop.

In the old days, that is at least until the mid-1990s, weekends were considered sacred in Norwegian working culture. Hundreds of thousands migrated to their cottages or country houses on Friday afternoons, and a main benefit of going out of town would consist in their being completely out of touch with the outside world for a few days. This is increasingly becoming illegitimate. Nowadays, it is far from rare to see Scandinavian tourists on beaches in the Canary Islands talking in animated voices with colleagues at work on their cellphones.

A few years ago, a lawyer interviewed by BBC World said that his firm was investigating the possibilities of passing a law protecting employees against being contacted by their bosses outside of working hours. In the old days, people could feel safe on the tube, in the pub and a number of other locations – indeed, not so many years ago, even phoning people at home was considered an intrusion into domestic life which should be avoided unless something urgent had come up. According to the lawyer, many employees now feel harassed by the feeling that they are never truly off work. Whenever and wherever the phone rings, it could be someone from work. The law is not likely to be passed, but it is significant that this kind of issue is now suddenly on the agenda.

Another issue, which might deserve an essay of its own at a later stage, is the interesting possibility that mobile and flexible work may not even enhance productivity. A Danish advertising firm has actually denied its employees access to the Internet, including e-mail, for the duration of the core working hours, because e-mail makes people very efficient at doing one thing, namely handling e-mail, which effectively prevents them from doing their work.

My point is a simple one: The new, flexible job arrangements based on mobile telecommunications and computers, have led to a real gain in flexibility regarding space: People can be anywhere and do their job. However, as Bateson might have predicted, there has been a concomitant loss of flexibility regarding time, since the omnipresent communications technology tends to fill all available gaps. I have written about this at some length in my book *Tyranny of the Moment* (2001), arguing also that in information society, the intensified competition for the attention of others implies the packaging of information in ever smaller packages, in order to make it fit the increasingly tiny gaps in the time budgets of the audiences.

There seems to be a classic Batesonian flexibility trade-off associated with the new information technologies: increased spatial flexibility entails decreased temporal flexibility. If inaccessibility and *empty time* are understood as scarce resources, the context of new work thus seems to be an appropriate context for a new economics as well. In fact, a main environmental challenge of our near future will consist in protecting slow time and gaps from environmental degradation. And not only that: Linear time as such is under threat. The late Neil Postman noted, in one of his last books (Postman 1996), that his students no longer used the term *because*. They were exceedingly clever at stacking sophisticated ideas on top of each other, but did not even try to link them together in causal, temporal chains. The there and then is sacrificed for the here and now. Increased spatial flexibility leads to a pollution of time.

For when something happens all the time, nothing in fact happens. All the gaps are filled. That, in effect, is why it is that it is only when nothing in particular happens that anything could happen. And this is what Bateson was trying to tell us.

Acknowledgments

I am grateful to Fred Steier for his very creative and valuable suggestions on the first draft.

References

Aunger, R. (Ed.). (2000). *Darwinizing culture: The status of memetics as a science*. Oxford: Oxford University Press.
Bateson, G. (1972a). Ecology and flexibility in urban civilization. In *Steps to an ecology of mind* (pp. 494–505). New York: Chandler.
Bateson, G. (1972b). Why do things have outlines? In *Steps to an ecology of mind* (pp. 27-32). New York: Chandler.
Bauman, Z. (1996). From pilgrim to tourist; or A short history of identity. In S. Hall & P. Du Gay (Eds.)., *Questions of cultural identity* (pp. 18–36). London: Sage.
Bloch, M. (2000). A well-disposed social anthropologist's problems with memes. In R. Aunger (Ed.), *Darwinizing Culture* (pp. 189-204). Oxford: Oxford University Press.
Bourdieu, P. (1977). *Outline of a theory of practice*. Cambridge: Cambridge University Press.
Eriksen, T. H. (2001). *Tyranny of the moment: Fast and slow time in the information age*. London: Pluto.
Eriksen, T. H. (2002). Ordets makt: The power of Wordô. In T. Slaatta, (Ed.), *Digital makt* [Digital power] (pp. 174-191). Oslo: Gyldendal.
Firth, R. (1951). *Elements of social organization*. London: Watts.
Harris, M. (1975). Why a perfect knowledge of all the rules that one must know in order to act like a native cannot lead to a knowledge of how natives act. *Journal of Anthropological Research, 30*, 242-251.
Gluckman, M., (Ed.). (1964). *Closed systems and open minds*. Chicago: Aldine.
Gould, S. J.(2002) *The structure of evolutionary theory*. Cambridge, MA: Belknap.
Gould, S. J., & Vrba, E. (1981). Exaptation: A missing term in the science of form. *Paleobiology, 8,* 4–15.
Ingold, T. (2001). Evolving skills. In H. Rose & S. Rose (Eds.), *Alas Poor Darwin: Arguments Against Evolutionary Psychology* (pp. 225-246). London: Vintage.
Kuper, A. (2001). If memes are the answer, what is the question? In Robert Aunger (Ed.), *Darwinizing Culture* (pp. 175-88). Oxford: Oxford University Press.
Nørretranders, T. (1999). *The user illusion*. London: Penguin.
O'Brien, S. J. et al. (1985). Genetic basis for species vulnerability in the cheetah. *Science, 227*, 1428-1434.
Postman, N. (1996). *The end of education*. New York: Vintage.
Rose, S. (1996). *Lifelines: Biology beyond determinism*. Oxford: Oxford University Press.
Sennett, R. (1998). *The corrosion of character*. New York: Norton.
Sperber, D. (1996). *Explaining culture: A naturalistic approach*. Oxford: Blackwell.
Sperber, D. (2000) An objection to the memetic approach to culture. In Robert Aunger, Ed., *Darwinizing Culture*, pp. 163-74. Oxford: Oxford University Press.
Sperber, D., & Wilson, D. (1986). *Relevance: communication and cognition*. Oxford: Blackwell.
Webb, J. (2004). Organizations, self-identity and the new economy. *Sociology*, 38(4): 719–738.
Zapffe, P. W. (1984). *Om det tragiske* [On tragedy]. Oslo: Universitetsforlaget. (Original work published in 1943)

Cybernetics And Human Knowing. Vol. 12, nos. 1-2, pp. 61-74

Understanding Ecological Aesthetics:
The Challenge Of Bateson

Peter Harries-Jones[1]

Aesthetics appears only fitfully in the literature on modern environmentalism; in Bateson's case it was an integral part of his epistemology of recursive systems. Bateson moves into ecology partly through concerns about the nuclear arms race and its potential for destruction. In this he fits with other concerned scientists during the 1960s. The difference was his continuing attention to aesthetics and its integration with scientific evidence, as a "second vision," to counter the "single vision" (cf. William Blake) of modern science, with its mechanistic approaches to living systems. The article considers the influence of Blake on Bateson but draws upon two post-modern writers, J.S. Coetzee and Suzi Gablik, in order to expand upon Bateson's aesthetic ideas. Finally, Bateson has been almost entirely neglected in the history of ecological ideas, yet. Recent research in the Arctic laments lack of knowledge about ecological feedbacks, Bateson's central focus, and possibilities of global climate change being abrupt, about which he warned.

1. Introduction: Aesthetics and Ecology [2]

Aesthetic response is often portrayed as being intrinsic to humanity's conceptions of nature and some of the evidence for this lies in the strong association of nature writing, photography and fine art with the aesthetics of landscape. These types of artistic representation of landscape conjoin easily with more formal representations of nature, especially those produced by natural historians in the 19th and early part of the 20th century. By contrast, aesthetics has had a somewhat fitful role in modern environmentalism, in North America, particularly as formal study of the environment moved from the representation of "nature as landscape" to a study of the ecology of ecosystems. On the side of continuity would be the example of the photography of Ansel Adams conjoining with the writing of the founder of the Sierra Club, John Muir. On the "somewhat fitful" side would be Aldo Leopold. In his early phase, when he was writing about "game management," aesthetics was of little concern to him. His revisionist ecology has only a few pages devoted to the subject and Leopold's followers have had to undertake detailed investigation of his writing in order to "work up" his aesthetic. Leopold drew connections between land and organic harmony, but was mostly concerned with rural economics and extending the notion of natural rights from humans to the land.

Rachel Carson is the important exception. The *Sea Around Us* (Carson, 1951) is a classic moulding of science with aesthetics and the success of her combination is an

---

1. Department of Anthropology, York University, Ontario, Canada. Email: peterhj@yorku.ca
2. A shortened version of this paper was originally prepared for a conference celebrating Bateson's centennial and his continued influence: Gregory Bateson Multiple Versions of the World at University of California, Berkeley, November 20, 2004.

evident reason for its resonance with readers. In the later part of her life, as a freelance science writer, she devoted even more time portraying the beauty and mystery in the sea while probing its ecology. There are many who have been inspired by her to acute aesthetic awareness and for these Carson is a tradition to be emulated.[3] Yet, after Carson, the task of melding aesthetics with ecological science became more difficult. Carson was a transitional figure. Nineteenth century natural historians wrote about their personal relationships with nature that, but that sense of private celebration of nature demonstrated in Thoreau's writing on Walden Pond, began to undergo a decisive shift in the mid- 20th century toward public engagement on environmental issues. *Silent Spring* (Carson, 1962) took issue with the profligacy of the post-World War Two industrial order and the consequences of degrading nature through unrestricted chemical use in agriculture. The underlying message of that book was the need for ethical change in the public at large. The prevailing spirit of conquest of nature had to become transformed into necessary respect for all forms of life plus a realization of our dependence on nature.

As Donald Worster tells us, this call for public engagement against the excesses of industrial practices, merged with another other trend, public concern about the testing of atomic weapons. The steadily increasing nuclear capability of the two superpowers, the USA and the USSR evoked fear of total destruction, even through a series of simple mistakes. "Under the threat of the atomic bomb a new moral consciousness called environmentalism began to take form whose purpose was to use the insights of ecology to restrain the use of modern science-based power over nature" (Worster, 1994, pp. 343-4). The growth of nuclear weaponry, the secrecy which surrounded its rapid development, the uncertainty surrounding the overall effects of nuclear fall-out from the testing sites, "cast doubt upon the entire project of the domination of nature that had been at the heart of modern history," and with it gave rise to doubts about the moral legitimacy of science, about the tumultuous pace of technology, about the Enlightenment dream of replacing religious faith by human rationality as the basis of material welfare.

This was a far-cry from the immediate post-World War Two perception of physicists, and natural science in general, as the leaders who would show nations how to increase their power and wealth. In this new age of atomic anxiety, ecologists emerged as the "guardians of fragile life" (Worster, 1994, pp. 340 & 343).

2. Bateson's Move into Ecology

By 1958 the probable ecological effects of nuclear fallout had become the focus of such public anxiety that a segment of United States scientists began organizing a

---

3. A recent example of the Carson tradition, a favourite of mine, is Sandra Steingraber's *Living Downstream,* a thorough investigation of the environmental factors behind the cancer epidemic in North America, while, at the same time presenting her own life as a story of living with nature. For attempts to "work up" Leopold's interest in aesthetics, while dealing with skimpy resources in Leopold's writing, see Callicott, *In Defense of the Land Ethic* (Callicott, 1989).

Committee for Nuclear Information. Its aim was to strip the secrecy away from the weapons programme and warn their fellow citizens of the dangers of further nuclear testing. In 1963 this Committee renamed itself the Committee for Environmental Information and launched a new magazine called *Environment*. A prominent leader of this Committee was Barry Commoner, who, later, was among the group of scientists whom Gregory Bateson called together at his 1968 conference in Burg Wartenstein, Austria on the "Effects of Conscious Purpose on Human Adaptation" and which, edited by his daughter, appeared as *Our Own Metaphor* (M.C. Bateson, 1972).

Political opposition to nuclear proliferation did not leave much room for an aesthetic appreciation of nature. For those who joined in with the various campaigns for nuclear disarmament, the immediate sensation was that of sore feet, and often a cold, stiff body. True, the prevailing emotions of those in a demonstration were of camaraderie and the warmth generated by collective response, yet warm feelings were overrun by a sense of great helplessness in the face of an unseeing, unfeeling power, and overall *angst* about the fate of the earth.

Throughout his career Bateson's had expressed his concerns about nuclear proliferation and there is little doubt that the close relationship between nuclear testing and the arms race was one of the factors that drew Bateson towards writing about ecology. He had studied the pattern of arms races before the war. Moreover, he knew quite a lot about the research into atomic particles that had being going on in Rutherford's laboratory at Cambridge University and even tried to use this knowledge in order to advocate the entry of the United States on the side of Great Britain into World War Two. It was his most active political phase. After the war he joined a committee of scientists that sought to understand the effects of nuclear weaponry on military defence strategies and international politics, a group that included Robert Oppenheimer, administrative head of the Manhattan Project, and even more unusually Alger Hiss, subsequently tried for espionage. He also published his views on "The Pattern of an Armaments Race" for the *Bulletin of Atomic Scientists* (Bateson, 1946a & 1946b). Even his ethnographic paper on Bali was a means for an attack on "Game Theory" which, at a theoretical level, underlay the early strategies of nuclear response of the United Sates towards the USSR (Bateson, 2000, pp. 107-127).

His shift towards ecology was also prompted by his research on dolphins conducted in the Caribbean and, subsequently, in Hawaii. The early stage of this research, conducted together with John Lilly, produced a withering attack on the behaviourist methodologies then used in the training of dolphins. Behaviourism was not the same as game theory, but there was an epistemological connection in the type of reductionist approaches that had produced them The epistemology of mechanism and reductionism became his overriding focus. At the end of his 1968 conference he spoke out for further epistemological investigation and against a call for political action. Given vocal support to the first "Earth Day" in 1970, he might have been safe in taking a political stance on behalf of the new environmentalism but did not, in contrast to his former spouse, Margaret Mead, who was a prominent figure at this mass demonstration in favour of ecology.

Bateson was more resolute a few years later when issues of ecology touched once again upon nuclear issues. Bateson resigned from the Board of Regents of the University of California when they expressed support for increasing research on nuclear weaponry in the university. He published his objections under the title "Nuclear Armament as Epistemological Error" (Bateson, 1979a & 1979b). His resignation letter repeats some of the themes of his earlier papers, notably that an attempt to initiate "trust" between the USA and the USSR would be much more likely to bring the nuclear arms race to an end than a constant escalation of the military capacity of the nuclear weapons.[4] Bateson was correct, though his position was only justified after his death; the talks in Iceland between Gorbachev and President Ronald Reagan did indeed initiate trust between the two countries and proved to be the beginning of the end of the Cold War.

Central epistemological issues had to be approached incrementally. Would the new science of ecology, in which so many now placed hope, prove any better than its forebears if ecological science still embraced the same framework of thinking about the pre-eminence of the material forces of nature? And what advance in thinking would an unreconstructed materialism bring about in the eco-management of nature? Even by 1970, Earth Day, there was sufficient new books and papers calling themselves "environmental" whose analyses exhibited little change from the approaches that dominated much of physics and chemistry. The influence of the two Odum brothers, Eugene and Howard, troubled Bateson, for while both of which spoke of the unity of nature and the necessity for an holistic approach to nature, they both held that "ecology must develop a unified theory of the ecosystem, described in precise mathematical and statistical terms, if the field was to be of any practical value" (Worster, 1994, p. 362). From an epistemological perspective, Bateson believed, their "holism" was as much an unreconstructed view of ecology as scientific reductionism to which all three were opposed. Eugene was wedded to the holism of nature by examining energy flux, concerning himself almost entirely with the analysis of biomass and bio-energy, while Howard examined the unity of nature as if it were a electro-mechanical circuit (Odum, E., 1963; Odum, H., 1971). Yet the academic world seemed to accept both brothers models as valid preliminaries for the eco-management of nature.[5]

The characterization of holism proposed by the Odum brothers had to be challenged, while the rhetoric of the new environmentalism introduced other epistemological quandaries. A phenomenon of the late nineteen sixties were the many who labelled themselves "ecologists" who joined the fashion to "drop out," and pull themselves entirely out of the realm of techno-science in protest against its destructive

---

4.   Heims draws attention to similar arguments put forward by Bateson's great friend, Norbert Wiener. Wiener's approach to nuclear issues and his models for decision making were characterized by "an emphasis on learning, communicating and the fulfillment of human possibilities." Wiener also proposed that the time scale of machines should be chosen so as to be appropriate for the time scales of the organisms with which they interact." Heims notes: "Wiener's emphasis concerning the element of time is ecological" (Heims, 1980, pp. 409-410).

5.   A more lengthy discussion of this point is contained in "Two Models of Ecology Compared: Odum and Bateson" (Harries Jones, 1995, Appendix 1, pp. 235-242)

consequences. Academia showed support suggesting a shift in ecological analysis towards spirituality and religion. There were, of course, may shades to this expression but some took root within "deep ecology." Bateson believed that the more appropriate route for was to challenge the "dualism" of natural science. Rather than "dropping out," ecologists should reform substitute epistemological propositions that arose from and were expressive of the forms of nature. Examples would be the way nature exhibits an overall pattern of recurrence; the perceptual abilities of all organisms engendered through their capacity for anticipatory response; and the way in which the evident interconnectedness of nature is not simply a phenomenon of physical interaction but is mediated through communication. The literature of cybernetics contained such insights and from there it became possible to build an epistemology of recursion. Only then could the new science of ecology put aside the apart-ness of natural science from natural order and deal with the unity of nature.

3. Why Aesthetics?: Bateson And Blake

The themes above suggest how and why Bateson moved into writing about ecology but not why he chose aesthetics as his major platform. One simple answer is that a science of nature attached to aesthetics is demonstrably more persuasive. Without mentioning Rachel Carson specifically, Bateson suggested this in several of his talks (Bateson, 1991, pp. 245-313). Nevertheless, Bateson's move towards aesthetics was unusual. Following Earth Day came the hope that ecology could offer not only interesting data but a path to moral enlightenment. Academic efforts of those in the humanities interested in ecology moved overwhelmingly towards a discussion of *the ethics of environment* that might accompany the new ecological science. As on prior occasions, the response to environment through aesthetics, rather than ethics, remained fitful.

A second answer, as varied publications have noted, was the influence of William Blake on Bateson. His interest in Blake stemmed from domestic circumstances; and, during his adolescence, he undertook formal research on the historical reception of Blake and the latter's artistic ideas. Though historians of art often dismissed Blake as being a mystic, Blake's aesthetic attack on Newton was both compelling and lasting, as anyone who has seen Blake's paintings of Newton will testify. Blake attacked Newton's science as a form of massive reductionism, a "single vision" of the world that foreshortened its complexity, and the beauty of its "minute particulars." In addition, the supposed universality of Newton's science radically undercut the ability of the human imagination to pursue the significance of these minute particulars. Blake had a comfortable relation with the Jehovah of his own artistic imagination and with Jehovah's angels, to whom he gave specific names, each name representing a particular quality. Yet, in striking contrast to the painters of the Renaissance, Blake rejected organized religion for much of his life.

Blake's aesthetic attack together with Blake's spiritual freedom from organized religion, had great appeal to Bateson. Blake, the supposed mystic, was free of the magical tricks of spiritualists, or the remnants of Theosophy, whom Bateson despised. Blake's visionary experiences were not fanciful performances, he stated. They derived from great self-discipline, a practised art inducing Blake's perception of transcendental figures. These self-induced visions were used in an artistic manner entirely distinct to the Theosophists or any other circle of spiritualism or the psychological pretensions of those who pursued the paranormal. [6]

His lifelong attachment to Blake is perhaps sufficient to account for Bateson's desire to initiate an aesthetic ecology, but Bateson had to move beyond Blake. Blake remains a fine exemplar of an aesthetic attack on the dualism of natural science but offers little by way of establishing rapport between aesthetics and a reconstructed science, which was Bateson's clear purpose. To explicate that purpose requires other exemplars but suggestive exemplars drawn from Bateson's own citations are fragmentary and difficult to pin down. For example one is even hard pressed to find in Bateson's publications any elaboration of Bateson's thinking about Blake. Poets such as Coleridge, C. S. Lewis, T. S. Eliot, Wallace Stevens, Lewis Carroll, and psychological philosophers such as Goethe, Bertrand Russell, and Carl Gustav Jung appear and disappear. In the case of Jung's study of archetype, Jungian conclusions are transformed. The same case could be made for Bateson's use of Russell's "logical types." Bateson usually hurried over issues of interpretation in their own writings as he elaborated his own scheme of thinking. Given this, I am going to take two living authors, J. M. Coetzee and Suzi Gablik, who, when brought into juxtaposition with Bateson, enlarge our understanding of Bateson's aesthetic vision.

4. J. M. Coetzee and the "True Challenge."

So far as I know neither J. M. Coetzee, 2003 Nobel Prize winner for literature, nor Suzi Gablik were influenced by Bateson. J. M. Coetzee was writing about a subject quite different from environmentalism, for his novels are based on South African dilemmas, stemming from South Africa's apartheid policy from 1950-1995. One of the most significant aspects of his novels is that they often do not carry any direct reference to everyday horrors of apartheid or of the totalitarianism that supported apartheid. Instead Coetzee portrays South Africa of the apartheid years as a nightmarish "out-of-time" dystopia, and the relationship between his characters, the curves in his plot and apartheid are left for the reader's imagination.

Coetzee was much criticized by other well known South African writers, such as Nadine Gordimer, for his seeming switch away from everyday reality and for creating art that did not clearly identify apartheid as a crime against humanity. Coetzee declared that there was a deeper problem:

---

6. An early example of Bateson's outrage against spiritualism is to be found in his diatribe against Alfred E. Craw-ley, a figure attached to the Theosophy circle, who had written a book on "primitive thought and its bearing on marriage." The diatribe is contained in a report to his mentors at St. John's College, Cambridge of his fieldwork on the Iatmul of New Guinea.

For the writer the deeper problem is not to allow himself to be impaled on the dilemma proposed by the state, namely, either to ignore its obscenities or else to produce representations of them. The true challenge is: how not to play the game by the rules of the state, how to establish one's own authority, how to imagine torture and death on one's own terms" (Coetzee, 1992, p. 364 cited in Jolly, 2004)

If one were to substitute the phrase *natural sciences* for *the state*, and *rhythms of life and death* for *torture and death* then they convey a setting for Bateson's ecological aesthetics. Thus, the deeper problem for the epistemologist is not to allow himself to be impaled on the dilemma proposed by natural science. The true challenge is how not to play the game by the rules of natural science, how to establish one's own authority, how to imagine the rhythms of life and death in different terms. That is, in not playing the game by the prevailing rules so firmly embedded in the scientific materialism of western society, how to establish an authority that enables the pursuit the possibilities of an altered science, one that is far less destructive. Ecological aesthetics has a key role to overcoming the apart-ness of the industrial sciences from the rhythms and patterns of biology and in awakening our senses to a perception of the destructiveness and obscenities of this apart-ness. Bateson challenges us to re-imagine the rhythms of life and death in a manner that accord with the unity of biological order for it is impossible to do this through conventional scientific research by attempting to put together again, like Humpty-Dumpty, all of its partitioned analyses.

We may draw other analogies. Coetzee has consistently refused to comment on the meaning of his novels, or to declare overtly his political affiliations. He is firm in the belief that it is an illusion to reduce political engagement to the aesthetics of literature or vice versa. In fact, Coetzee has said that he is alienated by all political language. He is alienated by "language that lays down the law, that is not provisional, that does not as one of its habitual motions glance back sceptically at its premises" (Killam & Rowe, 2003). So too with Bateson.

Coetzee tries to examine basic premises by transmuting political concerns into imaginative landscapes. This is accomplished without for a moment denying the political implication of his own presence within apartheid: "The whites of South Africa participated, in various degrees, actively or passively, in an audacious and well-planned crime against Africa....Is it in my power to withdraw from the gang? I think not." (Coetzee, 1992, p. 343; cited in Jolly, 2004)

This was exactly the point that Bateson made about ecological understanding. You cannot withdraw. You are part of the gang. If you are a part of a whole, there is no possibility to jump over a higher boundary and look down at your own actions as if this act enabled you to revert to a position of mere observer and somehow absolve yourself from participation within it. All ecological observers are also participants and this includes those within that observer's paradise of rationality, the Enlightenment and its postulates of Enlightenment science. An ecological observer cannot withdraw either actively or passively from the whole of which he or she is a part. How then to talk about all this? An ecological aesthetic creates a series of settings which verify participation. It registers a relation between the parts and the whole, in a manner very different from an observer pretending to be outside the setting, engaged in an exercise of eco-management.

Coetzee in his discussion of apart-ness in the land of apartheid had to invent a form in which the whole premises of apart-ness were transposed and once transposed, apart-ness appears in the self-reflexiveness of his characters in their individual situations. By this means the assumptions and basic premises of the "language that lays down the law" are examined. The post-modernists use phrases like "meta-fictions" and "examining discourse" to portray such transpositions and argue that this marks a general trend in fiction. However, Coetzee lets the aesthetic form in his writing engage the reader and through the reader's aesthetic imagination reveal his, Coetzee's, epistemological intent, that is grasping the obscene assumptions of racial apart-ness foisted on them by the state.[7] The same situation arises with Bateson. While he can be characterized as post-modern scientist, Bateson's metalogues and his introduction of "parables," as he called them, are unlike post-modern aesthetics. They are about system-ness. His metalogues are dialogues through which Bateson transposes personal narrative to inter-subjective encounter and from there pursues non-linearity in systemic interaction. The metalogues catch recursive relationships in human communication, characterizing that which they observe. They observe the apart-ness of modern science from biological order, through its highly linear logic and methodology.

5. Suzi Gablik and the Re-enchantment Thesis

A great deal of artistic response in the western world to environmental predicament has been effusively spiritual and other-worldly. It has evoked comparison between embodied cultural practices of "other peoples" where spirituality in the relationship between humanity and environment is very evident. Western sensibility about the environment that surrounds us nowhere near approaches that of North American hunter-gatherers. Other examples include the spirituality in agricultural practises of peoples who live in the high plains of the Andes; the way Australian Aboriginals demonstrate interrelationship between spirit and land in their expression of "dreaming." Yet others chosen to represent a way of life whose spiritual basis we, the industrial west, should try to emulate include Nepalese Buddhists, the various sorts of Japanese or Chinese martial arts connected with Taoism, followers of Hindu texts, and the Brazilian Rainforest peoples.

The handling of such cultural comparisons about spirituality is certainly controversial (Callicott, 1997). Suzi Gablik in her incisive study of artistic engagement with the ecological in the west, which she provocatively entitles *The Re-*

---

7.   With regard to "the language that lays down the law" Coetzee's autobiographical book, *Youth* (Coetzee, 2002), is
      an account of how he, Coetzee, was unable to resolve the personal issues of "apart-ness," of science and aesthet-
      ics in the time he spent as a computer programmer in Britain as a young man. At that time he had neither the aes-
      thetic form nor the self-reflexiveness to come to terms with this systems programming and see in what manner
      the new types of intellectual technology was contributing to the personal apart-ness which plagued his life.

Enchantment of Art, proposes: "The sacredness of both life and art does not have to mean something other than cosmic and otherworldly—it emerges quite naturally when we cultivate compassionate responsive modes of relating to the world and each other" (Gablik 1991, p. 181). She continues: "The sub-text of all art should therefore be restoring the balance, attunement to nature, together with the idea that all things are linked together in the cyclical processes of nature" (pp. 90-91). So far, I would argue that Bateson's position supports her re-enchantment thesis. He would also support her notion that the word *ecological* should replace the word *metaphysical* as the task of restoring awareness of our symbiotic relationship with nature.

Yet even Gablik encourages the western artist to emerge as some kind of shaman, who cultivates the visionary mode in order to interpret myths from cultures that are available to us and enable us, the artist's public, to touch that which emanates from arousal of the mysterious and the sacred (Gablik 1991, p. 50). Her viewpoint comes close to the position of organized religion, both Catholic and Protestant, on ecology and the search for grace. While Bateson's writings sometimes express an affinity with the human search for grace, he held a very different point of view about the realm of the sacred. Proponents of organized religion often proceed to argue that not only is re-enchantment a necessary condition for its rescue but a search for grace implies an abandonment of secularism. For Bateson, a leap from mechanism and materialism to an ill-considered spiritualism is a leap out of the industrial frying-pan into ethereal fire (Bateson & Bateson, 1987, pp. 50-64). Understanding unity and holism in environment should not result in a western embrace of other-worldly spirituality. Rather, we should recognize how our mechanistic civilization becomes overwhelmed, and thrown into epistemological panic, when confronting unity and holism in the biosphere, and does not know how to proceed (Bateson, 1991, pp. 268, 311).

Bateson opens up a dialectic between secularism and the thinking of organized religion by being critical of both. Ecology is an immanent feature of our existence. Bateson is firm about this. Therefore, to embrace an ecological aesthetic that is rooted in transcendent deities is to confuse a cultural mapping with the territory of ecological patterning. At the same time, Bateson expresses his displeasure with ecological science. Biological science had yet to become aware of the consequences of its continued insistence on the premises of dualism, borrowed from physics, and how this had led to increasing ignorance about the unity of biological organization over the years. Like any self-recursive communication system, biology must become aware of disruption brought about by misunderstanding natural harmony. We become that which we pretend (Bateson and Bateson, 1987, pp. 167-182). Biologists must learn, scientifically, that what humans do in this world to biological order will, in a circular manner, always comes around to stab them in the back. The recursive nature of biological order must be adopted as a primary focus in ecology. This will, in turn, alter current conceptions about continuity and discontinuity in ecological order as well as give us a better understanding of adaptation, both human and non-human in relation to each other.

Such was Bateson's ecological message embedded in a much broader aesthetic of holism.

6. Abrupt Change and Free-fall

For Bateson, a major difficulty in any ecological aesthetics is to find ways of delving beneath the surface of direct sensory experience of nature to include the less immediately visible aspects of natural history, such as diversity, complexity, and species interactions in ecosystems. This, of course is true of any aesthetic endeavour but ecosystems present special complexities. Their coherence rests on a common pattern—feedback—which, in turn, exhibits myriad couplings between sentient forms, each with hidden significance. Further, the conjoining patterns of change that make up biological order, make it difficult for any observer to construct any single point of reference and to rely upon that point of reference in order to appraise unity and interconnection in natural order. Not only are there multiple levels of connection in an ecosystem which have to be taken into account, but no observer is able to step outside an ecosystem and look back at it from above and so achieve some sort of visual look at its unity. How then do scientific observers or artists, who are themselves part of the field that they are observing construct points of reference, or registers?

Holism is shorthand for "that special sort of holism generated by feedback and recursiveness," (Bateson, 1991, p. 221). Such an interpretation requires the generation of quite different standards of reference that would enable rigorous statements to be made about unity and integration, slow change or abrupt change, in a holistic order such as the biosphere. Needless to say, these standards of reference would be quite different from the "registers" of sentience of Hume, Locke and other empiricists.

At one point he drew upon a striking image, that of "free fall." Without any register or standard of reference about feedback, ecologists are in the same situation as that of a parachutist jumping out of a plane with no instruments with which they can establish a relationship to the ground. They are floating into free fall, not knowing what their proper orientation to earth might be…up…or down. Our civilization is in free fall because it knows little or nothing about the holism of its eco-dynamics nor the recursive processes of ecology. Hence, as Bateson reminds us, if we are unable to adjust our ideas of adaptation to the dynamics of eco-systems we will be unable to come to any judgement about the patterns of continuity and discontinuity in ecological order. (Harries-Jones, 1995, p. 64).

At the time he wrote about "free fall," his metaphor seemed a remote and removed from empirical demonstration. But not today. We are now in a condition of climate change that may exhibit runaway. The thinness of the ice is already causing major problems in the Arctic and carving frozen glaciers into huge icebergs in the Antarctic; the loss of the polar ice cap in Greenland is suggestive of runaway effects. Whether "the great melt" will produce a set of climate changes which permit humans to adopt a relatively slow pace to climate change, or whether humans, animals, insects and other organisms face abrupt climate change, has suddenly become the major issue of climate research.

Consider the recent evidence of an ecologist attached to the Intergovernmental Panel on Climate Change:

> Feedback mechanisms in changing [ecological] systems are poorly understood....Feedback of interactions between humans and the environment in the face of climate change are likely to be negative and are expected to increase. As humans have to take adaptive actions to preserve their systems in the face of climate change and sea level rise, there is a risk that impacts on the environment will increase, despite better awareness of the issues. The short-term needs of humans are likely to take precedence over longer-term needs, which are intimately tied up with the environment. This could mean greater-than-expected and unpredictable indirect impacts resulting from climate change and sea-level rise. (McCarthy et al. 2001. Section 17.41.1 online)

Or let us take the study of the impact of global warming sponsored by the Pentagon. The authors of the United States National Research Council study argue against a complacent views of global warming, insisting that this does not take sufficient account of the discontinuities that may arise as warming crosses various temperature thresholds. Change driven by feedback is not the same driven by continuous adaptation (U.S. National Research Council, 2002, pp. 4-5). Darwinian images of change as continuous variation—which is what the public has been taught to be the case—is inaccurate. Evolutionary changes, both large and small, have also been characterised by abrupt change or discontinuity. Bateson could not have put it better himself.

Bateson knew about the potential for runaway in climate change for quite some time, having investigated this issue in the mid-1960s and had come to the conclusion that its effects, including the first signs of melting icebergs in the Antarctic, were likely to be much more grave than the ecologists of the time suggested (Harries-Jones, 1995, p. 29). One argument current during the 1960s which he spent some time examining, was that an increase in carbon dioxide in the atmosphere will be beneficial because it will aid growth of forests! He records that initially, he accepted the thesis that global warming would be good for the world's biomes because greater densities of carbon dioxide would promote thicker vegetative cover. Then he realized that such a hypothesis took no account of feedback and was, therefore, a dangerous misconstruction. He began writing that the scientific world had about twenty years to make this correction about recognizing anthropogenic influence and acting on it or the results of ignoring the correction would be ominous.

It is interesting that in the 1960s, Bateson did not add his voice to calls for improving quantitative analysis of ecological patterns. To him this was an inadequate resolution to the study of global warming. Bateson was pointing his aesthetics to second order patterns of feedback rather than tying scientific investigation to experimental data (first order patterning). His decision can certainly be challenged, but the study of feedback, Bateson maintained, goes beyond numbers, primarily because of a study of second order patterns of feedback combines continuous variation with discontinuous feedback, or runaway, and make this combination integral to an understanding of ecological change. Second, studying feedback in a recursive system is always very difficult, but a study made far more difficult by ignoring the study of feedback thresholds. Third, he well knew from his work in psycho-therapy that there would be both indecisiveness about probable effects with a strong possibility of denial of adverse effects of climate change.[8]

7. The Bateson Challenge In *Angels Fear*

It was another 20 years before national governments unequivocally recognized global warming, 30 years before the Kyoto Protocol was put forward to world leaders. Bateson's aesthetics arrives at a time when global ecology is no longer stable, no longer kind or munificent. We face great uncertainty for an indefinite period of time, very different from the regularities of global climate present when the science of the industrial age flourished, proclaiming itself as the harbinger of human progress. At the very moment of the ratification of Kyoto we are moving into the first hot period that humanity has ever experienced.

The themes of indefinite conditions, uncertain grasp of change, indeterminacy and the myriad deceptions of our conception of progress is built into all of Bateson's writing, none more so than in *Angles Fear,* his posthumous publication (Bateson & Bateson, 1987). There his attachment of aesthetics to ecology can be read in at least two ways. The first is that of increasing aesthetic sensibility to pattern and modulation of natural pattern: this is the material for dream and poetry (Bateson, 1991, p. 256). The other comes about through deepening a connection between epistemology and aesthetics. Bateson drew the connection in terms of a forked riddle: "What is man that he may recognize disease or disruption or ugliness?" "What is disease or disruption or ugliness that a man may know it?" The riddle's two aspects derive on the one side from perceptual acuity in recognizing a difference between beauty and ugliness, and on the other an observer's knowledge of pattern of disease, and disruption.

The pattern of the percept does not flow easily into the pattern of the other and numerous tensions lie in the fork between the two. Bateson admits this. At the outset there are issues of perception stemming from seeming contradictions in perceiving pattern flow. Next there is the tension between appearance and descriptions of reality conceptualized through recursive forms. This set of tensions become a problem of epistemology. Bateson suggests that working away at the fork of contradictions, the interface between aesthetics and epistemology, will likely promote a new conception of holism, and perceptually will draw us toward an awareness of beauty in a larger more inclusive system. As mentioned above, we must become more aware of the

---

8.   I admit to interpolating evidence from the Bateson archives at this point, but the interpolation is reasonable given 1968 correspondence, especially surrounding the conference published as *Our Own Metaphor.* In the numbers category, the Scientific Advisor to the United Kingdom Government recently commented we now know that carbon dioxide concentrations in the atmosphere over the last several million years have varied from 200 parts per million at the depths of the ice ages to 270 parts per million during the warming periods between them. We have now reached 379 parts per million and that figure is going up by 3 ppm per year (Sir David King quoted in *Toronto Star*, October 5, 2004).

myths by which we live. The myths of dualism, mind separate from matter, body separate from mind, environment separate from cultural tradition are among the most conspicuous of these myths in both science and the humanities. So too is the practice in science of separating of parts from the whole. Incorporating aesthetics meant neither a return to a mediaeval realm of the sacred, nor uncritical acceptance of any particular spirituality or world-view of peoples either inside or outside major religions. Instead, it fostered the idea that holism, unity and beauty were coincident with each other and should be an integral part of any modern science investigating the game of life. Wherever we begin to have intimate appreciation of form, shape, pattern in nature, there we should also generate and affirm aesthetic notions of how parts fit in relation to wholes

All recursive communication systems must become aware of disruption in its own relations, and, at the same time, must acknowledge systemic discrepancies which necessarily exist between what we can say and what we are trying to describe (Bateson & Bateson, 1987, pp. 151-156) So too, any epistemological work attached to aesthetics must examine how mind creates its mapping of the world, and how often the map is mistaken for territory (Bateson & Bateson, 1987, pp. 16-30).

Thus aesthetics offers a contrasting balance to rationalist conceptions of consciousness, of the particular, and the universal. The following exchange is indicative and is drawn from a discussion with the ecologist Henryk Skolimowski and others at Dartington Hall, England in October 1979, a few months before his death (Bateson, 1991, p. 300):

> Q. Would it be correct to suggest that the aesthetic is this unifying glimpse that makes us aware of the unity of things which is not [in the limited sphere of] consciousness?
> G.B. That is right; that is what I am getting at. The flash which appears in consciousness as a disturbance of consciousness is the thing that I am talking about.

It becomes a disturbance of consciousness because consciousness as a manifestation of scientific description tends to focus inwards, whereas notions like the sacred and the beautiful tend to be always looking outward for the whole. The logical types of descriptive prose are disturbed by the aesthetics of symmetry and ratio, rhythms and resonance inherent in metaphor, poetry and ecosystem integration. The two are not separate from each other. and they can become conjoined aspects of our ability to understand. Aesthetics, the unifying glimpse, provides a medium through which humanity can begin to communicate about how to understand wholes and thus the unity of the biosphere. Otherwise a science of ecology will lack a spiritual sense of its own immanence, and Bateson's *modus vivendi,* an ecology of mind, will be bad science.

References

Bateson, G. (1946a, September). The Pattern of an Armaments Race: An Anthropological Approach, Part 1. *Bulletin of the Atomic Scientists, 2*(5-6), 10-11.

Bateson, G. (1946b, October). The Pattern of an Armaments Race: An Anthropological Approach, Part 2. *Bulletin of the Atomic Scientists, 2*(7-8), 26-28.

Bateson, G. (1979a). Nuclear armament as epistemological error: Letters to the California Board of Regents." *Zero, 3,* 34-41.

Bateson, G. (1979b). Letters to the Regents of the University of California. *Co-Evolution Quarterly,* 24 (Winter), 22-23.

Bateson, G. (1991). *A sacred unity: Further steps to an ecology of mind* (Rodney Donaldson, Ed.) New York: Harper Collins.

Bateson, G. (2000). Bali: The Value System of a Steady State. In *Steps to an Ecology of Mind* (pp. 107-127). Chicago: Chicago University Press. [article originally published in 1949; book originally published in 1972]

Bateson, G. & Bateson, M. C. (1987). *Angels fear: Towards an epistemology of the sacred.* New York: Macmillan.

Bateson, M. C. (1972). *Our own metaphor: A personal account of a conference on the effects of conscious purpose on human adaptation.* New York: Alfred Knopf.

Berman, M. (1984). *The Re-enchantment of the World.* New York: Bantam New Age Books.

Callicott, J. B. (1989). *In defense of the land ethic.* Albany: SUNY.

Callicott, J. B. (1997). In Defense of Earth's Insights. *Worldviews: Environment, Culture and Religion, 1,* 169-182.

Carson, R. (1951). *The sea around us.* New York: Oxford University Press.

Carson, R. (1962). *Silent Spring.* Cambridge, MA: Riverside Press

Coetzee, J. M. (1992). *Doubling the point: Essays and interview* (David Attwell, Ed.). Cambridge: Harvard University Press.

Coetzee, J. M. (2002). *Youth.* London: Secker and Warburg

Gablik, S. (1991). *The Re-enchantment of Art.* New York: Thames and Hudson

Harries-Jones, P. (1995). *A recursive vision: Ecological understanding and Gregory Bateson.* Toronto: Toronto University Press.

Heims, S. J. (1980) *John von Neumann and Norbert Wiener: From mathematics to the technologies of life and death.* Cambridge, MA: The MIT Press

Jolly, R. (2004). Exploding the rules of the game: J.M. Coetzee writing South Africa. *Queen's Quarterly, 111/13* (Fall 2004), 462-466.

Killam, D. & Rowe, R. (2003). *Contemporary African Database.* (Retrieved January 11, 2005 from http://people.africadatabase.org/en/person/2259.html)

McCarthy, J. J. (Ed.). (2001). *Climate change 2001: Impacts, adaptation, and vulnerability: Contribution of Working Group II to the third assessment report of the Intergovernmental Panel on Climate Change.* Cambridge: Cambridge University Press. (Working Group 2: Feedback, Interactions and Resilience. Retrieved January 11, 2005 from http://grida.no/climate/ipcc_tar/wg2/638.htm#1741)

Odum, E. P. (1963). *Ecology.* Philadelphia: W. B. Saunders.

Odum, H. T. (1971). *Environment, Power and Society.* New York and London: Wiley Interscience.

Steingraber, S. (1998). *Living downstream: A scientist's personal investigation of cancer and the environment.* New York: Vintage Books.

U. S. National Research Council. (2002). *Abrupt climate change: Inevitable surprises.* Committee on Abrupt Climate Change. Washington, D.C.: National Academy Press.

Worster, D. (1994). *Nature's Economy: A History of Ecological Ideas.* Cambridge: Cambridge University Press. (Originally published in 1977)

Cybernetics And Human Knowing. Vol. 12, nos. 1-2, pp. 75-89

Circular Epistemology and the Bushman Shamans:
A Kalahari Challenge to the Hegemony of Narrative

Bradford Keeney, Ph.D.[1]

The Kalahari Bushmen shamans of southern Africa practice an implicit cybernetic epistemology based on the idea of *thuru,* referring to the never ending shape-shifting aspect of nature. It is argued that their way of thinking and being in relationship demonstrates how difficult it is to express any understanding of circularity and systemic process through narrative means. Challenging the hegemony of literacy and narrative, Bushman epistemology points toward different interactional forms of evoking sacred knowing. Social science and psychotherapy disciplines, most notably the field of family therapy, though historically influenced by cybernetic thinking, too easily abandon Gregory Bateson's call for the importance of circular and ecosystemic understanding. With an imaginary dialogue between Bateson and a Bushman shaman, scholars and therapists are encouraged to re-instate *dynamic* circularity as the heart of human encounter.

Like the thematic focus that organized the historic Macy conference meetings during the 1940's, Gregory Bateson was far more interested in the ideas associated with "circularity" than any of the phenomena he examined. Whether observing otters at play, learning of an octopus, therapeutic communication, cultural initiation rites, or William Blake's poetry, he looked through the surface appearances to find his way to the systemic forms that held the beholden.

In this same spirit, I first engaged with the field of family therapy, looking for ways it could illustrate systemic process. For a very brief moment, family therapy held a fascination with the systemic organization of family communication and a circular way of construing its practice, re-thinking and re-orchestrating everything from diagnosis to intervention. My contributions to the family therapy field were concerned with clarifying how cybernetic epistemology could deliver a more circularly (and improvisationally) involved therapist (and client). The systemic days of family therapy have since passed and it is now difficult to find family therapists who remember (let alone practice or teach) how to work with families rather than aggregates of individuals or brokered pieces of stories.

I left family therapy to pursue field research in a variety of cultures, including Japan, Bali, Amazonian and North American Indian tribes, Africa, the Caribbean, Brazil, Mexico, among other settings. I continued looking for how cultural phenomena, particularly the practices of shamans and indigenous practitioners of traditional medicine, were organized by circular epistemology. Unlike Euro-American psychotherapy and medicine, the majority of other folk healing traditions are more

---

1. Distinguished Scholar of Cultural Studies, Ringing Rocks Foundation. Email: bkeeney@ringingrocks.org

intimately and historically connected to circular thinking. Arguably influenced by their closer and more intimate relationship to nature, they began with a systemic view of the world and found the lineal thinking of outsiders to be dangerously limited (whether the visitors meant to exploit or help them, including those outsiders protecting them from the other colonialists).

The Bushman of the Kalahari, living in Botswana and Namibia, are often said to constitute our oldest living culture. I have spent over twelve years learning from their elders and this essay is a presentation of how some of their ideas may contribute to our conception of circularity. On the surface, this essay may appear as aimed toward family therapists who have lost their way, seduced by linear causality and power mythologies, often re-cast in the trendy metaphors of postmodernist or narrative orientations. However, what I have to say is not limited to family therapists, but applies equally to all practitioners of the so-called social sciences. Although the practiced ideas of cybernetic epistemology are implicit in diverse indigenous cultures, we have yet to achieve a firm grasp on how these ideas can radically transform contemporary human practices and understandings. This essay invites a glimpse at one of the oldest wisdom traditions with the hope that it may renew and deepen our interest in the difference that a respect for circularity may make in the practicalities of everyday life.

For decades, the Kalahari Bushmen (also called San) of Namibia and Botswana have been studied by anthropologists. It has been widely believed that

> one fundamental feature about…the belief patterns of Bushmen in general, is its multifarious, inchoate, and amorphous quality…a confusing triangle of ideas and beliefs, marked by contradictions, inconsistencies, vagueness, and lack of culture-wide standardization. (Guenther, 1999, p. 126)

My fieldwork has found that each Bushman shaman's beliefs change and are often inconsistent. However, my research (1999; 2003; 2005) also reports consistency, specificity, and clarity in talking with Bushmen from diverse communities and language groups with respect to what they describe taking place with their body when they engage in the process of healing others.

What varies and highlights inconsistencies are the Bushman's *explanations* of their physical experiences. The variation is not only true among different Bushman shamans, but within the ongoing accounts of each shaman. Most important to acknowledge is that a consistent and logic-tight articulation and explanation of experiences in language is not accorded a high value in Bushman culture. What is taken more seriously is what is felt—the body's expression, dialogue and interaction of movement that is triggered and orchestrated by what Bushmen regard as spiritual power, called *n/om,* most often displayed in their community healing dances.

Traditional academic and therapeutic ways of knowing emphasize rhetoric over somatic expression and thereby entail numerous blind spots to the most important experiences that take place in Bushman healing practices. To a Kalahari shaman, no "right" questions lead to understanding their way of being. Knowledge of the dance cannot be gleamed in conversation and cannot be held by narrative means. It's truths can't be seen or heard, but must be corporally felt. Although Bushmen do not have a high regard for clear and consistent descriptions and explanations, they spend considerable time reflecting on their healing ways and being entertained by discussing it. There are no official custodians of their knowledge or social institutions for maintaining any philosophical tradition. Lorna Marshall, in her classic paper, "The Medicine Dance of the !Kung Bushmen," makes this conclusion, "The !Kung are not concerned with carefully preserving the knowledge of their past, and they do not teach it systematically to their young; consequently, much is lost to memory" (Marshall, 1969, p. 351).

Fully bodied spiritual experience is most valued by Bushmen healers. This experience is born and expressed by the movement of their muscles and skin, not from the ruminations of reflective discourse. From the Bushman shaman's perspective, none of their sacred knowledge has been lost. It is encoded in the orally preserved songs and muscle memories of kinesthetic movements and postures. Its expression is sparked by a presumed natural/spiritual presence that moves their bodies to perform ecstatic choreographies of healing movement inseparable from intimate touch.

Given this different posture and stance about what is regarded as significant knowledge, how can we best communicate with Bushmen about their most sacred matters? Questions that aim to evoke a narrative are out of the question. They lead to Bushman word play at the inquirer's expense. Modern or postmodern skills in rhetoric, conversational politics, and narrative understanding are easily out of place, that is, out of context, when over-emphasized in a Bushman encounter.

I learned to interact in their preferred way, to embody an epistemology that placed me on their ground. Specifically, Bushmen want to see, hear, and feel our bodies move in relationship to the way they occupy and perform with their bodies. You might say that Bushmen are about as interested in the participatory making of semantic understandings and psychological (or cultural) theories as we are interested in knowing and describing their world through the sensation and metaphors of smell. To more fully know, appreciate, and respect the Bushman healing dance requires that we move forward and dare to enter their spirited world with both our body and mind—but foremost our body.

I have been dancing with the Bushmen for more than a decade and have been taught and initiated by many Bushman elders, both men and women. They believe they have turned me into a Bushman shaman who experiences first hand their spiritual universe. As Megan Biesele, an anthropologist with the former Harvard Kalahari Research Project, writes: "Brad spoke to healers like /Kunta Boo and =Oma Dahm after dancing with them for many hours. There was no question in their minds but that his strength and purposes were coterminous with theirs. I know this not only from the book [*Ropes to God*] but from talking myself, a year or two later, with /Kunta, =Oma, and others who had danced with Brad. They affirmed his power as a healer and their enjoyment of dancing with him."

From my perspective, I have learned to participate in their healing dance in a way that is recognized as a Bushman shaman's way of interacting. This engagement of contact and movement has brought me to the edge of what they affirm as their spiritual universe and at times has arguably allowed me to step inside. I learned that there is a rationale behind their shifting names and meanings, and the slippery and amorphous ways they speak of deities, devils, and spirits that comprise their spiritual universe.

Bushmen have a way of knowing that derives from the constantly changing forms they see in nature as well as the transformational experiences that arise in their healing dance and dreams. Like Gregory Bateson (1972; 1979), they build their understanding through observing the circular processes they experience in the natural world, such as changing weather and shifting patterns of plant and animal ecosystemic interaction. For a Bushman, change and transformation are the most constant aspects of life. The endless recycling and changing of forms constitute the central premise of their spiritual understanding.

For a shaman, the process of shifting forms, for example, a shaman shape-shifting into a (mythopoetic, dreamtime) lion, has a name—*thuru*. The same notion also applies to their conceptualization of a supreme being: the Big God exercises *thuru*, enabling the creation of many forms. With this in mind, the whole circle (or sphere) that holds the tracings of all imaginable (and unimaginable) forms is *G//aoan*, but it is a name the Bushmen use to indicate God, devil, and ancestral spirit. On the surface, it may appear confusing and contradictory to have one word attached to these different referents. But if we recognize that *devil* is simply a way of pointing to the trickster aspect of their spiritual universe (rather than marking an opposition between good and evil), we find that their understanding is neither dualistic nor illogical. It is circular or recursive, with different aspects or forms (over different phenomenal domains) brought forth by ever-changing processes of transformation.

In a way, *G//aoan* is the supreme shaman who never stops practicing *thuru*, first changing into its most encompassing forms—a stable sky god (as well as stable underground god) along with the constantly changing trickster gods. Subsequently, as we step down an order of abstraction, at another level of process, *G//aoan* brings forth lesser forms—the benevolent and malevolent spiritual ancestors *(g//aoansi)*, entities, and forces. And finally, on the human level, *G//aoan* evokes the realizations of a Bushman shaman. As a shaman opens herself or himself to receive and activate *n/om*, the power that transforms, she or he can become the arms and hands of *G//aoan*, or become indistinguishable from an ancestor or even the Big God.

Bushmen elders told me that *G//aoan* brings forth both the Big God and the trickster god (the latter being what they believe the missionaries call "Satan" or "the devil"). If you think of *G//aoan* as inseparable from the primal process of transformation, then Bushman spiritual discourse reveals circular (recursive) logic. Transformation, at the highest order of abstraction, brings forth both a stable form (the Big God) and a changing form (trickster god). The Big God lives in the sky (and is mirrored underground) and is described in similar ways by different Bushmen—it is a shaman/teacher in the sky with a family that dances and lives like all other Bushmen.

Its description is stable with minor variations in detail. Megan Biesele (1993, p. 27) astutely notes that there are few Bushmen tales that refer to the sky god. There are very few details and virtually no mythological stories and accounts of their Big God. On the other hand, *G//aoan* has the trickster side, a mercurial source of trouble and sickness that has many names including Satan. It can also be helpful at times. The problem with anything that can change in any aspect, direction, or connotation, is that it is nearly impossible to know when to trust it. Bushman life is filled with many stories and descriptions of this trickster side of *G//aoan*.

The fact that *G//aoan* is the same name given to both these aspects again underscores the inseparability and complementarity between them. Discussions of Bushman spirituality suggest, on the surface, a dynamic dualism between good and evil, with evil cast as a trickster character often in the form of a jackal. As a trickster, evil can assume many forms, none of which can be seen as a singular, permanent manifestation. It then follows that the Bushmen's stories, descriptions, and explanations of evil and causes of bad outcomes and disease necessarily will be inconsistent and variable. It is the trickster's nature to change its identity, perhaps disguising itself as the spirit of a bad ancestor, or as a shade, ghost, or other ambiguous aspects. However, at a deeper level, the jackal is found to be an aspect of the Big God. Here we find a unity, rather than a dichotomy of opposing forces. In this view, good and evil interact to form a more encompassing complementarity.

On the everyday level of life, the Bushmen see every human being as manifesting the recursive interaction of a stable identity brought forth by changing trickster forms. Here the shifting forms cover the wide range of human feelings including happiness, sadness, jealousy, altruism, love, and hate. Bushman shamans understand the mercurial side of our emotional lives and our shape-shifting relational patterns. All married couples, for example, go through one form after another, shifting emotions and patterns of interaction. Passion and intimacy shift to anger and withdrawal, interspersed with caring, parenting, friendship, and so forth. For Bushmen, health and well-being are defined as the ever present transformative action of *thuru*. As long as the forms keep shifting or moving along the circular path, there is life in the relationship. All the forms, taken as a whole, constitute a stable healthy relationship. Family therapists with a systemic view have tried to articulate the same understanding (see Keeney, *Aesthetics of Change*). For the Bushman shaman, any effort to maximize any particular form (or minimize another) is to block *thuru's* life-giving movement.

Bushmen see all of life, from the presence of the gods, ancestral spirits, and their living community, as requiring never-ending change. Their view echoes the wisdom of cybernetician, Heinz von Foerster (1981; 2003), "If you want to find yourself, change!" Whenever the circle of transforms stops moving, Bushmen say that "a circular string has been broken." This is when healing is necessary.

Bushman shamans are capable of other orders of transformative process. In addition to experiencing the recycling climates of human emotional life, they have learned to transform themselves into the experiential domains of the ancestral spirits and the gods. As their bodies express an awareness of the possibility of these shifts, an inner movement of dancing around life's differences and oppositions is let loose. This is when *thuru* takes hold of their inside and outside, transforming one opposite into another, doing so as the body shakes, jerks, and trembles. The movements are an enactment and realization of *thuru*, a Kalahari version of the dance of Shiva. Sharing the shaking touch helps activate *thuru* in others. In this whirling mix, problems, symptoms, and illness are exchanged and interchanged with healing, inspiration, and vitality.

The shaman can not do this work alone. He or she must interact with the ancestral spirits and gods. This, in turn, takes them to the heart of the Big God's love. There they merge with a divine love, with hands trembling and delivering spiritual birth, death, and resurrection. When shared with another person who is open to full participation, both are taken into a moment of ecstatic communion and union. The most basic premise of the Bushman's philosophy is the recursive (cybernetic) relationship between change (shifting forms brought about by *thuru*) and stability (never ending presence of identity). In cybernetics, the stability (identity, organizational closure, autonomy, wholeness) of a system is brought about by the never-ending processes of change (re-cycling of differences making differences, moving along a Batesonian circular trail).

With this well rounded perspective, the circle of life is an unbroken circle of transformed states, identities, and particularities. The lines that connect all forms, the stable identity of the whole, is a circle of circles, a sphere like Mother Earth. This is arguably the "mind of nature," to follow Gregory Bateson's metaphor: When mind is defined as a conversational pattern ["a fixed point in the infinite recursion of interactions between a set of participants," as Varela (1976) defined it], then we may speak of: (*conversational pattern/participants of the conversation*).

Here we are participants in the vast conversations of the biosphere. This recursive understanding, in turn, frees us from the bondage of the mind-body duality, where we now have: *mind (conversational pattern)/bodies (expression of the participants)*.

In the Kalahari, the conversational domain of the dance (with no words spoken), is understood as: (healing dance/shaking, interacting bodies) where the expression of *thuru* though a shaking body brings forth the world of the dance, an eternal moment when all ancestors and creation are present through the evoked lines of love that connect and interchange.

The process underlying life's interconnectivity and wholeness is generated by the circularity of ever-changing forms. Like Ezekiel's wheel, n/om, kundalini, chi, and the holy ghost power are all brought about by the constantly turning circle. Here the circle swallows itself, then gives birth to the same process that created it. In this circulation, the mind of nature is not separate from the body of nature. They are joined by the formless form, no-mind, absent-body of *thuru*, the pleroma behind creatura, as Jung (1961) articulated it. It is nothing less than the mystery which can not be named or known outside of being in its embrace.

If *thuru* comes to a stop and the trickster is unable to keep changing its wardrobe, the circular string will break. This is equivalent to saying that the opposite sides of a relationship have pulled themselves apart. My Bushmen friends tell me that other cultures have broken the string with them, suggesting that the interaction has been a unilateral push and pull, rather than circularly reciprocal. These same cultures, black and white, have broken their strings with the animals and plants, where there is no co-respect, co-learning, co-operation, and co-love. Bushmen seek to live within the circles of life. Their shamans surrender to *thuru* as a way of being in *G//aoan.*

A Bushman shaman is a master of *thuru,* capable of dancing across the realms. Here there is an awareness that good can give birth to evil and vice versa. Knowing this, the shaman sees the suffering of others brought about by the laws of rigid dualisms, where evil and good, devil and God, are held as separate and in holy war, one side determined to destroy the other. Whether articulated as saving the world from infidels, heathens, racists, or colonialists, this is the folly of the human world. It is the grand illusion and mass spell that must be broken. The way out is to see the world circularly, that is, realizing that all things are related and created through their interaction. Destroy one side and the string is broken while all sides perish.

In Bali I learned that the tension between good and evil is called *sakti.* The Balinese shamans believe that no one really has *sakti* in the sense of having a force or power inside of them. It is more accurate to say that a spiritual person is "fighting for *sakti"* rather than say that they "have *sakti.*" As my Balinese colleagues put it, if we say that you have *sakti* it really means that you are in a battle for it. If there is no evil attacking you, there is no *sakti* in the situation. But if someone is trying to kill you and you are still alive, you are in *sakti.* This is an important concept to the Balinese and outsiders who study their culture usually don't understand it. You never win a battle because the important fights keep going on. If you are winning, then there is *sakti.*

The shaman's body holds on to all imaginable contraries and differences, embracing all sides and voices. Inside these polarities, a whirling wind originates, whipping the shaman from side to side. Waves of energy express the inner contradictions and contraries of human existence. Love and hate are held next to each other, neither side allowed to run away. The wheel turns. Altruism and selfishness face off, but neither crosses the line. The wheel turns again. Good and evil stand their ground, facing one another. Again the wheel turns. *In contraries lies progression.* In the body of the shaman, the wheel of life (and death) turns and spiritual electricity is generated.

Bushman shamans vary in their depth of discerning, understanding, and articulating the ambiguities, paradoxes, and complexities of life. Some see a simple battle between good and evil, while others have a more complex view of the interpenetration of contrasting sides of a conceptual relationship. An individual Bushman doctor may also alternate between these simple and complex outlooks within the course of a lifetime or within a single conversation.

The scholar who studies Bushman culture is caught in a dilemma. Namely, conversations with Bushmen are being transformed into theoretical discourses that attempt to explain and account for their unique way of life. The outcomes of this transformation include scholarly papers, books, formal conferences, additional research funding, and organizations that try to further understand, help, and relate to Bushman life. What is seldom asked is whether such transformations and outcomes are resonant with Bushman culture. Do Bushmen give any importance to textual understanding? Are Bushman tales about the dance simply a form of storytelling made for the moment of entertainment? Is it the Bushman or the anthropologist who is more invested in the political correctness of using "correct" metaphors (and theories) when describing their culture?

Imagine a group of Bushman traveling to a psychotherapy or social science (or cybernetics) conference, saying that a dream had inspired them to visit. Instead of asking any questions and holding any well- formed conversations, an invitation to dance is extended. The Bushmen dance and then go home and talk to their friends about how they danced with the therapists. No explanations. Only stories. Stories that changed with each telling. And they dance to celebrate the great journey.

Meanwhile the scholarly therapists write academic papers on what the Bushman said after they danced. A specially organized conference is quickly assembled for colleagues to announce their findings. Phrases like "non-colonial encounter" and "Bushman narratives" are bantered about. None of the therapists consider dancing at the gathering.

Historically, authoritative psychotherapists are prone to the laborious production of textual accounts. In the process of creating these formal stories, a scholar-therapist's body sits or stands still while trying to manipulate words into stable semantic chains and nets of understanding. This is true for all textual renderings, including those of the postmodern writers. (Is there a postmodern therapist who has stopped writing and talking, teaching solely through improvisational touch and dance?) Meanwhile, back in the Kalahari, the Bushman's body moves and the fluidic stories are encouraged to change with each telling. What is stable in the Bushman's experience is the process of movement itself—dancing feet, swaying bodies, trembling hands, pumping bellies, convulsing heads, as well as the ever-changing stories and jokes that are shared underneath the afternoon shade of a camelthorn tree.

In the Kalahari, I found that Bushmen shamans do not place a rigid value on any stable or dominant story. Narratives are not the primary basis for organizing everyday life in their spiritual universe. Bushmen rely on their immediate experience—what they smell, taste, feel, hear, and see. The more that sensory experience is amplified and combined in a holistic way, the closer they are to their truths. It follows that any shaman, in the moment of realizing full-blown synesthesia, is the carrier of big truths. These truths are not held in the telling, but in the webs of multi-sensory polyphony that express the rhythms, music, movements, and touch.

Anthropologists and therapists, on the other hand, come equipped with a narrative view of the universe—believing that what people do is organized by the understandings brought forth by dominant stories carried in individual and social conversations. Imagine how semantic-oriented psychotherapists and social scientists of Euro-American culture would be driven mad by any attempt to conduct conversational work with a Bushman. When a classic psychoanalyst or a contemporary narrative therapist or researcher (incidentally, both are arguably of the same logical type) attempts to uncover dominant motifs and underlying stories and re-construe "therapeutic" life stories, it is like trying to mark a spot on the ocean with a cork, to borrow a phrase from the Zen Buddhists. Bushman epistemology is not a marking of constants in a sea of discourse. It is more akin to the movements of the rising and falling tides themselves. Their ocean of sand is alive with cycles of movement, marked not by words, but by the furrows of dancing feet that are immediately blown away by the wind. Bushman talk, like their dance, moves round and round a circle. It may start in one direction, but can shift to the opposite direction at any moment. The only stability in this universe of experience is the constancy of change and movement itself.

Bushman shamans know that understanding the mysteries of the Big God's creation is less important than participating in it. They want us to dance more and talk less. They want us to feel with our hearts rather than fill our minds. The Bushman way is more polyphonic, improvisational, performative, playful, and biological than the textually ruled world that anthropologists and therapists inhabit. They prefer shape-shifting in and out of a polychromal and polyphonic spiritual universe over word-shifting onto monochromal academic paper. Their truths mirror the truths of the sky, earth, plants, and animals that surround them. Their epistemology and way of life can only be understood in the smell of sweat, the experienced warmth of blood flowing out of a hunted animal, the bare handling of roots and earth, and the tender embrace of one another through hearts and hands that flutter.

One of the reasons I report these particular fieldwork findings is to set up an intellectual tease, enabling me to say that perhaps the Bushman shamans and the systemically oriented elders of early family therapy (among others with circular orientations) are similarly misunderstood by the plethora of semantic-driven onlookers (outside observers/judgers) who over-emphasize meaning while maintaining a blind spot for the circularities of interactive process. As we used to say many years ago, they deal with *content* while being ignorant of real-time *process*. By process, I am referring to the patterns and connective logics that hold together one's way of knowing, where epistemology is an inseparable loop of cognition and behavior, played out in relationship with others, whether present or elsewhere.

In 1975, Gregory Bateson was invited to a gathering of humanistic psychologists in Tucson, Arizona. Bateson listened to them define humanistic psychology as a radically different paradigm than behaviorism and then proceeded to shock everyone by suggesting that both humanistic and behavioristic approaches belonged to the same paradigm. Each embodied linear logic, maintained rigid dualisms, and emphasized metaphors of power over metaphors of pattern. Rollo May was shaken and transformed by the trickster contributions of Bateson, writing about it in his essay, "Gregory Bateson and Humanistic Psychology" (in Brockman, 1977). Bateson proposed, and I agree with him, that cybernetics pointed the way to an epistemology that was paradigmatically distinct from the old Newtonian way of maximizing and minimizing variables with its zero sum game played by adversarial (read hierarchical) opponents.

I recall lecturing in Adelaide, Australia quite a few years ago and hearing a social worker sitting in the back row saying, "I don't like Gregory Bateson anymore because he is too behavioristic. I have moved on to the importance of narrative." At the time I was giving a talk on postmodern rhetoric, which must have been misheard, but being in the spirit of postmodern polyphony (rather than postmodern totalitarianism), it did not initially disturb me. However, he and others later proclaimed that they found a new world of meanings and understandings, emphasizing the power differentials between various cultural stories and their interlocutors. Looking (and listening) back, I now hear that the Australian's comment was not voiced in the spirit of play, but was the one-up positioning of a new hegemony, a monocular view as ignorant and potentially empty-headed as the paucity of epistemological blindness Bateson had many years earlier pointed out to his American humanistic audience.

Logic, whether circular or linear, is a different order of abstraction than behavior, interaction, therapy, gender, or culture. Yet all theories of gender, culture, therapy, and justice are held together by inherent logics, patterns of relationship that link its different concepts, argue its various proposals, and so on. The narrative and postmodern therapy movement(s) in family therapy and social science (but not necessarily elsewhere), I dare say, seldom, if ever, embrace a circular logic, but provide yet another relapse into power talk with hardened dualisms, void of little wisdom of systemic process, circular relationship, and ecological interaction. I can imagine Bateson turning over in his grave and fantasize hearing him grumble (if he were able) about the mess others have made.

My imagined Gregory speaks: *The time is ripe for clarity in a discourse run amok with muddle and empty-headed talk that perpetuates rigid posturings of political correctness (the new dominant and one-up moral hierarchy). I eagerly await its collapse and the fresh air of liberation that will follow when its towering tower of pretentious babble is tumbled to the observable ground of everyday interaction and the natural cycles of biological process from which it was given birth.*

The interactional view of the Mental Research Institute in Palo Alto began with Don Jackson's desire to continue the research project of Gregory Bateson. Although its members had differences, some not insignificant, it has historically attempted to articulate an interactionally focused therapy, based on an understanding of the recursive relation of problems and attempted solutions. Other schools of family therapy, looking back after all these years, were more often than not, conceptual muddles of psychology talk with a little sociology thrown in from time to time. Now that muddle has broadened, as the reifications of gender and culture (rather than their relational definitions) have been thrown into the mix, along with a dose of diagnostic nomenclature and brain chemistry. Similarly, other social science disciplines, previously inspired by visions of circularity, have been brought back into the non-circular fold. No one promised it would be easy to hold onto the slippery tail of Ourobourous.

I propose that participation in other cultural ways of healing will encourage for others, as it has for me, that many of the world's indigenous cultures are more related to circular forms of understanding and less interested in the dualisms that seem to latch on to therapeutic and Euro-American discourse. My fieldwork with the Bushmen, Himba, Zulu, and other tribal groups in Africa, along with work in Bali, Japan, Thailand, Amazonia, Brazil, Paraguay, Argentina, Mexico, Australia, the Dine (Navajo), Lakota, Ojibway, Cree, and Micmac, among others, has repeatedly found the circular way (see www.ringingrocks.org). It is held by most of the elders who remember the old ways of wisdom.

Sometimes the younger generations, more influenced by missionaries, social workers, Euro-American universities, and popular radio/television culture, lose the circular wisdom. They find a new enemy to fight and in their tireless condemnation of the other (as enemy, terrorist, perpetrator, sexist, racist, colonialist, intervenist), destroy the wisdom formally held when differences marked the turning of a wheel, whether in conversation or ecological interaction, rather than the destruction of the possibility of the other.

The elders, wisdom keepers of the circles of networked rather than demarcated life, lament the absurd follies of those seduced by the mirages of power, whether they see themselves with it or without it. They wait for *thuru* to change the climate, which they know will inevitably take place in the greater natural cycles. Then the healing may begin. Shamans, practiced in the passages of existential death and resurrection, won't belittle or say "we told you so," but with open arms, invite the "once elevated, but now down-trodden" to recognize their equality with all, including good and bad, wise and foolish. In this bringing down, a dance is possible. Here everyone is deconstructed, then re-constructed, changing forms, like the trickster gods of old. At the altar of *thuru,* we find ourselves in the differences with others. We learn to embrace our enemies, knowing that without them there can be nothing but ruined interaction and hierarchical isolation. In our interacting contraries are truth, circular progression, and celebratory dance.

Too many Euro-American therapists (and social scientists) have drifted from the circular wisdom and interactional skills of their cybernetic elders. Many of them, like religious zealots conducting courts of inquisition, they lazily march to and from, sentencing those who research, intervene and practice variant ways, awarding banishment for any trickster free of dualistic answers and absent of politically ordained clichés. They shout: "Down with interventions!" "Deconstruct one and all who dare voice a contrary view or practice!" "Shun those crude problem-solving therapists (and their mirror-imaged solution-focused therapists) who knowingly influence others." Blind to their authoritative one-way patterns of influence, held by hierarchical positions of feigned humility, we find creative process, playful exploration, and timeless wisdom trampled and removed from sight and sound.

The postmodernists and narrativists have something to learn from the oldest custodians of healing on the planet. They, too, can benefit from silencing their talk, quieting their minds, and stepping down from their bully pulpits. Their oldest ancestral spirits invite them to enter the dance and feel the freedom of crazy wisdom, coyote, jackal discourse that enables the wrong thing to be said for the right reason.

The shamans cry forth, "Loosen up, shake your body, laugh at your necessary stupidity, and join the oldest healing circle. Inside the dance, become your body and forget pre, post, old, and modern. The eternal return carries the wisdom unattainable by contrived narrative."

Round and round the dance, a furrow of sand is dug, reminding us that the cyclical nature of all living process assures that therapists will tire of the infinite regress of verbal discourse and the rigidity of over-inflated understandings. Turn and return to the indigenous fires and circles of unspoken mysteries. There the ancestors continue their teaching.

In our imagination, we can construe dialogues that help bring back the circles. In dreams our mentors may return and become present with voice and direction. They remind us that we carry an ecology of differences within ourselves and that we must play out many variations to rescue ourselves from any form of hegemony, whether it be the tyranny of literacy or illiteracy, the hold of static dogmas or frozen bodies, the trap of fixed image or cliched music. We must go inside to find the corrective influence of the natural world as we must venture into the wild to loosen our inner entrapment. Into the imaginary dialogues we can enter:

Bateson: William Blake, who outlined the changing forms, spoke of Creative Imagination. I dare say that this is another way of speaking of *thuru*.
Bushman shaman: For a moment we can see *thuru* and the creative force as the same. But as we ponder their similarity, they will become different. As I speak, I am already aware that *thuru* embraces being noncreative.
Bateson: And your proposed difference between these notions evokes yet another similarity, different than the one before. Namely, behind *thuru* and creative imagination is the elemental form of difference. It enables both the conception of an idea as well as putting the idea into motion.
Bushman shaman: But difference is preceded by the absence of difference and form.
Bateson: Yes, that must be so. As G. Spencer Brown was fond of sketching it, we must start with space before we can cleave/project any identity within it.
Bushman shaman: Spencer Brown's marked forms, Blake's outlines, and Gregory, your so-called "differences that make a difference" point to the vaporous trails left behind as *thuru* dances us through many changed identities. We are more similar than different, although you dance the ideas in your conversations whereas I am more found of dancing it around an evening fire. But, in spite of you're appearing to be more in your mind and my appearing to be more in my body, we are more similar than what meets the eyes or ears.
Bateson: I think my intellect's desire to mend the body and mind divide is matched my your dance's desire to mend the same. We both belong to the dance, a dance greater than what is seen as limited to movement in physical or mental space.

Bushman shaman: I remember your talking last week about your insistence upon maintaining multiple descriptions in order to help achieve more relational understandings of any given situation. My Bushman colleagues see that job as being carried out by the trickster god, the jackal who is always presenting us with changing descriptions.

Bateson: But for the jackal to do its shape-shifting, she must borrow you from time to time. You and your shamans step into the jackal's role and shake things up, whether in your own movements in the dance or in the changing stories you tell one another.

Bushman shaman: Similarly, you dance from one logical level of abstraction to another in your own discourse. Sometimes you pretend to be serious about keeping the abstractions nice and tidy so as to help Alice get her mind straight in Wonderland. To paraphrase your quote attributed to Lewis Carroll, "the name of the dance's name is neither the name of the dance nor the dance."

Bateson: Now you're really making me want to dance! Let me show you what I mean. [Bateson stands and leans over, stomping his feet on the ground, dancing around an imaginary circle. As he dances he continues speaking.] With each step I take, I remain a dancer and confirm my place within the circle. But the deeper my entry into the dance, the less I am the dancer and the more I am simply the dance. As the dance, I shed my skin and my mind, and can become many forms, understandings, and relations.

Bushman shaman: You are ready to dance tonight, Gregory! Please join us as I call forth the village in the sky to make a great fire.

Bateson: I'm still an old stick in the mud, but I don't mind sticking one foot into the mud or sand. But I can't help being mindful of my observational self, the other leg that stands outside the circle.

Bushman shaman: I don't think you should ever spend too much effort trying to stop your observing. It would be the kind of first order dance that maintains your presence in the same place. Didn't you and your colleagues imply that "the more you try to stop observing, the more you observe"?

Bateson: You're taking me into Milton Erickson's territory. I can imagine that old trickster encouraging me to be more of an observer, thereby making it more likely to fall into the dance and forget my ever having had a leg outside the circle.

Bushman shaman: I am so happy that I am a Bushman. We don't have to worry about using talk to free ourselves from the constraints that talk can construct. We simply dance.

Bateson: But from time to time, some of your Bushman shamans don't let the dance grab them in the way you desire. They dance it with too much purpose and even start practicing sorcery, the craft of trying to bring about a maximization or minimization of a particular variable in the ecosystem. As you put it, they break a string.

Bushman shaman: As you fear breaking a leg in our dance as you try to hold one leg on the outside and one on the inside.

Bateson: I concede that you have a point there.

Bushman shaman: So whether we aim to straddle the dance circle, remain outside, or fall inside, we somehow face the same challenges: to not break a leg or string. We want to nurture the relationships, not harm them.

Bateson: As ecological custodians, we must be careful to not break the connections. I devoted my life to helping others have this understanding.

Bushman shaman: As I devoted mine to helping others participate in this practice.

Bateson: What, my dear friend, might we do for the therapists who are trying to be healers of relationship? What can we do to help them see their blind spots, to loosen them up to participate in trickster movement and have deeper respect for the necessary paradoxes, ambiguities, and inconsistencies of human existence?

Bushman shaman: I knew it. Gregory, you want to be a shaman!

Bateson: I would prefer saying that you desire becoming a cybernetic epistemologist.

Bushman shaman: Yes, but only for a split second because then I must become something else!

Bateson: Now back to our parting words for therapists. And that includes the cyberneticians, who are also therapists mending the broken strings, trying to make lines become circles again. Therapy always needs therapy. Like everyone and everything else, it gets stuck in a particular outline or form. Then, with the delusions of certainty, consistency, clarity, and purpose, it becomes a toxic presence to others. It is toxic in the sense that it blocks the natural progressions of change and tightens the grip on *thuru's* expression. For example, I see today that many therapists and social scientists have lost their view of interaction, relationship, and ecology.

Bushman shaman: And they still haven't learned to dance with us. We Bushman don't believe that anything said can make a difference. Talk is first-order change, my friend. We speak to demonstrate the futility of talk, but we do so as an amusement. I'd say your overly serious therapists need some teasing. Didn't you once tease them with that muddled notion of double bind?

Bateson: You had to bring up that double bind business. I regret ever publishing the damned thing. Everyone saw it as a thing to be counted.

Bushman shaman: You gave it to the wrong people. If you had spoken to the Bushmen, we would have never been seduced into any pious act of reification, but would have joyfully danced it. We would have known, without being able to specify this knowing, that how we dance with the idea is the very means by which we give the idea its meaning. And that meaning would be encouraged to morph as we continued dancing with it.

Bateson: Perhaps I should regret having gone to New Guinea. Things may have been different had I headed to the Kalahari. I can now assume that it would have made a difference in how I interacted with the therapists.

Bushman shaman: You may have danced a bit more and talked somewhat less seriously.

Bateson: I certainly would have encouraged others to have taken your dance more seriously and encouraged them to surrender their words to a greater dance. I would, however, have to count on you to provide the trickster play, the merciless teasing, the endless shape-shifting.

Bushman shaman: And so we have done a bit of this, Gregory. And so we shall ever continue dancing together throughout eternity, being both above and below.

Bateson: It appears that the women have gathered for the dance. It's time for our dance to speak for itself.

[The two ancestral friends walk toward the fire, singing different songs, punctuated by synchopated clapping and polyphonic singing of the community.]

References

Bateson, G. (1972). *Steps to an ecology of mind*. New York: Ballantine.
Bateson, G. (1979). *Mind and nature: A necessary unity*. New York: E. P. Dutton.
Bateson, G. & Bateson, M. C. (1987). *Angels fear: Towards an epistemology of the sacred*. New York: Macmillan Publishing Company.
Biesele, M. (1993). *Women like meat: The folklore and foraging ideology of the Kalahari Ju/'hoansi*. Johanessburg: Witwatersrand University Press.
Brockman, J. (Ed.). (1977). *About Bateson*. New York: E.P. Dutton.
Erickson, B. A. & Keeney, B. (Eds.). (2005). *Milton H. Erickson, M.D.: An American healer*. Philadelphia: Ringing Rocks Press.
Guenther, M. (1999). *Tricksters and trancers*. Bloomington: Indiana University Press.
Jung, C. (1961). *Memories, dreams, reflections*. New York: Vintage Books.
Kottler, J.,Carlson, J., & Keeney, B (2004). *American shaman: An odyssey of global healing traditions,* New York: Brunner-Routledge.
Keeney, B. (1983). *Aesthetics of change*. New York: The Guilford Press.
Keeney, B. (1999). *Kalahari Bushman healers*. Philadelphia: Ringing Rocks Press.
Keeney, B. (2003). *Ropes to God: Experiencing the Bushman spiritual universe*. Philadelphia: Ringing Rocks Press.
Keeney, B. (2005). *Bushman shaman: Awakening the spirit through ecstatic dance*. Rochester, VT: Destiny Books.
Marshall, L. (1969). The medicine dance of the !Kung Bushmen. *Africa, 39,* 347-38.
Spencer-Brown, G. (1973). *Laws of form*. New York: Bantam.
Varela, F. (1976). Not one, not two. *CoEvolution Quarterly, 1976, 11,* 62-67.
Von Foerster, H. (1981). *Observing systems*. Seaside, California: Intersystems Publications.
Von Foerster, H. (2003). *Understanding understanding: Essays on cybernetics and cognition*. New York: Springer-Verlag.

we accept it
assuming time -
assuming time as
a fundamental resource
a strict increment
metered out
by god or cosmos
we spend time
and name the spending
cost

what if time
was not limiting?
What if time
was not,
was nought
But our invention?

Cybernetics And Human Knowing. Vol. 12, nos. 1-2, pp. 91-101

May the Pattern be With You

Douglas Flemons, Ph.D.[1]

This article is infused with the mindful presence of Gregor-wan Batesoni, the pattern-spinning alter-ego of Star Wars' Obi-wan Kenobi. The author, a Skywalker wannabe, careens through 25 years of Bateson-inspired ideas and practices, zigzagging between descriptions of his work and a thinking-out-loud search for an appropriate metaphor for classifying who he is and what he's been up to. Along the way, he introduces readers to a self-referential distinction that opens the door to whole-part relationships; to a new way of thinking about therapeutic change; to a relational understanding of hypnosis; and to a fresh approach for teaching composition.

> The Force is what gives the Jedi his power. It's an energy field created by all living things. It surrounds us and penetrates us. It binds the galaxy together.
> —*Obi-wan Kenobi*

> The Pattern is what makes the Jedi's mind possible. It's an information network characteristic of all ecosystems. It frames us and evolves with and through us. Differentiating, classifying, self-regulating, it is the weaving of life.
> —*Gregor-wan Batesoni*

For the last quarter century, I've been wielding Gregory Bateson's ideas as if they were something of a light saber, using them to slice through sources of professional and personal confusion, to illuminate a relational understanding of various relational conundrums. The writing hasn't been easy. Thinking clearly on paper takes me much time and multiple drafts. But every once in a while, in the quiet of the early morning, I'll hear Gregor-wan Batesoni grumble, "May the Pattern be with you,"[2] and I'll get inspired to keep going.

Okay, okay, I can imagine what you're thinking. "Douglas," you're saying to yourself, "I served with the Jedi knight Luke Skywalker. I knew Luke Skywalker. Luke Skywalker was a friend of mine. Douglas, you're no Luke Skywalker."[3]

What can I say to such a charge? I'm certainly not going to go symmetrical with you. How about a complementary response? "You're right, Reader. Though my 11-year-old son, Eric, would love to claim 'Douglas Skywalker' as his dad, I don't have the wherewithal to pull off the image of 'cyber-warrior.' I'm just a therapist, a supervisor, a teacher of ideas and writing. So allow me to drop my saber and start again.[4] I'll tell you some personal stories, stir in some ideas, and try to spin some more apt metaphors."

---

1. Professor of Family Therapy; Director, Brief Therapy Institute; Director, NSU Student Counseling, Nova South-eastern University. Email: douglas@nsu.nova.edu
2. In *Star Wars,* which came out two years before *Mind and Nature,* the blessing was, "May the Force be with you."
3. Lloyd Bentsen, the 1988 Democratic nominee for Vice President, famously said to Dan Quayle, who had just compared himself to JFK, "Senator, I served with Jack Kennedy. I knew Jack Kennedy. Jack Kennedy was a friend of mine. Senator, you're no Jack Kennedy."

In 1980, a friend gave me a copy of Bateson's (1979) *Mind and Nature*, and it changed my life. I'd already dipped into *Steps to an Ecology of Mind* (Bateson, 2000), but I didn't, at the time, make it beyond the metalogues (it never occurred to me to read the damn essays out of order). I'd gleaned something from *Pragmatics of Human Communication* (Watzlawick, Beavin, & Jackson, 1967), but it wasn't until I encountered *Mind and Nature* that I got hooked. Like no other book before or since, it grabbed me and wouldn't let go. I still find this curious, given that I'd never been much of a science guy. Five years earlier, unnerved by my Biology 101 class—the auditorium seating, the smell and paraphernalia of the lab, the creepiness of the assignments—I'd retreated from my vague plan to eventually study dolphins or monkeys and meandered my way into the study of poetry, Chinese philosophy, and communication.

In those days, I lived in Vancouver, British Columbia, and I rode the bus everywhere. For a couple of years, *Mind and Nature* was my constant companion. Talk about circular process! As soon as I finished reading it, I started again at the beginning. In time, notions such as difference, classification, circular causality, stochastic process, communication, context, learning, relationship, cybernetics, and mind started making sense, and then, and *then*, when I was able to make connections *between* the ideas, to get a feel for the tautological network linking them,[5] then something significant shifted in my style of engagement.

Perhaps the best way to explain what happened is to invoke Bateson's (1979) description of moiré phenomena, which he defined as the "enrichment of information" that occurs when "two or more rhythmic patterns are combined" (p. 79). He used this definition to raise questions about perception and cognition:

> Do we...carry around with us (like the blind person's sonar) samples of various sorts of regularity against which we can try the information...that comes in from outside? Do we, for example, use our habits of what is called "dependency" to test the characteristics of other persons? (p. 80)

As always, he didn't restrict his focus to the merely human. He was interested in *all* of *Creatura*: "Do animals (and even plants) have characteristics such that in a given niche there is a testing of that niche by something like the moiré phenomenon?" (p. 80).

At first with much intent, but gradually with automatic ease, I started treating the tautological web of Bateson's fundamental premises as a "receiving pattern," a pattern of regularity with which to test—to approach, question, think through, and act in response to—whatever piece of Creatura was intriguing me at the time. In the beginning, I used the web to help me sort out such patterns as Taoist and Zen thought,

---

4. Notice that by saying this, I manage to discount the criticism that I'm refusing to defend myself against: Who but a Jedi would have a light saber to lay down? Don't you love paradox?

5. Bateson, giving a nod to the necessity of self-referential (i.e., tautological) integration in complex systems (including systems of thought), defined explanation as the "mapping of the pieces of a description onto a tautology" (1979, p. 93). He characterized tautology as "a body of propositions so linked together that the links *between the propositions* are necessarily valid" (p. 93).

jazz theory, and American and Soviet nuclear posturing. The resulting moirés taught me much, not only about the phenomena in question, but also about Bateson and about myself.

In 1984, I decided to head back to school to study family therapy. During my master's and doctoral studies, Bateson's network of assumptions helped me think through issues about research (Flemons, 1985, 1987), power (Flemons, 1989b), violence (1989a), and correspondences between Taoism and therapeutic change (Flemons, 1991). And during the last 15 years of teaching, seeing clients, and supervising, it has organized my exploration of hypnosis and brief therapy (Flemons, 1998a, 2002; Flemons & Shulimson, 1997), relationships with clients (Flemons, 2002; Flemons & Gale, 1997), supervision (Flemons, Green, & Rambo, 1997), sex therapy (Flemons & Green, 2004), false memory (Flemons & Wright, 1999), meditation (Flemons 2004b), reading and writing (Flemons, 1998b), and qualitative research (Flemons, 2004a; Flemons & Green, 2002; Ellis & Flemons, 2002; Matthews & Flemons, 1999; Wright & Flemons, 2002). Rather than brandishing a sword, I've been casting out this net of fundamentals, seeing what I can catch and discover. Hey, wait a minute! I'm no Jedi knight—I'm a Batesonian fisherman!

But that's not it, either. Bateson's premises don't allow me to snag pre-existing notions and bring them to the surface of consciousness; rather, they alter my focus, my attention and intention, as I tease a lump of something into strands of relational interaction. His fundamentals have allowed me to think relationally about relational phenomena, so, in a sense, they are more like paint choices for sketching a landscape, or like the notes of a scale with which to compose pieces of music.[6]

But again—bummer!—these art-based metaphors also don't quite cut it. The self-referential nature of Bateson's meta-ideas—ideas *about* ideas, thoughts about how to think about thought—can't be captured by media that don't lend themselves so easily to irony, to the paradox of self-awareness. It is perhaps inevitable that every painting can be viewed not only as a work of art but also as a commentary *about* art, and something analogous is true also of music.[7] But despite such meta-capabilities, neither medium is able to support the articulation of a *theory* of art creation or appreciation. Such theoretical musing requires at least another level of self-reference—the meta-meta-capability to comment on the meta-capability to comment on an invention.

Notice that in considering and rejecting these various metaphors for characterizing what I am and how Bateson has influenced me, I've been oscillating between loose and strict thinking (Bateson, 2000, pp. 73-87), and I've been zigzagging between classifications of form (the ontological question of what I am) and descriptions of process (the details of what I've been up to) (Bateson, 1979, pp. 209-224). This behind-the-scenes narrative gives you a good idea of the extent to which

---

6. I like that a *piece* of music—a chunk—is made up of *patterns* of notes.
7. This is most evident in the compositions of P.D.Q. Bach (a.k.a. Peter Schickele), such as "The Short-Tempered Clavier and Other Dysfunctional Works for Keyboard."

Bateson's ideas have affected—hell, *in*fected—my thought patterns. Later, I'll zig back to nailing down a metaphor that can adequately classify my doing-and-being, but first I'd like to zag into a more in-depth discussion of my process, offering illustrations of ideas and applications—Batesonian moirés—I've managed to develop over the years.

The first moiré I want to touch on is an abstraction, a distinction that has allowed me to think clearly about whole-part relationships, recursion, and context, as well as about the vexing nature of therapeutic problems and the freeing quality of therapeutic change.

Connection/Separation

Closely examine any distinction—front/back; pattern/scatter; old/young—and you'll discover something curious. The slash (/) serves as a boundary, separating the terms on either side of it. But the distinctiveness of each term depends on its being juxtaposed with its complement. Thus, the slash does double duty—it both separates the two sides *and* connects them.

I don't remember just when or quite how I happened onto this realization. Bateson never said it directly, though it is implicit in his writings. When I got my hands on it, I had the sense that it could serve as a key to the multi-layered, both-and logic of his relational world, but it was actually my next mini-epiphany that allowed me to unlock and open the door.

Tinkering with this notion that boundaries connect whatever they separate, I got the idea to create a self-referential distinction, one that would fold back on itself, doing to itself what it describes itself doing. Out popped *connection/separation,* where "the reflexivity pivots on the identity between the terms used to describe the function of the slash (/) and those that comprise the distinction itself: that is, the slash *connects and separates connection and separation*" (Flemons, 1991, p. 34).

Although the two sides of this distinction—the act of connecting and the act of separating—are the same logical type or level of abstraction, the *results* of these actions create conditions of different logical type. Connections string parts into wholes (systems, contexts, categories), and separations render wholes into seemingly independent chunks or things. If you consider each component of the distinction as an isolated idea—*connection* on the one side and *separation* on the other—you can recognize the fundamentally divergent root inspirations of holistic and analytic (or reductionistic) thinking, respectively. However, if you attend to the necessary link between the two sides, you can see how *linking-together* and *teasing-apart* are mutually dependent processes of mind (Flemons, 1991; 2002). This realization has been invaluable in my designing a relational approach to therapy.

Relational Freedom

My clients just want to be free of their problem. Whether they are struggling against physical pain, bursts of anger, intrusive thoughts, a life-sapping relationship, or spirals of panic, depression, or addiction, they are frightened and exhausted by doing battle with something that seems to have a mind of its own. Understandably, they want me to help them get it under control or, better yet, out of their lives completely. But this desire and the actions it engenders only make matters worse.

The problem starts with everyday conscious awareness. Although mind is composed of relationships established by differences (Bateson, 1979; 2000, pp. 454-471), the connections that these boundaries establish are not the stuff of conscious awareness. Indeed, they generally remain unconscious until we isolate them as objects of scrutiny. For example, I've worked with clients who were confused and depressed about feeling profoundly sad, until they realized (i.e., became conscious of the fact) that the emotion overwhelming them had welled up on or near the anniversary of a loved one's death. The absence (separation) of an important person on a particular date established an unrecognized (unnamed, unconscious) connection, which was experienced emotionally, but not with conscious recognition.

Typically, we consciously notice only the results of our boundary marking, the what-appear-to-be discrete entities—whether external objects or internal thoughts, images, or feeling states—that are demarcated and circumscribed by the distinctions we draw. So although the whole system of mind is woven of relationships, our conscious thought and action proceed as if it were constructed of things.

If you've had it with a problematic object in your personal space—that lime-green sweater from the in-laws, the broken coffee maker, a pair of worn out shoes—you toss it in the trash and never give it another thought. So it makes sense that you would, with your mind-as-a-repository-of-things assumption firmly in place, attempt the same operation when faced with a problematic piece of personal experience. However, since the experience itself and your act of demarcating it are both relationally defined, it doesn't obey the laws of unwanted physical objects. If you slam-dunk your shoes into the trash can, they stay there until the garbage collector drives up.[8] But try chucking your anxiety in there, and you'll quickly discover that it behaves much less like shoes than it does a boomerang—the harder you throw, the quicker it returns.[9]

In the mental world, where information is news of difference, taking action against anything for which you have strong feelings only binds you to it, underscoring, rather than erasing, its importance. The relational nature of mind accounts for the vicious circles clients create whenever they try to control or eradicate something they consider *Other*. The more they attempt to fence off or banish their problem, the more it

---

8. There is, of course, no ecological free throw. The shoes don't just disappear; they end up on some trash heap. Our approach to garbage displays an analogous ignorance to our approach to personal problems.
9. The physical analogy perhaps confuses the issue. A boomerang returns for aerodynamic reasons; the personal experience, for relational ones. And if an object is meaningful to you, its relational importance may well be heightened by your throwing it away.

gloms onto them, which, of course, increases their distress. Such purposeful separations create unintended (and usually unpleasant) binds and double binds. I call them "separated connections."

Therapy involves transforming such separated connections into connected separations—rather than trying to get free *of* a problem, it involves getting free *in relation to* it. So rather than helping my clients *counter* their problem, I invite them to *en*counter it—to become curious about the micro-dynamics of their experience and to experiment with and learn from it. To this end, I ask loads of detailed questions about how and when their symptom appears; I piece together a play-by-play description of how they, and those around them, recognize and react to it, and I suggest possibilities for participating differently in what happens. Therapeutic change is always a species of relational freedom—the freedom to connect to the very thing from which clients have tried to keep separate, the freedom to respond comfortably and unpredictably to whatever provocation their symptom offers up. When clients are able to transform their relationship with their problem, they free it up to unravel, allowing it to change in a variety of ways: duration, location, intensity, quality, frequency, and/or significance.

Concordance

Hypnosis theorists continue to argue back and forth about whether hypnosis constitutes a "special state" and to what degree clients' "hypnotic susceptibility" or "suggestibility" is a stable "trait" and a determining factor of experimental or therapeutic outcomes. The participants in these discussions share the assumption that hypnosis involves one or more individuals whose minds reside inside their skulls and who possess localizable, concrete attributes (traits) that can be quantitatively measured.

If my daughter, Jenna, were to hear their arguments, she would caution, "Don't even go there, Daddy." And I would reassure her, "Don't worry, Sweetheart, I wouldn't be caught dead entertaining such assumptions." Years ago, I headed off in another direction, entirely.

To make sense of hypnosis, I don't need to invoke the notion of a special state. Instead, I sketch it as constituted by two special relationships—one between the client and the hypnotist, and the other between the client and him or herself. Both occasion a shift in the client's experience of *self*.

If you and I started talking about the current state of the world, we'd pretty quickly be scoping out each other's political sensibilities. If we discovered significant divergence, we might not resort to arguing, but we'd be acutely aware of our own integrity in contradistinction to the other, and we'd be silently intoning, "I'm sure as hell not you."

But if we discovered, as we talked, that we held remarkably similar political views on everything from Roe v. Wade and environmental policy to health care and capital punishment, then our remarkable agreement would tend to render whatever differences there were between us—gender, appearance, religion, nationality, and so on—unremarkable. Our political accord would, at least for the duration of our conversation, hold sway over any non-similarities. We would become *of one mind*.

As a hypnotherapist, I strive to become of one mind with my clients. I don't get there by finding out about and adopting their political views; rather, I ask them questions about their experience, and I listen closely to both what they say and how they say it. As we talk, I offer empathic statements, based on what I've gleaned, and I venture hunches about what their situation must be like for them. When I'm accurate in both my reflections and inferences, they let me know, both verbally and non-verbally, that I *get* them.

My family and I frequent a restaurant where the chef simultaneously ladles two different thick soups, one cream colored and the other dark brown, into a bowl. The result is visually surprising and appealing—a straight line down the middle of the two liquids. Now, if the chef were to pour the *same* soup out of both ladles, the bowl would still arrive at our table with its two halves, but we'd be unable to notice the line between them, so we'd see nothing remarkable—just a regular bowl of soup.[10] If you place identical information on both sides of a boundary, the boundary disappears from your perception.

When the information I'm offering back to my clients matches what they're telling me, they stop noticing the differences between us. We become, for a time, of one mind—one bowl of soup. This is the first of the two special relationships that constitute hypnosis. The second is similar, in that it involves the de-signifying of a boundary, but the change happens across the mind-body divide separating their conscious awareness—their "Observing-I"—and the rest of their experience. The easiest way to facilitate this shift is to invite them to notice and acknowledge whatever makes it into their awareness. If their Observing-I is making note of whatever is happening non-volitionally—sensations, images, their breathing, sounds in or outside the office, thoughts that pop up, and so on—then it creates the same information on both sides of the mind-body boundary, and the boundary becomes insignificant.

This is the process by which clients become of one mind—one bowl of soup—with themselves. When their Observing-I is no longer setting itself apart from the rest of their experience, there is no insular consciousness taking credit for whatever is happening, and they are able to experience non-volitional changes in their thoughts, emotions, and body processes. Such "hypnotic phenomena" provide openings into the non-volitional change of symptoms.

The word *hypnosis,* from the Greek *hupnos,* meaning sleep, is a lousy choice for such dynamic boundary-erasures. A far better coinage for what goes on in my office would be *concordance,* the Latin root of which—*concorde*—the *O.E.D.* defines as "of one mind" (from *con,* together + *cord-,* heart: *concorda-re,* to be of one mind). My clients and I enter into concordance so they can be in concordance with themselves,

---

10. Of course, if we knew in advance that the chef would be using two ladles to create the appearance of uniformity, then when the soup arrived, we would notice ourselves not noticing the line down the middle—an instance of second-order noticing.

and once that is happening, they are able to discover the transformational properties of their symptom.

Sentence as Story

Early on in my teaching career, despairing at the quality of my students' writing, I assigned Strunk and White's *Elements of Style* as a required text in every class. I just knew that the students would closely read it and then methodically and effectively apply what they learned to their assignments. They'd improve their writing, and I'd be able to stop gnashing my teeth: A win-win solution.

Yeah, okay, you're right. I *was* naïve, wasn't I? But hey, it only took me a few semesters (well, maybe a bit longer) to recognize that my lazy intervention was a dismal failure. In any event, I needed a Plan B.

I talked to my dean about creating a graduate-level writing course, and when I got the go-ahead, I turned to Bateson for guidance on how to design it. He once commented, in *Mind and Nature*, that the standard way of teaching grammar—that is, that "a noun is the name of a person, place, or thing, and a verb is an action word" (1979, p. 16)—is nonsense, for it defines each part of the sentence by isolating it. Children "are taught…that the way to define something is by what it supposedly *is* in itself, not by its relation to other things" (pp. 16-17). However, if *relationship* were used as the basis for definition, then "any child could…see that there is something wrong with the sentence '"Go' is a verb" (p. 17). This resonated strongly with me, as did a notion he had dangled a few pages earlier—that all minds think in terms of stories (1979, p. 13).

Relationship and story. I had what I needed—an organizing principle and central metaphor that I could use to orient myself and the students as I toured all aspects of composition, from sentence construction, punctuation, and tenses, to idea development, aesthetic issues, and writing strategies (brainstorming and editing). Fortunately, no one had yet mapped a relational way of teaching writing (Bateson having been, as far as I could tell, silent beyond these little ticklers in *Mind and Nature*), so I got to make it all up from scratch.[11]

I had three reasons for not wanting to teach a standard composition class. First, whenever I'd even whisper the word *grammar,* my students' eyes would either glaze over or narrow with fear. Most of them had failed to thrive in high school or undergrad English classes. Second, although I knew how to write reasonably well, the last time I'd formally studied grammar was in seventh grade, so I would have been hard pressed to offer up a credible impersonation of someone who knew what he was talking about. Third, I recognized that I would lose *relationship* as my organizing principle (and lose the participation of the students) the moment I started in on parsing sentences.

So rather than subject my students (and myself) to the drudgery of memorizing a bunch of decontextualized rules coded in grammarianese, I decided to engage them in

---

11. And write it all down. A book detailing the approach, *Writing Between the Lines*, came out in 1998.

a process of discovery. To learn how to write, I told them, you have to learn the microdynamics of how you and others *read*. That is, you have to understand how sentences *work*—how they, like melodies, unfold their patterned meaning through time.

You can't inhale a sentence the way you can a painting; you have to make your way along it; you must follow its course.[12] The meaning happens in the encountering of the relationships between words and the relationships between sentences. The part of the sentence you've just finished reading contextualizes what you are seeing at this very instant, but the opposite is also true: The words you're reading right now may change or nuance the meaning of the words you've just left behind.

Given such complexity, how do readers not get bogged down or lost? For a sentence to function properly as a sentence, it has to accomplish two tasks. It has to tell a story, a narrative involving a main character (or two or three), perhaps some props, and some action (though sometimes what happens in a sentence is so laid back, it comes across more as a state of being than a process of change). And simultaneously, the sentence has to provide the reader with implicit directions for how to follow along, for how to keep track of the relationships that are getting created. Such directional cuing is the responsibility of punctuation marks and various sorts of "guiding words."

Because the meaning in sentences is so time-dependent, readers need to be continually cued to anticipate and remember: "Get ready," announces the colon, "here comes an explanation, elucidation, or elaboration of what you just read." "Heads up," says the conjunction, "what you're about to read is parallel to some earlier part of the sentence, and the next word or two will specify precisely which earlier cluster of words to recall and include in the comparison."[13]

One of the benefits of learning a relational approach to writing is that the ideas are relevant at all levels of complexity. Once you get the hang of how to guide readers through a sentence, you can apply the same principles (if not the precise techniques) to constructing and interrelating coherent and captivating paragraphs, sections, and chapters.

Batesonian Invention

As I sometimes tell my clients, figuring out who you are is closely linked to your defining who you aren't. Clearly not a Batesonian Jedi, I'm also not a Batesonian fisherman, painter or composer. None of these metaphors hold together under close checking for internal consistency (or what Bateson might call tautological integrity). But in rejecting them, I've arrived at another description of myself, or, better yet, of

---

12. When it comes to art, you might claim, à la Bill Clinton, that you never inhale. Okay, fair enough. But a painting, unlike a sentence, doesn't demand that you take it in sequentially. You can let your eyes wander over it.

13. I call the words that appear just after conjunctions and/or punctuation marks *retrace cues* (Flemons, 1998, pp. 102-107)

what I've been up to. I've been having the time of my life absorbed in Batesonian invention.

According to the *O.E.D.*, the source of the word *invent* is the Latin *invenire,* to come upon, discover, find out, devise, contrive. My inventions—the ideas and applications I've contrived, tinkered with, and implemented—are infused with and patterned by Bateson's fundamental assumptions. I shudder to think where I'd be now if I hadn't discovered his work. The images that suggest themselves are not nearly as pretty as the Batesonian moirés I've managed to create.

Recognizing Bateson's profound influence on my professional and personal life, I've needed to stay mindful of how to keep my edge, how not to lose myself. A Batesonian inventor is one thing; a Batesonian drone is quite another. To manage the challenge, I hold tightly to my relational freedom.

I work like crazy to connect with my clients *and* I protect like crazy my freedom to joke, question, let go, improvise, change direction. Likewise with Bateson. Twenty-five years ago I swallowed his work whole, and I've spit up precious little since. Indeed, my regard for his ideas borders on belief. This has created an interesting dilemma for me, given what I know of his reservations about hypnosis and therapy. If he were still alive, would he write me off as just another "social engineer"? I'm not sure. My response is to practice with devotion to integrity—"responsive to the pattern which connects" (Bateson, 1979, p. 8)—but also a devotion to improvisation. To preserve my relational freedom, I'm happy to embrace Bateson while telling him to go to hell.

As any jazz musician (and Bateson) could tell you, good improvisation requires an ear for pattern and an inclination for chaos—a mischievous reach for the unexpected note or chord, for a syncopation that messes with the rhythm section. So wait! Maybe I'm not so much an inventor as I am a Batesonian improviser!

In which case, May the Pattern and Scatter—the Pattern/Scatter—be with you.

Acknowledgements

I'm grateful to Fred Steier and Shelley Green for their insightful suggestions on earlier drafts of this article.

References

Bateson, G. (1979). *Mind and nature*. New York: Bantam.
Bateson, G. (1991). *A sacred unity: Further steps to an ecology of mind* (R. Donaldson, Ed.). New York: HarperCollins.
Bateson, G. (2000). *Steps to an ecology of mind*. Chicago: University of Chicago Press.
Ellis, C., & Flemons, D. (2002). High noon: A fictional dialogue. In A. Bochner & C. Ellis (Eds.), *Ethnographically speaking: Autoethnography, literature, and aesthetics* (pp. 346-358). Walnut Creek, CA: Altamira Press.
Flemons, D. (1985). The hump in the Gaussian curve: Wandering through the labyrinth. *B.C. Journal of Special Education, 9,* 193-202.
Flemons, D. (1987). Zucchini mush as a misguided way of knowing. *Canadian Journal of Counselling, 21*(2 & 3), 161-164.
Flemons, D. (1989a). An eco-systemic view of family violence. *Family Therapy, 16,* 1-10.

Flemons, D. (1989b). Consensus/Dissensus: A relational alternative to the metaphor of power. *Journal of Strategic and Systemic Therapies, 8*(2 & 3), 58-64.

Flemons, D. (1991). *Completing distinctions: Interweaving the ideas of Gregory Bateson and Taoism into a unique approach to therapy.* Boston: Shambhala.

Flemons, D. (1998a). The strength to swallow death. In F. Thomas & T. Nelson (Eds.), *Tales from treating families* (pp. 125-132). New York: Haworth Press.

Flemons, D. (1998b). *Writing between the lines: Composition in the social sciences.* New York: W. W. Norton.

Flemons, D. (2002). *Of one mind: The logic of hypnosis, the practice of therapy.* New York: W. W. Norton.

Flemons, D. (2003, Jan./Feb.). The psychology of the sandpit. *Psychotherapy Networker, 27*(1), 32-37.

Flemons, D. (2004a). Spinning warm stories: The wholehearted scholarship of Arthur Bochner. *American Communication Journal, 7. http://www.acjournal.org/holdings/vol7/special/Flemons/index.html*

Flemons, D. (2004b, May/June) The Tao of therapy. *Psychotherapy Networker, 28*(3), 44-47, 68.

Flemons, D. G., & Gale, J. (Eds.). (1997). Attending to relationships [Special issue]. *Journal of Systemic Therapies, 16* (2).

Flemons, D., & Green, S. (2002). Stories that conform / stories that transform: A conversation in 4 parts. In A. Bochner & C. Ellis (Eds.), *Ethnographically speaking: Autoethnography, literature, and aesthetics* (pp. 87-94; 115-121; 167-171; 189-192). Walnut Creek, CA: Altamira Press.

Flemons, D., & Green, S. (2004). Just between us: A relational approach to sex therapy. In S. Green & D. Flemons (Eds.), *Quickies: The handbook of brief sex therapy* (pp. 126-170). New York: W. W. Norton.

Flemons, D., Green, S., & Rambo, A. (1996). Evaluating therapists' practices in a postmodern world: A discussion and a scheme. *Family Process, 35,* 43-56.

Flemons, D. G., & Shulimson, J. (1997). Participating in the culture of cancer: A demilitarized approach to treatment. *Contemporary Hypnosis, 14*(3), 182-188.

Flemons, D., & Wright K. (1999). Many lives, many traumas: The hypnotic construction of memory. In W. J. Matthews & J. H. Edgette (Eds.), *Current thinking and research in brief therapy, Vol. 3* (pp. 179-195). Philadelphia: Taylor & Francis.

Matthews, W. J., & Flemons, D. (1999). Rejoinder. One case study, many conversations: An E-mail correspondence on research. In W. J. Matthews & J. H. Edgette (Eds.), *Current thinking and research in brief therapy, Vol. 3* (pp. 195-206). Philadelphia: Taylor & Francis.

Wright, K., & Flemons, D. (2002). Dying to know: Qualitative research with terminally ill persons and their families. *Death Studies, 26*(3), 255-271.

Cybernetics And Human Knowing. Vol. 12, nos. 1-2, pp. 102-119

Steps to an Ecology of Emergence

Thomas E. Malloy,[1] Carmen Bostic St. Clair,[2] and John Grinder[2]

To begin to take steps to a mental ecology of emergence we first establish two fundamental assumptions from the methodology of transformational grammar—the centrality of human judgment based on direct experience and the proposition that the systematic nature of human behavior is algorithmically driven. We then set a double criterion for understanding any formalism such as emergence: What is formalism X, that a human may know it; and a human, that a human may know formalism X? In the cybernetic sense, the two are defined in relation to each other. In answer to the first question, we examine emergence as a formalism, using Turing's work as a defining case and an NK Boolean system as a specific working model. In answer to the second question, we frame the knowing of emergence in a Batesonian epistemological approach informed by modern developments in discrete dynamic systems. This epistemology specifies mental process as the transformation of differences across a richly connected network. The relational reference point which integrates the two sides of the cybernetic question is human judgment of perceptual similarity which links emergent hierarchies in a formal NK Boolean model to hierarchies of perceptual similarity based on direct experience.

KEYWORDS: Emergence, Perceptual Categories, Dynamic Constancy, Hierarchies, Boolean Models, Epistemology, Knowledge, Bateson, Kauffman

I have said that what gets from territory to map is transforms of differences and that these (somehow selected) differences are elementary ideas.

But there are differences between differences. Every effective difference denotes a demarcation, a line of classification, and all classifications are hierarchic. In other words, differences are themselves to be differentiated and classified. In this context I will only touch lightly on the matter of classes of difference, because to carry the matter further would land us in the problems of *Principia Mathematica.*

Let me invite you to a psychological experience, if only to demonstrate the frailty of the human computer. First note that differences in texture are different (a) from differences in color. Now note that differences in size are different (b) from differences in shape. Similarly ratios are different (c) from subtractive differences.

Now let me invite you... to define the differences between "different (a)," "different (b)," and "different (c)" in the above paragraph.

The computer in the human head boggles at the task.

—Gregory Bateson (1972), pp. 463, 464.

Model-based Intuitions about Emergence

In 1952 Alan Turing, in study of embryology, published a ground-breaking paper that laid the foundation for the concept of emergence. Within the constraints of a formal mathematical symbol system, he derived insights into morphogenesis—how

---

1. Department of Psychology, University of Utah, 380 South 1530 East Room 502, Salt Lake City, Utah 84112-0251. Email: malloy@psych.utah.edu
2. Quantum Leap: http://www.quantum-leap.com/

form self-organizes from the interactions among well-defined processes. He found that forms observed in nature (dappled patterns, radial whorls seen in leaves around stems) resulted naturally from the interplay of coupled nonlinear equations that in themselves had no hints of the higher order characteristics of the emergent forms. Turning's paper has become among the most seminal of the twentieth century (Keller, 2002, p. 108). Fifty years later this insight can now be more easily understood through more accessible formalisms, often derived from the languages of computing (e.g., Holland, 1998, p. 103, p. 125). For example, the gliders generated by simple rules in Conway's cellular automaton, *Life* (e.g., Holland, 1998, p. 138) skate across a computer screen, transforming and reforming as they interact. Gliders have become a canonical example of emergence. Furthermore, simple cellular automaton rules can produce gliders that generate other gliders (see http://llk.media.mit.edu/projects/emergence/index.html).

The distinction between the level of generating processes and the level of wholes that emerge is the basis of the idea of emergent hierarchies. If interacting processes produce wholes with novel characteristics not found in those lower level processes and if the wholes are themselves processes that can interact and so produce even higher level wholes with yet again novel characteristics, then we have an outline of a process for emergent hierarchies. Candidates for emergence were fundamental to Bateson's epistemology (1979/2002, chapter 3), although he did not use that term. The case of difference, that "there must be two entities such that the difference between them… can be immanent in their relationship" (1979/2002, p. 64), is particularly relevant to this discussion. Other candidates discussed by Bateson for what might now be called emergence are binocular vision, beats and moiré patterns.

Boolean Dynamic Systems

To specify how emergent levels develop in a model and, more critically, how those model-defined levels relate to human perception of those emergent levels we will use a computer simulation, E42, which generates NK Boolean dynamic systems (Kauffman, 1993, p. 188). NK Boolean systems are a network of N nodes (the "entities" whose relationship generates difference in Bateson's terms) each of which takes input from K other nodes in the network. These systems are Boolean because each node has only two possible states (0 or 1) and therefore are based on difference. As such, NK Boolean systems create a simulation context which can be mapped to the fundamentals of Bateson's difference-based epistemology (see Malloy, Jensen, & Song, 2005). Moreover, E42 is capable of differentiating differences in differences thereby generating emergent model-based hierarchies corresponding to those in the opening quote.

Under very broad constraints the reverberation of differences in NK Boolean networks falls into repetitive cycles called basins or attractors—that is, the system will cycle back to the same overall state in a given number of iterations. The number of iterations in such a cycle is called the basin length. This spontaneous falling into cycles is what Kauffman (1995) calls "order for free." That is, if you grant that biology can be construed as a vast network of transformations of difference, then under certain general conditions it will self-organize into complex cyclic patterns. As Turing demonstrated, these cyclic patterns can be expressed as form; and their emergence from the interactions of lower-level processes is what he meant by morphogenesis. Figure 1 shows static snapshots of basin patterns from two small Boolean systems generated pseudo-randomly by E42. Note that these patterns are dynamic and result from the system cycling over and over in the same basin. Panels (a) through (d) are all from the same dynamic system. Panel (e) shows a basin from a different pseudo-randomly generated system; panel (e) is included merely to show that there are many pseudo-randomly generated ways to getting the appearance of striped camouflage. Figure 1 shows the sort of camouflage pattern found by Turing but generated from a very different mathematical basis.

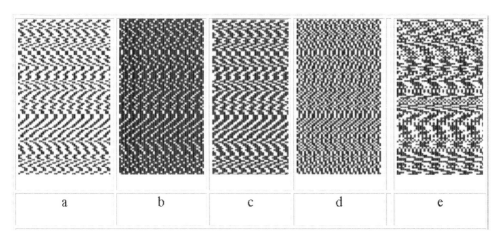

| a | b | c | d | e |

Figure 1: Camouflage-like striped patterns. The first four columns (a to d) are four basins from the same dynamic system. The fifth column (e) is a basin from a different dynamic system.

This approach to form as a self-organized persistent whole generated by the interplay of underlying processes pioneered by Turing has been a prime basis for defining emergence as a phenomenon and is still consistent with modern criteria (e.g., Holland, 1998, p. 225). Forms, in this tradition, are not things but rather processes, although as with leaf patterns or animal spots, forms may be persistent enough to be taken as if they are things. In fact, as Turing indicated, they are ongoing processes, more like a stationary wave in a mountain stream which may appear to stable, even static, but is in each moment holding its form by the interactions of fluid processes.

Kauffman (1993) proposes that, along with natural selection, the self-organization of emergent form is a co-principle in the evolution of life. As an example of how this might work, note that the forms in panels (a) through (d) in Figure 1 all self-organize from interaction of Boolean processes and are from the same dynamic system. Let these forms represent four kinds of camouflage that self-organize from the Boolean idealization of genetic interaction (Kauffman, 1995, p. 74, 104). Given that these forms can emerge from the interaction of genes, then natural selection, depending on environmental pressures, would act to favor one form over another; the lighter camouflage (a) might be favored in areas with long winters while the zebra-like striping (c) may be favored in open grasslands. If something like the Boolean idealization is what happens in genetic interaction, then the rich patterning observed in life is not the improbable result of chance acting in long random walks of natural selection but the inevitable and expected result of self organization (Kauffman, 1995, p. 71ff). Natural selection, in such a model, has only to explain which form survives; it does not have to explain the genesis of form, which as Turing in 1952 demonstrated, can emerge from process interactions.

Critiques of Emergence

More elusive and more controversial has been the use of these model-generated insights and definitions as explanatory devices for "actual" phenomena. Keller (2002) provides a convincing history of the lack of success in developmental biology of mathematical models in general and of Turing's morphogenic ideas in particular. In short, the contention is that the processes that generate the patterns of hair on a zebra are nothing like the processes underlying Turing's derivations or E42's simulations. That is, the processes which generate levels in a model are sometimes conflated with processes that generate corresponding levels in the phenomena (Goldstein, 2002). Goldstein also summarizes other issues in the definition of emergence. Emergence is often characterized negatively (an emergent characteristic is not found in the processes that generate it). Frequently emergent levels seem arbitrary due to a lack of detailed specification of how processes generate emergent levels; it is one thing to say that cells interact to produce tissues; but without detailed process specification, tissues may be an arbitrarily chosen emergent whole for the interaction of cells. Finally, Goldstein (2002) and others have noted that emergent phenomena of interest arise naturally while models such as glider guns are carefully designed and therefore unlike natural phenomena. We will return to these issues later, after our ideas are more developed.

Intuition as a Legitimate Methodology

We are primarily concerned here with epistemology and with Bateson's notion of ecology of mind. How might hierarchies of differences (see quote which begins this paper) and therefore hierarchies of pattern emerge in a mental system? There are several crucial epistemological frames to establish in answering that question. As a start, our epistemological approach has two fundamental assumptions (Bostic-St. Clair & Grinder, 2001). Both of these assumptions are explicit in Chomsky's transformational grammar.

Let us first focus on the paradigmatic centrality of human judgment based on direct experience (what Chomsky calls intuition). As an example, consider the sentence, "This pig is ready to eat." Is the sentence ambiguous, that is, does it have more than one meaning? Both the answer to that question and the definition of the linguistic phenomenon of ambiguity in Chomsky's paradigm depend on the linguistic intuitions of native speakers of English as they experience that sentence.

The second assumption (also explicit in Chomsky's paradigm) is that human behavior is systematic in the sense of being rule-based; moreover, in the linguistic paradigm, it is assumed that native speakers have internalized the grammatical rules of their native language so that their intuitive judgments are based on these rules. A monolingual speaker of English, while able to make judgments about important linguistic phenomena in English, would fail to do so when presented with Spanish or Chinese sentences. The grammatical rules of a language must be well-learned before a person's direct experience with a sentence leads to appropriate natural language intuitions.

Chomsky's transformational grammar is a mapping from natural language phenomena such as ambiguity onto explicit models, namely, recursive rule systems of great simplicity and formal power. It is worthy of note that learning and internalizing these mathematical rule systems produced model-based intuitions which allowed researchers to determine with little effort what the actual claims of the model are and what would constitute a counterexample to the model's claims so as to make mapping from rule system to linguistic phenomena open to challenge and refinement based on intuition. Notice that there are two kinds of intuitions in this discussion: Those resulting from internalizing the grammatical rules of a natural language and those resulting from internalizing the rules of a mathematical model (which Chomsky then mapped onto the language phenomena). In this epistemological framework, the intuitions about emergence based on Turing's math required a deep commitment to learning the symbolic language system he used. The same is true in the more accessible ideas based on neural nets and their generalization to emergence, (e.g., Holland, 1998). Even the relatively simple logic of a Boolean system (see Appendix) requires a fair commitment to learning its formal language (Kauffman, 1993). In any case, intuition, be it based on internalizing grammars or internalizing formal models, is a key element of our epistemology.

In this paper we propose NK Boolean systems as a simple set of recursive rules that generate hierarchies of differences in differences which can be mapped onto visual forms and validated against perceptual intuitions. We will not ask you, the reader, to generate model-based intuitions by internalizing the rules of Boolean math (equivalent to Chomsky's recursive rules); we will, however, ask you to check your natural perceptual intuitions about emergent hierarchies of visual forms (equivalent to linguistic phenomena like ambiguity). If you want to develop model-based intuitions for Boolean systems examine the Appendix or see Malloy, Jensen, and Song (2005) where we lay out the requisite logic of such systems at some length. Our strategy here is to let computer simulations do the work of realizing the Boolean models' processes by mapping their logic onto visual forms and then allowing you to check your own natural perceptual experience about the emergent hierarchies which result.

The Embodiment of Mind

How can we address emergence within an epistemology soundly rooted in systems framework? Warren McCulloch (1965) suggested a possible direction. The cybernetic conceptualization of neural nets as a basis for mental process was pioneered (Varela, Thompson, & Rosch, 1993, p. 38) by McCulloch and Pitts (1943). Later, enmeshed in a culture which deeply presupposed the Cartesian mind-body split, in our era manifested as the hidden homunculus of cognitivist theories, McCulloch articulated a general framework for the embodiment of mind (1965). He revised the Psalmist spiritual question, "What is a man that Thou shouldst know him?" to a stringent double criterion (1961): "What is a number, that a man may know it, and a man, that he may know a number?" Here, in this question stated in cybernetic form, a formalism and a description of human epistemology are known in relation to each other. Properly to define emergence by this relational criteria is to propose formalisms for emergence in relation to a description of human knowledge.

McCulloch (1965, p. 6) uses Russell's definition of a number: "A number is the class of all those classes that can be put into one-to-one correspondence with it." As an example, he notes that "7 is the class of all those classes that can be put into one-to-correspondence with the days of the week, which are 7." He further notes that while some mathematicians may question whether this is all that a number means, it is sufficient for his purposes which is to define a number in such a way that, like linguistic ambiguity, most people can have intuitions about it since most people have internalized rules of mathematics well enough to generate intuitions about such a definition of number. For the other side of his question, he refers to his earlier work with Pitts and summarizes the theoretical importance of it. He maps people's intuitions about number onto a recursive rule system of great power. In doing so he lays the ground-work for the now familiar argument that the logic of neural nets is sufficient for knowing in general and for knowing numbers in particular. Both Holland (1998, p. 96ff) and Varela, Thompson, and Rosch (1993, p. 155ff) develop examples of models (neural nets, cellular automata) clearly enough that most people can have model-based intuitions about them.

McCulloch proposed and then met a stringent double standard: He specified a double—(a) a description of what is known (a number) and (b) a model of the epistemology of the knower (neural nets)—in such a way that both terms of the double could be mapped to each other. McCulloch's double requirement that we be explicit about the relationship between a formalism and a description of human knowledge is critical. What are the *processes* which underlie formalism X that it may be known by a human, and the *processes* of human knowing that a human may know formalism X? To meta-frame this discussion in Turing's metaphor, and to point at what we think McCulloch and later Bateson were asking us to think about, we ask, "What forms emerge from the coupled interactions of *the above processes*?"

That a Human May Know It

What is the formalism named E42? We will aim here for an intuitive answer to that question. The details of how Boolean systems work along with their correspondences to Bateson's epistemology can be found in Malloy, Jensen and Song (2005). As a start, let us examine how the images in Figures 1 and 2 represent the behavior of E42. Recall that an NK Boolean system consists of N nodes, each taking input from K other nodes. This input consists of either a 0 indicating that the other node is OFF or a 1 indicating that the other node is ON. At any time, T, every node in the system uses a logical operator whose arguments are its inputs to decide if it will be ON or OFF for the next iteration (T+1). For example, if a node has two inputs and its operator is the logical AND operator, then it will be ON during the next iteration (T+1) only if both its inputs are ON during the current iteration (T). If another node is using the logical INCLUSIVE OR operator then it will be ON at T+1 if either one input or the other or both are ON at time T. If a node is using the logical EXCLUSIVE OR (XOR) operator then at T+1 it will be ON if its two inputs are the different (that is, either {0,1} or {1,0}); conversely it will be OFF if its two inputs are the same (that is, either {0,0} or {1,1}). The XOR operator thus detects difference and is related to Bateson's difference-based epistemology in important ways. Any logical operator can be used a system constructed by E42 and which operator actually is used by each node is decided pseudo-randomly when the system is first built. For more details see the Appendix or Malloy, Jensen and Song (2005).

The behavior of an E42-generated Boolean system can be represented as a historical trace of the states (ON or OFF) of all its nodes across time. Examine Figure 2, which has finer detail than Figure 1, and shows output from a different pseudo-randomly generated dynamic system than those that generated Figure 1. This system has N = 35 nodes. The 35 nodes run up vertical axis while time (iterations) runs along the horizontal axis. Look at Figure 2 (a), basin 40. The first column shows the state (ON = black square and OFF = white square) for each the 35 nodes arrayed as a vertical vector. The second column shows the state of each node for the next iteration, and so on. Figure 2 (a) shows one particular basin, basin 40, into which that the system falls. Panel (a) shows 24 iterations on the horizontal axis; this is enough for the system to cycle through "basin 40" four times—that is, the length of the basin cycle happens to be six iterations, and we have four cycles through that basin. Six iterations per cycle times four cycles yields 24 iterations on the horizontal axis of Figure 2 (a). Once in a basin such as that shown in Figure 2 (a) the system will stay there forever unless it is perturbed. Figure 2 panels (b) through (d) show three other basins (each cycling 4 times).

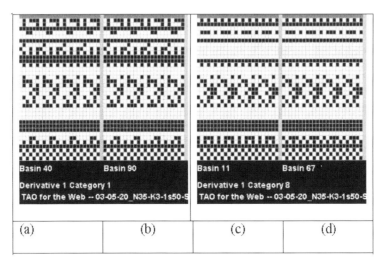

Figure 2: Four basins from a pseudo-randomly generated dynamic system. Panels (a) and (b) are perceived as similar as are panels (c) and (d).

The representation of dynamics as a historical trace generates a pattern resulting from the behavior of a system across time; more specifically, it shows the differences in the states of the full set of nodes (vertical axis) as they change across time (horizontal axis). These changes over time are the dynamic component of system's behavior. The 2-D patterns generated by changes in the states of an array of nodes (ordinate) over time (abscissa) are perceptible to humans as coherent wholes when a system is cycling in a basin. In Figure 1, these patterns are evocative of the visual experience of striped camouflage, and it was this sort of coming-into-being of form a cross time which was the central point of Turing's paper. In Figure 2, the patterns are more abstract.

Recall that we described two kinds of intuitions, those that come from internalizing a model (such as Chomsky's) and those that come from encountering phenomena such as linguistic ambiguity. The intention here is to represent the workings of the Boolean model in a way that you may have intuitions from the model without the considerable effort of internalizing its rules. We are examining here the first half of McCulloch's questions: What is (one example, at least, of) a dynamic system that a human may know it? Representing the processes of a Boolean model as a visual historical trace allows you to have visual intuitions about the logic of the model without needing to internalize that logic. On that basis, we will later ask you to check your intuitions about visual hierarchies which are candidates for emergence.

Dynamic Constancies for Differences in Differences over Time

An interesting aspect of Figure 2 is that, in the judgment of humans, patterns generated by basins 40 and 90, panels (a) and (b), resemble each other but are distinct from the patterns of basins 11 and 67, panels (c) and (d), which in turn resemble each other. Here we are using the linguistic methodology and you are asked to examine Figure 2 and make your own judgments.

For a discussion of the nature of emergent hierarchies, these obvious perceptual judgments are crucial. Before we examine that issue, we first will consider one more issue that is technical—the discrete first derivative. The E42 system can perform operations parallel to the thought experiment proposed by Bateson (1972, p. 463, 464) involving hierarchies of difference. Figure 2 shows four basin patterns that result from the historical trace of the differences in a system across time. Change over time implies the possibility of a change in change over time (that is, the discrete analogue of the first derivative). In essence, E42 takes the discrete first derivative to determine whether the differences over time that generate one basin are themselves the same or different than the differences over time that generate another basin. The details of this process are found in Malloy, Jensen, and Song (2005).

The discrete first derivatives of the basins in Figure 2 (a) and (b) are identical; so too are the derivatives of the basins shown in Figure 2 (c) and (d). That is, the differences in differences over time are the same in panels (a) and (b) and likewise are the same in panels (c) and (d). Patterns that have the same first derivative—panels (a) and (b) or, alternately, panels (c) and (d)—look similar to humans.

Emergent Hierarchies in Model and in Perception

In Figure 2 we have two possible levels of a proposed emergent hierarchy. The first level is realized by the basin patterns (zebra stripes in Figure 1 or the more abstract patterns in Figure 2) that are generated by the interaction of the Boolean processes. This level of emergence is the one proposed by Turing in his study of morphogenesis and is essentially the same level of emergent form as Conway's gliders in the game of Life. The second proposed emergent level is realized by the appearance in Figure 2 of categories of form generated by the model using the first derivatives taken on those forms. In our methodology, these model-generated levels are calibrated against the reader's perceptual judgments.

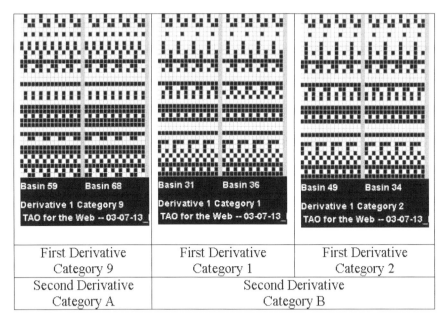

First Derivative Category 9	First Derivative Category 1	First Derivative Category 2
Second Derivative Category A	Second Derivative Category B	

**Figure 3: Dynamic Constancy. Six visual forms placed into three categories
based on identical first derivatives. The three categories are themselves
placed into two meta-categories based on identical second derivatives.**

Figure 3 shows a more interesting example consisting of six basins from yet another pseudo-randomly generated dynamic system that has 36 nodes. The length of a basin in Figure 3 is four iterations; so four times through four iterations yields the 16 iterations shown on the horizontal axis for each basin. Based on identical first derivatives, the model places the six basins into three categories of two basins each: category 9 (basins 59 & 68), category 1 (basins 31 & 36) and category 2 (basins 49 & 34). (The system has more basins and more categories, which are not shown here.) All basins in the same category have identical discrete first derivatives; and all basins in different categories have different first derivatives.

Using the criterion of human intuition akin to the linguistic paradigm you are asked to examine your own perceptual judgments about two interesting perceptual observations with implications for the concept of emergent hierarchies. Both perceptual observations are related to what we will define as the principle of dynamic constancy. First, basins within a category are more similar to each other than they are to basins in other categories; this is the same point noted above in Figure 2. This first point is particularly applicable in category 9 where basins 59 and 68 are perceptually hard to distinguish and in category 2 where basins 49 and 34 are nearly as difficult to distinguish. The only weakening of this point is in category 1 where basins 31 and 36 have some elements that are perceptually quite distinct, distinct enough that some people might not put them in the same category. In fact, there are boundary conditions for this phenomenon (that categories based on first derivatives correspond to human perceptual judgments); these boundary conditions, while important, do not invalidate the phenomenon and are discussed in depth at www.psych.utah.edu/dysys.

Second, and of great interest for conceptualizing emergent hierarchies, is that, taken as a whole, some categories are more similar to each other than they are to other categories. To be concrete, notice that the basins in category 9, while closely resembling each other, are quite distinct from the basins in categories 1 and 2. In contrast, the four basins in categories 1 and 2, taken together, are relatively similar to each other. They certainly resemble each other more than they do the basins in category 9. It is as if there is a possibility of meta-categories consisting of categories that are similar to each other. Could not the four basins in categories 1 and 2 be placed together, all in the same higher-level category? The answer, at least the answer provided by the Boolean model, is yes. How would the model do this?

A first derivative implies a second derivative. Up to this point we have used the first derivative to examine the differences in the differences of the states of a system as it iterates across time. Now we will use the second derivative to examine the differences in the differences in the differences in the states of the system across time. In doing so what we find is that categories 1 and 2 (meta-category B in Figure 3) have identical second derivatives, while category 9 (meta-category A in Figure 3) has a distinct second derivative. This model-based processing of differences in the states of the system over time once again generates categories that correspond to human perceptual judgments.

Now we have three potential levels in a candidate for an emergent hierarchy. The first level is the genesis of form from the interaction of generating processes. The next level is the emergence of categories of form generated by the processes involved in taking differences in differences over time. The third level is the emergence of meta-categories of form based on taking differences in differences in differences over time. These levels, precisely defined in the realm of the model, correspond to human perceptual judgments. We propose that this is one way to operationalize Bateson's hierarchy of differences outlined in the opening quote.

The categories are examples of cases where changes over time themselves do not change. We call the perceptual similarity of patterns in such categories the principle of dynamic constancy and propose it as a new principle of perceptual grouping to be added to the well-known Gestalt principles of grouping (for a modern discussion, see Palmer, 1999).

We have now discussed in general terms what E42 is that a human may know it. The answer, then, to McCulloch's first criterion is that E42 is a formal model whose differences over time generate forms such that the differences in the differences in those forms generate a hierarchy of levels that can be known by humans through judgments of perceptual similarity.

The Human Reference Point

Let us return to our epistemological frame with a quote from Bostic St. Clair and Grinder (2001, p. 76):

> The linguist manipulates the syntactic, phonological, and semantic forms and judges and/or asks native speakers to judge whether the consequences are a well-formed sentence in the language, an ambiguous string or any one of an array of numerous other possibilities. The relevant reference point by the very nature of the research is internal to the bearer of the internal grammar—the native speaker himself.
>
> To put the matter in a somewhat different form, suppose that we succeeded in constructing an instrument that purportedly arrived at the same judgments for visual inputs as those possessed by normally sighted people.
>
> How would we know whether the instrument worked?
>
> The answer clearly is that we would accept the instrument as accurate if and only if the responses of the instrument matched those of normally sighted people. In other words, we would calibrate the instrument by using precisely the same set of judgments (intuitions) reported by the people involved that we presently use in the absence of such an instrument.
>
> Thus in fields where the patterning under scrutiny is patterning of the behavior of human beings, the reference point and the source of the judgments will necessarily be the human being.

How could it be otherwise?

In this framework, the correspondence between the hierarchical levels of the model and human perceptual judgments integrates the two sides of McCulloch's relational loop. It is the human that is the relational center when formalisms are generated and known.

What is Human Knowledge that a Human May Know Dynamic Systems?

We now address epistemological issues in the second part of McCulloch's question: What is a human that s/he may know a formalism? We will present one thread of thought in this regard.

The conceptualization of knowledge in terms of the "all or none" character of "difference" goes back in its modern computationally-based form at least to McCulloch and Pitts (1943). The fundamentals of neural nets that they laid down have undergone various stages of elaboration and development by theorists like Hebb (1949), Holland (1975) and Varela, Thompson and Rosch (1993) among many others. And the rigorous focus on difference as the defining epistemological relationship was developed extensively by Bateson (1972, 1979/2002), and continued in our own work by DeLozier and Grinder (1987) with application as a teaching method by Malloy (2001).

Influenced by McCulloch's thinking (see M. C. Bateson, 1991), Gregory Bateson proposes that difference is the basis of mental process which itself has six criteria:

> (1) Mind is an aggregate of interacting parts or components. (2) The interaction between parts of mind is triggered by difference. (3) Mental process requires collateral energy. (4) Mental process

requires circular (or more complex) chains of determination. (5) In mental process the effects of difference are to be regarded as transforms (i.e., coded versions) of the difference which preceded them. (6) The description and classification of these processes of transformation discloses a hierarchy of logical types immanent in the phenomena. (Bateson, 1979/2002, pp. 89, 102, 106)

The second, fourth, fifth, and sixth criteria are particularly relevant to emergent hierarchies of a mental ecology as operationalized here by perceptual categories resulting from the analysis of differences in differences.

McCulloch directs our attention to the relationship between any formalism and the specification of an epistemology within which that formalism could be known. Bateson's descriptions of mental process, connected as they are to McCulloch's foundations of neural network theory, act as a starting point for an epistemology that would allow humans to know emergent phenomena. Based on that starting point we have given Bateson's descriptions more specificity by modeling them with a Boolean system. This modeling allowed the specification of what is meant by taking differences in difference and produced model-based hierarchies of visual pattern. This model-based hierarchy in turn corresponds to human judgments of similarity—the reference point for connecting model-based emergent hierarchies with emergent hierarchies in perception.

Critical Concerns Revisited

Earlier, we focused on three critiques of emergence as a concept. One is that the processes that underlie hierarchies can be under-specified, vague and post hoc with the result that the emergent levels which are named are arbitrary. In the case of the perceptual categories presented here, the Boolean generating processes, including discrete derivatives, produce hierarchies in the visual output of E42 model that are well-specified, thus the model-based categories which emerge are not arbitrary but a deterministic result of Boolean logical processes. The second critique is that the levels in model and the levels in the actual phenomena are conflated and then the processes that generated the emergent levels in the model are assumed to be the same as the processes that generate the levels in the actual phenomenon. This is a deeper scientific issue, applying to all models and theories whether they address emergence or other concepts. It amounts to confusing the map with the territory. In our case this would be equivalent to assuming that the transforms of differences generated the E42 model are the same as the transformations taking place in a human perceptual system which generate corresponding levels of similarity judgments. This critique cannot, indeed should not, be dismissed in any definitive sense. It is crucial to keep a well-defined distinction between, on one hand, a model, and how it works, and, on the other hand, the phenomenon, and how it works.

A productive and positive approach to this second issue is offered by Bateson (1979/2002, p. 76) who defines explanation as the mapping of a tautology onto a description of some phenomenon. Bateson considers such a mapping from tautology to description as an example of the gains in knowledge that result from multiple versions of the world. What we have offered here is a (Boolean) logical tautological system mapped onto Bateson's description of a hierarchy of differences which opened this paper. The intent is not to confuse the tautology with Bateson's descriptions nor with the processes of human perceptual physiology. Rather the intent is to generate gains in insight and utility that could result from putting the two into relationship, much in the spirit of McCulloch double-sided question. Thus the formal hierarchies of emergence based on differences in differences in the model are set into relationship with a Bateson's description of a human as knower; and, finally, human perceptual judgments are used as the reference point for evaluating the utility of that relationship itself.

The third critical concern was that emergent phenomena of interest arise naturally while models are carefully designed. Taking Bateson's framing of explanation as a mapping of a tautology onto a description of a phenomenon this will always be the case. Verbal or mathematical, the model or the theory that we map onto our descriptions of the world are by definition a human artifice. The hope is that some utility emerges from such mapping from artifice to nature. In this discussion hierarchies of differences in differences generated by E42 have been mapped onto visual form and hierarchies of perceptual similarity in those forms. The utility of gliders and glider guns in cellular automata theory depends on what they are mapped onto and how the mapping is done. But even if gliders are taken as a general metaphor, they may be of great value.

Emergence as Metaphor

The importance of metaphor's function in a mental ecology is both pervasive and useful. An important metaphor, at least in western civilization, which is proper to religion and certain areas of philosophy and metaphysics, is the designer metaphor—that an all-knowing, all-powerful being designed the universe. Something, split off from and separate from the biological world, designs the biological world. Proper as it may be in religion and other disciplines, the designer metaphor is not proper to science. Turing set out to defeat the "argument from design," in the life sciences. The concept of emergence which his work eventually led to is a powerful metaphorical alternative to the metaphor of designer. In this function it allows discourse about many human ideas and experiences without the necessity of proposing a designer. Keller (2002, p. 90) documents that Turing intended for once and for all to "Defeat the argument from Design." He provoked an alternative framework to theories and discourses that presupposed life needed ultimately to be explained by a designer. As we've argued in the previous section, there is no paradox here; a mathematical proof that form can emerge from the interplay of processes is no more paradoxical in its use as a tautology to map onto natural phenomena than are other tautologies, whether they be the idea of a designer or idea of reductionist causality (see below).

The power of the emergence insight is that wholes self-organize themselves as a natural function of the interplay of the processes that make them up. Turing and others have, at least within the realm of logic and mathematics, offered proofs of this. This is a logico-mathematical concept of great generality and power. Science doesn't follow the chain of causality back to the being, who external to the world, designed and created the world. It does use, however, a reductionist metaphor to follow causality down to sub-atomic particles or back through time to the big bang. While such chains might well someday be literal, tracing every link rigorously, in fact currently that is not possible; and the reductionist chain is primarily metaphorical, coloring in the background the way we think about what is important in theory and data. The metaphorical frame of emergence offers an alternative background, supplanting long chains of metaphorical reductionist causality with local neighborhoods of process levels within which phenomena of interest self-organize into emergent wholes to be studied and understood in relation to those neighborhoods of process. As Keller (2002, p. 102) summarizes it, "Turing's work… offered a way out of the infinite regress…" In fact, within the emergence metaphor, the reductionist chain can never be complete because there will always be gaps in that chain where sub-processes self-organize into higher-level processes whose characteristics cannot be found in the sub-processes.

As Kauffman argues, the underlying concepts of science influence scientists and nonscientists alike every day in metaphorical ways.

> The vast mystery of biology is that life should have emerged at all, that the order we see should have come to pass. A theory of emergence would account for the creation of the stunning order out our windows as a natural expression of some underlying laws. It would tell us if we are at home in the universe, expected in it, rather than present despite overwhelming odds (Kauffman, 1995, p. 23).

In a general day to day context, having a way of understanding that leaves can form in an elegant whorl around a plant's stem as a natural consequence of the processes of plant physiology or that organs might emerge out of tissues and tissues out of cells is a useful alternative both to thinking about life as designed by an external entity and to thinking in the materialist tradition of biology as a machine, a linear sequence of cause and effect. If formalisms, such as numbers, emerge as characteristics of neural networks, then, by metaphorical generalization, mental processes, ideas, the whole of mental ecology can be cast as an emergent characteristic of the processes of human (and all) biology—mind and body are an integrated whole. And they are integrated as a whole both in a metaphorical way and in a way that is susceptible to study through formal models, in whatever degree of specificity is required by a scientific question. They are integrated in a way which is "neither mechanical nor supernatural" (Bateson & Bateson, 1987, chapter 5). As such, the metaphor of emergence serves as a functional addition to the mental ecology of western society, with potential for contributing to integrating the mind-body split and moving toward mind and nature as a necessary unity (Bateson, 1979/2002).

A final gain of great potential value which results from using dynamic systems tautologies like E42 to map onto descriptions of knowledge is that in a dynamic systems approach mental process will self-organize. If ideas are thought of as dynamic basins, then knowledge need not always be learned incrementally; rather, interactions with the environment within such a model are likely to provoke mental process to self-organize into ideas. The flash of insight is what is expected and works hand in hand with incremental learning. Insight and incremental learning might correspond in a general way to the modern insight that evolution is shaped by both self-organization and by natural selection.

Steps to an Ecology of Emergence

How might hierarchies emerge in a mental ecology? To answer that question we have used McCulloch's double criteria: What is emergence, that humans may know it, and human knowledge, that they may know emergence? In the cybernetic sense, the two are defined in relation to each other. In answer to the first question, we have examined emergence as a formalism, using Turing's work as a defining case and an NK Boolean system as a specific working model. In answer to the second question, we have framed the knowing of emergence in a broad Batesonian epistemological approach informed by modern developments in neural nets and discrete dynamic systems models. This epistemology specifies mental process, both verbally and in computer simulations, as the transformation of differences across a richly connected network. As the relational reference point which integrates the two sides of McCulloch's cybernetic question, we have used human judgments of perceptual similarity to link emergent hierarchies formally found in an NK Boolean model to hierarchies of perceptual similarity in human knowledge.

References

Bateson, G. (1972). *Steps to an ecology of mind*. Chicago: Chicago University Press.
Bateson, G. (2002). *Mind and nature: A necessary unity*. Cresskill, N.J.: Hampton Press. (Originally published in 1979 by Bantam Books in New York City).
Bateson, G. & Bateson, M. C. (1987). *Angels fear: Toward an epistemology of the sacred*. New York: MacMillan.
Bateson, M. C. (1991). *Our own metaphor*. Washington, D. C.: The Smithsonian Press.
Bostic-St. Clair, C. & Grinder, J. (2001). *Whispering in the wind*. Scotts Valley, CA: J & C Enterprises.
DeLozier, J. & Grinder, J. (1987). *Turtles all the way down*. Bonny Doon, CA: Grinder, DeLozier Associates.
Goldstein, J. (2002). The singular nature of emergent levels: Suggestions for a theory of emergence. *Nonlinear Dynamics, Psychology and Life Sciences, 6*, 293-309.
Hebb, D. O. (1949). *The organization of behavior*. New York: John Wiley & Sons.
Holland, J. H. (1975). *Adaptation in natural and artificial systems*. Ann Arbor, MI: University of Michigan Press.
Holland, J. H. (1998). *Emergence: From chaos to order*. Reading, MA: Addison-Wesley Publishing.
Kauffman, S. A. (1993). *The origins of order: Self-organization and selection in evolution*. Oxford: Oxford University Press.
Kauffman, S. A. (1995). *At home in the universe: The search for the laws of self-organization and complexity*. Oxford: Oxford University Press.
Keller, H. F. (2002). *Making sense of life*. Cambridge, MA: Harvard University Press.
Malloy, T. E. (2001). Difference to Inference: Teaching logical and statistical reasoning through online interactivity. *Behavior Research Methods Instruments & Computers, 33*, 270-273.
Malloy, T. E., Jensen, G. C., & Song, T. (2005). Epistemology and evolution: Expressing Bateson's epistemology with Boolean networks. *Nonlinear Dynamics, Psychology, and the Life Sciences, 9*, 37-60.
McCulloch, W. S. (1961). What is a number, that a man may know it, and a man, that he may know a number? *General Semantics Bulletin*, nos. 26, 27, pp. 7-18.
McCulloch, W. S. (1965). *The embodiment of mind*. Cambridge, MA: The MIT. Press.
McCulloch, W. S., & Pitts, W. H. (1943). A logical calculus of the ideas immanent in nervous activity. *Bulletin of Mathematical Biophysics, 3*, 115-133.
Palmer, S. E. (1999). *Vision Science: Photons to phenomenology*. Cambridge, MA: The MIT Press.

Turing, A. M. (1952). The chemical basis of morphogenesis. *Philosophical Transactions of the Royal Society of London. Series B, Biological Sciences, 237,* 37-72.

Varela, F. J., Thompson, E., & Rosch, E. (1993). *The embodied mind.* Cambridge, MA: The MIT Press.

Appendix

E42 builds Boolean systems consisting of N ($4 \le N \le 400$) binary nodes (0, 1). On any iteration (T), each node accepts input (either 0 or 1) from K ($2 \le K \le 5$) other nodes in the system. Let the Boolean value "1" mean a node is "ON" and "0" mean a node is "OFF." Each node has a logical truth table which determines what its value will be on iteration T+1 as a function of the inputs it receives on iteration T. **NODES**. Consider as an arbitrary example a minimal system that has N=4 nodes and K=2 inputs to each node. Name the four nodes, in order, A, B, C, D. **WIRING**. Let node A take input from nodes C and D; let B also take input from C and D. Let nodes C and D each take input from nodes A and B. **LOGICAL OPERATORS**. Node A uses an *OR* gate to determine if it is ON at T+1; that is, it will be ON at T+1 if either C or D or both are ON at T. Node B uses an *EXCLUSIVE OR (XOR)* gate; that is, it will be ON at T+1 if either node C or node D (but not both) are ON at T. Node C uses an *AND* gate; that is, it will be ON at T+1 only if nodes C and D are both ON at T. Node D uses an OR gate. The operators in this example are arbitrary. **STATE VECTORS**. To keep track of the changing states for all four nodes we define a state vector. At time T, the state vector, **S**(T), is defined such that the first position in the vector represents the state of A, the second position the state of B, and so on. In this way the expression **S**(1) = {1100} means that, at time T=1, A = 1, B = 1, C = 0, and D = 0. Define a state space as a matrix of all possible state vectors; in this example the state space is the set of vectors from {0000} to {1111}. **STATE TRANSITIONS**. As a dynamic system, the system's state vectors can change over time (T). These changes are deterministically derived from the wiring and logical operators of the system. For example, if at T the system is in state vector {1000}, where only node A is in state 1, then at T+1 the system will go to {0001} where only node D is in state 1, where 1 = ON. This transition can be derived using the logical operators acting on inputs. Given {1000} at T, at T+1 node A will change to 0 (since nodes C and D are both 0 at T). On the other hand, node D will change from state 0 at T to state 1 at T+1 because D takes on state 1 if either A or B or both are a 1, which is the case at time T. By similar reasoning, nodes B and C do not change states. Other state transitions are left to the inspection of the reader. For convenience, we list all state transitions: {0000} => {0000}; {0001} => {1100}; {0010} => {1100};{0011} => {1000};{0100} => {0001};{0101} => {1101};{0110} => {1101};{0111} => {1001};{1000} => {0001};{1001} => {1101};{1010} => {1101};{1011} => {1001};{1100} => {0011};{1101} => {1111};{1110} => {1111};{1111} => {1011}. **BASINS**. From this list of all possible state transitions we can start the system in any state vector and follow the flow of its deterministic process from one state vector to another. For example, starting with vector {0111}, we find the following flow: {0111} => {1001} => {1101} => {1111} => {1011} => {1001)... Note that {1001} has now repeated;

therefore the system will loop back to {1001} every four iterations, cycling endlessly through {1001} => {1101} => {1111} => {1011} => {1001}... This is called an attractor cycle or basin of length 4. Call this Basin 1. The first vector in this example, {0111}, is called a tributary because if the system falls into that vector it will only pass through it once on its way to Basin 1. Basin 1 has four other tributaries: {0101}, {0110}, {1010}, {1110}. The reader can confirm that this minimal system has two other basins. Basin 2 = [{0001} => {1100} => {0011} => {1000} => {0001}...]. Basin 2 has two tributaries: {0100}, {0010}. Basin 3 = [{0000} => {0000} => ...]. External or internal "perturbations" are required to provoke the system to escape from a basin. In confirming the above logic, we recommend that the reader create truth tables for the logical operators, make a table of state transitions, and visualize both the wiring and the basin structure with sketches.

Cybernetics And Human Knowing. Vol. 12, nos. 1-2, pp. 120-136

A Failed Dialogue?
Revisiting the 1975 Meeting of Gregory Bateson and Carl Rogers

Kenneth N. Cissna[1] and Rob Anderson[2]

This study of the 1975 public "dialogue" between Gregory Bateson and Carl Rogers shows that, far from "talking past each other" in a "fiasco" of misunderstanding and "debate" that some (including Bateson and Rogers) have taken it for, the two men accomplished at least two of the important functions of dialogue: *extending* common ideas in new directions and *distinguishing* significant and realistic differences. Bateson, in particular, clarified his use of *context* and provided a number of insightful examples of this important concept.

When the Marin Association for Mental Health decided in February 1975 to invite Gregory Bateson and Carl Rogers to be the primary speakers for a fund-raising event, they had very high hopes for its success.[3] The organizers billed the meeting as a "dialogue," and they hoped it might have the impact of the Buber-Rogers and Rogers-Skinner dialogues from earlier decades (see Kirschenbaum & Henderson, 1989). Unfortunately, their May 28, 1975, conversation did not work out quite as anyone had hoped. Two weeks later, in a June 11 letter to Rogers and existential psychotherapist Rollo May, Bateson described it as "a dreadful event": "two hours under klieg lights in front of fifteen hundred people, trying to talk and trying not to talk." In July 1 letters to Bateson and to Richard Farson, who served as moderator of the dialogue, Rogers agreed that it was "dreadful," a "fiasco," even, and said that he was embarrassed that the dialogue would be "available in cassette form for people to listen to and shake their heads at."[4]

As far as we have been able to determine, neither Bateson nor Rogers ever mentioned the dialogue or the other in print, nor do their biographies refer to the other or to their dialogue (Bateson, 1984; Donaldson, 1991; Harries-Jones, 1995;

---

1. Department of Communication, University of South Florida, Tampa, Florida. Email: kcissna@luna.cas.usf.edu
2. Department of Communication, Saint Louis University, St. Louis, MO. Email: anderro@slu.edu
3. In a February 21, 1975, letter, program organizer Richard Farson wrote to Rogers, "Bateson said *yes*—he's enthusiastic about the possibility. And so am I." Earlier, though, in a handwritten note to Rogers, Bateson referred to their prospective encounter as a "gladiatorial show" arranged by the "busy bees of money-raising and public relations."
4. Our work on the Bateson-Rogers dialogue was informed by the papers, notes, and letters in the Rogers Collection of the Library of Congress and by materials from the Bateson Archive at the University of California at Santa Cruz. We acknowledge the invaluable assistance of Martha and Lee Mathis in helping us obtain documents from the Library of Congress and Christine Bunting, head of Special Collections at the University of California at Santa Cruz Library, who provided us letters and two audio recordings of the dialogue from the Bateson Archive. The materials from the Rogers Collection are from box 93, folders 9 and 12, and box 28, folder 1. The materials from the Bateson Archive were used by permission of Mary Catherine Bateson and the Institute for Intercultural Study.

Kirschenbaum, 1979, 1995; Lipset, 1982; Rogers & Russell, 2002; Thorne, 1992). In the only works we could locate that refer to their dialogue, Rollo May, on the basis of the letter he and Rogers received from Bateson, called the Bateson-Rogers meeting a "notorious debate" (1977, p. 96), and Snyder (1989) also referred to it as "their debate" (p. 362). Farson, at least, had such high hopes for their dialogue—now, if it is mentioned at all, it is called a debate. How could such a propitious event have gone so wrong? Or did it? What happened in this dialogue, and why it has been so neglected, are the central questions guiding this study.

After reviewing the historical record, including evidently never-before-transcribed portions of the audiotape, we conclude that—far from the fiasco some have assumed it to be—the Bateson-Rogers meeting was surprisingly insightful and helpful in clarifying the positions of the two thinkers, and in satisfying two of the most important expectations for dialogic communication: that important ideas are extended into new shapes and territories, and that important distinctions between ideas are recognized and taken into account. In effect, we seek to reclaim a nearly-lost artifact of twentieth century intellectual history. We present our argument in three stages. First, we review the relevant background to the dialogue, including its genesis and the decisions concerning its structure. Second, we trace the conversation the two men actually had that evening, not just the one they thought they had and recalled with disappointment. We show how the themes they explored illustrated important extensions and distinctions in precisely the spirit of dialogic surprise they had hoped for. Finally, we conclude by showing how the dialogue can be considered a central text especially for clarifying differences between theoretical and applied communication and between personal and relational/ecological concepts of the self, and for clarifying the relationship between Bateson's concept of context and Rogers's significant learning.

Background to the Dialogue

The dialogue in Marin was not the first meeting of Bateson and Rogers. A month earlier, they were among two dozen participants in a three-day conference in Tucson, Arizona, sponsored by the Association for Humanistic Psychology and devoted to the development of theory in humanistic psychology. One of the most "stimulating discussions," according to one reporter, followed a presentation on choice and decision. Bateson, Rogers, and Jonas Salk compared their understandings of free will and determinism, and agreed, "as much as the group agreed on anything," that this was a false dichotomy (Gilbert, 1975, p. 2). Over breakfast one morning, Bateson and Rogers discussed their meeting in Marin the following month. Rogers said jokingly that they planned the event "at great length—I think almost ten minutes perhaps,"[5] and they agreed that they would start with the topic of learning, which concerned them both; that both would give opening statements of approximately 10 minutes; and that Rogers would go first.

Shortly after the Tucson conference and a couple of weeks before the Marin meeting, Rogers sent a memo to all of the participants in the theory conference, thereby also initiating a correspondence with Bateson. He called the conference "stimulating and exciting" and said that he "learned a great deal," yet upon his return felt a growing sense of disappointment. The reason for this was that the conference had been antithetical to humanistic psychology's emphasis on the "whole person" by focusing exclusively on the intellect without taking time to consider the feelings of the participants. Although Rogers said that he was as much responsible as anyone for this, "as I think back, I believe I was profoundly mistaken."

So Bateson and Rogers both came to the College of Marin to discuss learning with some recent shared history,[6] and they also brought their own personal histories, which moderator Richard Farson briefly described. Rogers, said Farson, was the only psychologist to have received both the Distinguished Scientific Award and the Distinguished Professional Contribution Award from the American Psychological Association. He was known through his many books and articles for his "revolutionary idea" that we can "trust the capacity and the resources for self direction in the people we're trying to help," which has, Farson continued, "transformed not only the mental health professions, but…has extended and generalized into all kinds of other fields—education, religion, medicine, business and industry, social welfare, [and] community planning."

Farson began his introduction of Bateson with what he called a "dirty trick for me to tag you with" by calling him "one of the great minds of the twentieth century." He noted that Bateson added new dimensions and enlightenment to a wide range of fields including cultural anthropology, psychiatry, and human and animal communication, but especially in the areas of "biological evolution and the new epistemology that comes from systems theory, from ecology, from cybernetics and the information sciences." Although Farson didn't mention Bateson's (1972) *Steps to an Ecology of Mind*, published only a few years earlier, he probably didn't have to, for most of the

---

5. Our quotations from the Bateson-Rogers dialogue come from the transcript we made, with the help of Zachary Flowerree of the Honors College at the University of South Florida, of the two-cassette audiotape from the Bateson Archive. This quotation comes from Rogers's opening statement. We reference quotations from the dialogue by noting the minute and second each utterance began as well as which tape the utterance occurred in (A is the first side of the first of the UCSC cassettes, B is the second side of the first cassette, and C is the first side of the second cassette). Our transcription of the audio tape recording is noticeably different than the transcript published in Kirschenbaum and Henderson (1989). We included 47 speaking turns that were omitted without indication or explanation from the published transcript and corrected a number of words that were mis-transcribed earlier (it seems to have been edited from what the men said to what someone thinks they ought to have said—probably with the goal of making it more readable). Such truncated and inaccurate transcriptions of public dialogues often does the principals a disservice—as we have discussed elsewhere (Anderson & Cissna, 1997, pp. 1-9).

6. Although neither mentioned it during the dialogue, each man surely knew of the other's awareness of his connections to Kresge College of University of California at Santa Cruz and to its new Provost, Robert Edgar. Edgar hired Bateson at Kresge because he thought the college was "troubled" and lacked a "major academic mission." Founded only four years earlier, Kresge was inspired by the humanistic psychology of Rogers and Abraham Maslow. A decade earlier, Edgar had been in an encounter group led by Rogers, which he described very positively, saying it changed his view of education (see Kirschenbaum, 1979, pp. 346-347; Lipset, 1982, pp. 279-282; Rogers & Russell, 1992, p. 203).

audience members were surely well aware of it. The book was hailed widely, and resulted in Bateson receiving many invitations to speak, perhaps including this one.

The "Bloody Hot" Evening and its Conversation

Scholars interested in the processes of public dialogue tend to be concerned with how public events can be structured to encourage two factors we term *extension* and *distinction*. While the former helps participants to move beyond current thinking to new combinations and fresh ideas, the latter keeps communicators focused on recognizing, valuing, and, when necessary, maintaining differences. *Extension* requires a structure allowing for the relatively free play and exploration of ideas as a consequence of the interaction—something like the transcendence that Farson said the participants had in mind for this dialogue when he noted that they wouldn't focus on debating but on a desire to "build on each other's ideas in a real dialogue" (34:06A). At the same time, *distinction* requires a structure of dialogue that discriminates—one that is true to the uniqueness of the positions articulated by dialogue partners. The conversation of dialogue involves the commitment to mutual cooperation implied by extension, but does not result in a complete merger of perspectives. The best dialogue is not necessarily the one that produces a unified agreement, nor does it submerge participants' personalities. Dialogue also involves the equally mutually committed recognition of difference implied by distinction. Understanding the Bateson-Rogers dialogue means that we must look at the agreed-upon structures intended to enhance extension, and well as the more emergent structure involved in the distinction processes.

Circumstances were difficult for Rogers and Bateson that evening. Both knew the other and the other's work only casually. They were crammed into a gymnasium, with an audience of, by different estimates, 1000 to 1500 people, a significant number of whom were sitting on the floor. Farson described the weather as hot. Referring to the bright klieg flood lights that were brought in to film or videotape the evening, Bateson called it a "bloody hot evening," and, if that wasn't bad enough, apparently his dinner left him nauseated. Nevertheless, the audience was surely looking forward to their conversation.

A Structure for Extending and Distinguishing Ideas in Public Dialogue

A month earlier, at the AHP conference in Tucson, Bateson and Rogers had agreed to a three-part division for their dialogue and to focus it, at least initially, on "learning," a topic about which each of them had written much, although in quite different venues and ways. After an introduction by Richard Farson, first, each man would make an opening statement of 10 minutes in which they lay out the issues related to learning that each man thought were important. Bateson evidently had asked Rogers to speak first. Then, Bateson and Rogers planned to converse for a time about the implications of their ideas—following up or extending some, questioning or contesting others. In their planning, they held open the possibility that the focus on learning could widen. Some of the more intriguing aspects of the dialogue were highlighted in this section. Finally, the speakers wanted to take questions from audience members. The tape recording of the evening captures a far wider range of audience response—and more clarification of issues—than is indicated in the only published transcript of their conversation (Kirschenbaum & Henderson, 1989, pp. 176-201).

Rogers began his statement by arguing that the "politics of education" mandated that knowledge be considered a commodity dispensed from the top down, and that this control structure reduced the opportunity for a more genuine kind of "whole-person" education—one that involves feelings as well as intellect, and one that leads to "self-initiated" discovery that has more personal meaning for the learner. When this "significant learning" is allowed, learners transcend what Rogers calls the "jug-and-mug" approach that pours knowledge into "passive, anxious students" (7:33A). Although Bateson might have predicted Rogers's issues to some extent, based upon their participation in the recent AHP-sponsored conference in Tucson, from that point on the dialogue became increasingly less predictable. The willingness of each man to be surprised by the other's positions in the conversation segment is exemplary for public dialogue, and the audience-oriented question-and-answer segment led to additional surprises of both extension and distinction, as we will see.

Distinction and Extension in the Bateson-Rogers Dialogue

Listeners who think the dialogue might illuminate the thought of Bateson or Rogers would do well to focus on those moments in which they acknowledged their own differences—providing evidence for a kind of distinction-based dialogue—and on the moments in which they extended one another's thought in interesting and creative ways. We discovered one significant extension and five major distinctions highlighted by Bateson and Rogers themselves. In a sense, these moments created the emergent idea-structure that was most critical for the audience gathered at the College of Marin. How did these two theorists, with such different personalities and interests, yet each associated with humanistic paradigms, relate to each other? In this section, we describe the extensions and distinctions roughly in the order in which each issue first arose in their conversation, and later we discuss their importance. Rogers's statements actually provided Bateson with a series of unexpectedly valuable foils with which to launch and reaffirm his own interests.

The Difference in "Natural History": "Action People" and "Theorists"
After Rogers concludes his introductory statement, Bateson's first words do not deal with their ideas but with how their backgrounds and approaches to their professions differ at an exceedingly fundamental level: "I guess there's a biggish difference in…natural history between me and Carl: one sort of animal; another sort of animal." Bateson goes on to describe himself as a "theorist," while Rogers is one of the "action people" who "believes what you do matters." Although Bateson allows that both

"have…uses in the world," he also observes—tongue at least partially in cheek—that he "never can quite understand the use of the action people," even though they "have a good time, and they improve the world, I guess" (19:21A).

Rogers frames this distinction as more powerful than a mere recognition of subtle shades of intellectual life, jotting in his notes that Bateson's distinction was "theorist vs. doer." That he describes the distinction as an opposition perhaps captures something of his own inclination, but more likely indicates how he heard Bateson's distinction. One of his rhetorical goals seems to be to claim that this is not necessarily an either/or proposition. Later, Rogers reminds Bateson and the audience that he's tried to "theorize" about context, too—that the Bateson dichotomy isn't as insurmountable as might be assumed by some. Thus, he extricates himself from his ascribed role of "action person" who presumably doesn't theorize and claims the intellectual versatility of being concerned with both thinking ideas through and putting them into practical application. At the same time, he acknowledges that Bateson is "somewhat more philosophically minded" (37:06A). He also distinguishes between an organism seen as "unified" (a positively loaded term for Rogers) and one seen as "a purely intellectual system" (a term with negative connotations for him) (12:32A). It is clear when he responds subsequently to their "different degree of faith in the intellect," as Bateson put it (20:36A & 20:49A), that he wants to distance himself from Bateson's intellectualism as much as Bateson wants to distance himself from Rogers's thin pragmatism. This interchange becomes grounded in the issue of human feelings and their role in so-called "significant" learning.

The Similarity in Politics of Significant Learning: "Person-Centered Learning" and Inevitable "Implications for Character"

Rogers addresses his prepared opening statement to the value of what he calls "significant learning," which is self-initiated, desired by the learner, and makes a "pervasive difference" in the learner's knowledge, behavior, and attitudes. Little, if any, of this goes on, Rogers says, in conventional education. By contrast, person-centered learning makes the teacher a facilitator and the student an active learner. Bateson, following his introductory remarks about their different backgrounds, immediately agrees with Rogers about what Bateson, perhaps somewhat deprecatingly, calls "the idea that's in the back of his [Rogers's] mind": "that the French gender systems, the comparative anatomy of the insect, the sequence and dates of the Kings of England" are not significant learning. Bateson then adds an important twist: "I cannot take a learning creature and have him learn [something such as] the anatomy of the beetles and *not* give him also significant learning…. Always and inevitably there is a significant learning that goes along with whatever it is that is being taught." This, he says, "is probably our subject of discussion," and it involves "a whole order of learning, quite different from the subjects being taught, inevitably always carrying implications for character, about what sort of world you think you're living in, about what sort of a world you think the relationship between you and the teacher springs out of" (19:21A).

These implications arise directly from one aspect of Bateson's theory of human communication—the concept that every message is actually a dual message, having "two sorts of meaning": "On the one hand, the message is a statement or report about events at a previous moment, and on the other it is a command—a cause or stimulus for events at a later moment" (Bateson, 1951, p. 179). In the case being discussed at the College of Marin, the report might be the topic of a class or lesson, perhaps the anatomy of the beetle or even the nature of human learning. The command part of the message deals with the relationship between the instructor and learner. So powerful is that part of the message for learning that Bateson says he could teach the anatomy of the beetle (or, presumably, almost anything else) "in a way which will make little Hitlers out of" the learners, or, if the learning is approached differently, "dancers or artists—even, perhaps, democratic citizens" (19:21A). Thus, significant learning, Bateson says, introducing one of his favorite concepts, is shaped by the *context* of learning.

Bateson uses Rogers's primary term (significant learning), but provides a broader theoretical context for it. Although they have somewhat different perspectives on significant learning, they seem to agree about the nature and importance of the concept. And they continue to use the "beetles" and the "Hitlers" to discuss this issue, with Bateson mentioning the beetles in 5:45B and Rogers at 22:33B and 23:42B, when he even refers to it as a "very meaningful" analogy.

Rogers was right—at least the analogy was very meaningful to the audience. Two of the first three questions from the audience dealt with this. The second questioner pushes Bateson on whether he could make fascists out of anybody (37:04B), to which Bateson responds, "I would hedge on the *anybody*, but I would say that you could have an educational system in a country which would make a great many." Rogers then supports Bateson, explaining: "If the teacher really models a dictatorial type of behavior, a great many of the students will pick that up as the way in which they should behave." To the consternation of many in the audience, Bateson and Rogers agree that this significant learning, an education for character that would result in a "great many" students learning to be "little Hitlers," could be taught by modeling a certain kind of behavior in the classroom.

The Difference in Attention to Feelings: "Emotional Personalized Meanings" and "Intellectual Processes"
Rogers's perspective in the 1960s and 1970s emphasized feelings far more than most previous theories of human behavior. That emphasis fuels his opening statement in the Bateson dialogue: In "significant learning," the "whole person" is engaged, and "feelings as well as…intellect" are "very deeply involved" (7:33A). Rogers identifies the extent to which he focuses on feelings as "one real difference" between himself and Bateson (43:25A); as he says in the dialogue, his conversation partner "justi[fies] the feelings that you have about it [the behaviorist approach] on the basis of your analysis of whether it is true or not…," although "it is just as valuable to be aware of feelings as it is to be aware of our intellectual processes." Rogers defines feelings here

as "emotionalized personal meanings" (:47B), but Bateson disagrees with the importance attached to this construct. Instead, Bateson argues that feelings—inasmuch as they can be conceptualized at all—should be related to slippage or contradictions of contexts:

> Suppose I attack you [addressing the audience] in terms of your understanding of the context in which you are here tonight: your respect, your amusement, your entertainment, your—all this weave of contextual themes, schemata, whatever you want to call it, in which we are here tonight: me, trying to find out how I relate to Carl; Carl, trying to find out how he relates to me; Dick, trying to ride two horses at the same moment, and all the rest of it. If, in, as participants in that dance, you suddenly find you put your foot through the floor, this is where feelings are. This is where, if you offer respect and respect isn't the thing that was asked for: "Unhh." If you offer amusement and amusement isn't it; if you are serious and you feel I am mocking you, "Unhh." Always at this point, which is essentially the question of being at ease in the content. The moment you are not at ease in the context, then you get unpleasant feelings. And the change towards ease within the context is a very large part of pleasantness of feelings.... This is what I call feelings. Maybe I am wrong. (1:02B)

Thus, Bateson does not filter feelings from his system, but defines them more ecologically in their interdependence with humans' experiences with contexts.

One interesting context for this interchange is, in fact, the meeting between Bateson and Rogers in Tucson just weeks prior to this dialogue. Following that AHP-sponsored conference, as we noted earlier, Rogers had written an open letter to other participants about his disappointment, "in myself and in the conference," that this group of humanistic psychologists had over-intellectualized, a habit they normally associated with more traditional psychological theorists. Tucson participants felt that this "was a time for *ideas*, not for searching of self as to the personal meanings *behind* those ideas":

> But, I ask myself, "Suppose you fantasize the conference as completely ideal, with every person being as aware of his immediate feelings as he was of his ideas, where would that have led, given the limited number of hours we had together?" I don't know the answer to that question. But I wish we had tried to find out.

Bateson, of course, received this April 15 letter, and probably heard Rogers's comments in the May dialogue as an extension of the same critique. Yet he didn't then respond to this point in Marin.

He did so later, in a June 11 letter to both Rogers and Rollo May regarding the AHP conference, Rogers's "disappointment" letter, and the dialogue with Rogers:

> Personally, I usually shut up when people talk about *feelings* or *intellect* or the conflict between, or *choice* between them, and so on. How can there be a choice, or a conflict, between two misconceptions? To make a choice would be to reinforce the error.

Bateson continued by asserting that this distinction, as well as the "whole stance" of so-called "third-force" psychology, is rooted and re-rooted (meta-rooted) in an unacceptable 17th century model—a materialism wedded to a supernaturalism—a worship of the "captain" who is the captain of somebody's "soul," which in turn (intermittently) inhabits somebody's mechanical "body," to make, by putting the pieces together, a sacred cow called a person. Or, even more sacred, a "whole person."

    Carl, you keep saying that the whole persons matter. No, no, no. In that gathering of fifteen hundred persons only the ideas mattered, and the ideas included such propositions as "it is a hot night," "only the ideas matter," "only the persons matter," and so on, because the monstrous thing is that in a world where only the ideas matter, contrary ideas can exist, and even incorrect ideas. And the incorrect ideas will commonly kill the people, leading them to kill each other, or to poison the water which they drink. But it is an idea that this killing (or life-giving) matters. Do not say that this is "only" an idea. What greater thing could it be?

Bateson extends this point further in a July 20 handwritten letter to Rogers in which he says he will "try to say in my language what I understand by the word *feelings* in yours." In six enumerated points, he describes and elaborates on feelings as a class of ideas (see Kirschenbaum & Henderson, 1989, pp. 200-201). Although the letter appears to break off in mid-sentence, in their dialogue and in the follow-up correspondence it is clear that Bateson believes that Rogers's claim about feelings reflects a fragmentary, reductive perspective on reality.

The Difference in How Learning Should Be Controlled: "Teaching" and "Seeking"
At one point in the dialogue, after a discussion of how learning can be, in Bateson's term, "pickled," Rogers calls attention to "one real difference that I sense in our approach to thinking about some of these issues," which is how the two of them appear to claim different roles in educational situations: "You are primarily a teacher," Rogers observes, whereas "I have come to value placing primary trust in the student as learner" (16:04B). Rogers evidently means that Bateson is more interested in making control-based decisions in educational contexts, whereas the kind of "significant learning" Rogers has in mind cannot be imposed on students from outside their experience. Bateson is more of a "teacher," whereas Rogers once famously asserted that "teaching…is a vastly overrated function" (1969, p. 103).

    Yet, concerning how to encourage and increase learning, if teaching is not the important process, then what is? For Rogers the emphasis should be on "seeking," which he argues is how people like Bateson (and himself) learn. This led to a good-natured if sharp disagreement after Bateson mentions that he learns by going to teachers. Uncharacteristically, Rogers bluntly responds that "No, you don't go to teachers. At least—let me challenge you on that.…I think that you pick up a book or you go to a person because *you* want to learn something, which is quite different from teaching in the ordinary sense. I don't want us to get all tied up on semantics here, but teaching usually does mean the imparting of information" (28:52B), which, as Bateson allows, is different "from being visited by a seeker" (29:29B). Ironically, as we shall see, it is Rogers's reluctance to make semantic distinctions that continues to prickle Bateson.

    Bateson had earlier acknowledged the teaching/seeking distinction to some extent, and ratified it. He took Rogers's negatively loaded connotation for "purely intellectual," and redefined the intellect as a context issue—distinguishing between significant and intellectual learning. Intellectual learning, Bateson says, is learning that occurs "under a context marker" and not just a marker but a box—"a semipermeable or impermeable box, so that what's learned from that box is nontransferable anywhere" (14:12B). He agrees that "I am setting a situation for [students] to discover," but insists that he is still "in an active role. I think that's true" (17:11). To this, Rogers replies that "I get the feeling that perhaps you do know some of the points you want the student to reach. I only know that I want to help him start on his own self-initiated path. And perhaps that makes a difference" (19:28). Whether this is an issue of educational epistemology or merely one of personality or personal style is not thoroughly explored here, although it is a potentially rich issue.

After a long pause, Bateson, perhaps getting to the basis of this distinction, asks Rogers thoughtfully, "How many students are seekers, I wonder? You assume they all are?" (30:32B). Rogers answers "many"—to which Bateson expresses surprise. Rogers explains that they are seekers until being "squelched" by the educational system, which "turns off that seeking" (30:49B). They agree that the educational system can turn students off and that the desire to learn can be "reawakened" (Rogers, 30:49B; Bateson, 32:00B), but Rogers, no doubt, continues to believe in the superiority of the person-centered approach to facilitate that reawakening.

The Difference in Explanatory Style: "Familiar Forms" and "Rigor"
Interwoven with the dialogue's development of the third distinction above, Bateson and Rogers also probe some differences in personal style, as Bateson highlights in a particularly revealing turn in which he revisits "the intellect." "I think we have a different degree of faith in the intellect," he asserts. His own "faith" or "creed" is that thinking with "very sharp rigor" is necessary in order to make sense of the forms of human relations that are usually discussed in "blinding and misleading language" and inappropriate metaphors. It turns out that he and Rogers have not merely a different degree of faith in the intellect, but a disconnect of language: "Now I think you, Carl, are more willing to use the familiar forms of speech than I am. You think you can get away with them and it'll be all right, and I sort of drag myself into either joking, clowning…or into being rather a bore, you see, in insisting on being pedantic" (20:49B).

Perhaps in part because of Bateson's self-deprecating irony, Rogers appears to misunderstand how deeply he's being critiqued here, responding that "Well, you see, you probably talk more than I do, which gives you…more of a chance to show any of those things" (22:33B). Then he brings the conversation back to his own point about trust in the individual. Bateson's distinction, however, was about not settling for familiar—non-rigorous—forms of speech when considering complex contextual levels of intellectual inquiry. Rogers might think Bateson had ignored his point about the need for a learning-based "pluralism," "initiating the learning" in a variety of students without telling them what to think—a point he reasserts in his next significant turn (23:42B, 24:42B). If Rogers thinks Bateson is too concerned with control-centered teaching, Bateson apparently is replying that Rogers's intellectual style offers too little substance, and that pluralism is not an adequate substitute for methodological and linguistic rigor. This same issue resonates also in the final distinction the participants mention that evening, a difference in the kind of advice they would give to loved ones trying to negotiate the problems of human communication.

The Difference in Approaches to Self: "Deepest Self" and "Clichés"
Considering the other issues, this one would not generate much attention were it not that it serves to capsulize their relevance and highlight a basic difference in how Bateson and Rogers approach discourse itself. In the audience participation phase of the dialogue, the next-to-last question asked by an audience member sought some advice based on "the richness of your total life cycle, both at a personal and at a professional level" (8:13C). The questioner continued: "Think of us as a family of grandchildren and there are just a couple of things that you feel are very, very important for you to share with all of us." Rogers answers first, jokingly but accurately referring to himself as the elder. His best advice is to trust the "deepest self," and he notes that many problems in the world can be traced back to people's unwillingness or inability to know themselves and to trust in their own resources (9:00C). Bateson might have used this as an opportunity to expand his earlier critique of how psychologists use the language. Instead, he refers to it only obliquely in a brief response:

> And, I suppose, on this side of the house, I would hope that you get an idea that it is possible to think feelingly and with some rigor about a great many of the problems that we have been talking about. They don't have to be dismissed either with clichés or with approximations. (10:03C)

Here Bateson refers both to the conceptual divisions he thinks divide the two men and to a process that may have emphasized debate more than dialogue ("on this side of the house"). Further, he implies that the self—at least as Rogers imagines it—might be an unprofitable cliché and one of the outmoded terms to which he referred earlier, a view he developed elsewhere in his writings. For example, in an address delivered two years later and subsequently anthologized, Bateson (1991) refers to self as an "epistemological monster" and a "mythological component" of a larger system, and in his next book, *Mind and Nature* (1979), "self" is a "heuristic concept, a ladder useful in climbing but perhaps to be thrown away or left behind at a later stage" (1979, p. 149). In other words, self is a concept that might be useful at times for "action people," but not for epistemologists who recognize that, ultimately, human experience has to be considered relationally and ecologically. Elsewhere we have argued that Rogers's concept of self is more relational and more process-oriented than he is often given credit for (Cissna & Anderson, 1990; Cissna & Anderson, 2002, pp. 68-78), but on this uncomfortably hot evening, neither man evidently wanted to prolong the point in order to explore such things.

A Final Similarity

After distinctions were probed, the conclusion of the dialogue offered an interesting and powerful instance of unexpected similarity, and it was Bateson who recognized it. As a way to cap audience questioning and conclude the dialogue, Farson, as moderator, took the liberty of phrasing the final inquiry and did so in a particularly intriguing way: "What kinds of things at this stage of your development are you having second thoughts about? Where are you wondering whether or not you said it in the right way the first time you said it? What would you erase if you had a chance to go back and erase the tape? Where have you misled us, you two, and what, if anything, do you have to say about that?" (12:46C). In one sense their answers were distinctive, but the question was rich enough to stimulate responses that also converged in creative ways. Bateson mentions regretting that his first double-bind paper (Bateson, Jackson, Haley, & Weakland, 1956) was published too soon—it reads, he says, as "too concretistic, and a lot of people have spent, wasted a lot of time trying to count double binds" (13:49C). For his part, Rogers admits that he and associated therapists initially "became too much focused on techniques" and "that has misled a great many people in the counseling field. I realize that" (14:48C).

To this, Bateson—ever alert to patterns—replies: "Interesting. It's almost the same..." (15:17C). How is it the same? Bateson perceives in both situations an impulse to serve something up too soon, a tendency to package, concretize, or technologize knowledge in ways that do not respect its full complexity. Although Bateson undoubtedly believes his more rigorous and theoretical approach to the reality of ideas was preferable, both men acknowledge here that ideas can be too readily reified, too prematurely "pickled," resulting in readers being misled. Their brief concluding interchange provides a rich counterpoint to earlier issues of how to define learning itself, and how to decide regarding the issues of control that are perhaps inherent in educational decision-making.

Reclaiming the Reputation of the Bateson-Rogers Dialogue

Some, including the participants themselves, have disparaged this event. When it has been mentioned in print, which hasn't been often, it has usually been called a debate rather than a dialogue. In a June 11 letter, Bateson called it "dreadful," as it involved "trying to talk and trying not to talk." In July 1 letters to Bateson and to Farson, Rogers said it was an "embarrassment" and a "fiasco" in which they were "shadow boxing." Nearly a decade later, in response to a West German woman inquiring about any contact he might have had with Bateson, Rogers mentioned this event and called it "one of the most unsatisfactory dialogues I have ever held. For some reason, Gregory and I simply talked past each other. We could not seem to really meet in our thought." He mentions to his correspondent in this October 19, 1983 letter that the dialogue was recorded, although, he says, "fortunately [it] was never transcribed or published. I honestly do not think it would be worth very much to you." Even one of the audience members prefaced a question by noting a "feeling of disappointment with the dialogue" [38:02B], and the author of a short article in the weekly newspaper in Marin County also notes that some in the audience were disappointed, quoting a psychologist as saying "They didn't say anything they haven't said before."[7]

Perhaps predictably, Richard Farson, organizer of the event and moderator, defends the dialogue and reassures his friend Rogers in a letter written a few days later on June 1st: "I know that you have concern about how it went, but I want to assure you that everyone I spoke to was quite interested." He continued, "It was what it was—an opportunity to witness an exchange between Rogers & Bateson, and it was surely that." In a subsequent letter on July 9, after receiving copies of some of the Bateson-Rogers exchange, Farson backs off a little: "No one I spoke to thought of it as a 'dreadful evening.' Most everyone seemed to like it." He recognizes that it didn't live up to Bateson's or Rogers's expectations, but insists that "it was no 'fiasco.'"

Our analysis reflects a far more encouraging interpretation of the dialogue, based on what Bateson and Rogers actually said that evening. Further, a second look at the event would be rewarding both to Bateson and to Rogers scholars, as well as to anyone interested in dialogue and communication. Was this an ideal dialogue? Decidedly not. But no dialogue is ideal—indeed, by its very nature, dialogue emerges, when it does, in the particular occasion and in response to the people and exigencies of that occasion. Dialogue is always and inevitably partial. Although it left the principals and some in the audience less than fully satisfied, we found much to learn from the Bateson-Rogers dialogue. In our view, they weren't as much talking past each other as they were disagreeing—and sometimes people find it hard to disagree well, especially in public. It can be convenient to say "we were talking past each other" when neither party finds itself to be persuasive to the other. Yet dialogue is not primarily about persuasion, as we've seen. Dialogue has its own life, which may not coincide with the intentions or hopes of the communicators. The tendency to want "meeting" and dialogue to result in agreement can obscure that dialogue can be as much about clarifying disagreement as about recognizing or achieving agreement. Bateson and Rogers did both. They found that they differed in a number of ways and disagreed about several issues:

- *Their orientations toward the world*—Bateson, the intellectual and theorist, strongly and unapologetically asserted the importance of theorizing and intellectual definition, while Rogers equally strongly asserted the importance of trusting everyday "research" and the value of application. Their meeting was an

---

7. Bateson and Rogers also responded to this issue during the dialogue itself. Asked what their purposes were for the evening, Bateson indicates that he had few, other than to see "what happened when two quite different languages about human behavior, different epistemologies, met" (39:27B). Rogers responds similarly, thinking that perhaps they "might strike sparks in each other which would be meaningful to us and therefore…to the audience" (40:26B). Bateson then surfaces what he calls the "carrier question" that lies behind the one that was asked—"Have we done so?" Rogers says, "Yeah, I feel that you've struck some sparks in me, and I think I've struck some sparks in you" (40:53B). Bateson responds, "Yeah, I think that maybe three months hence I shall say something differently because of this evening" (41:11B). Rogers concludes this interchange with "And I will think more about the broader context of what I do" (41:30).

exceptionally clear enactment of this ongoing controversy in the human sciences.

- *The role of feelings in human relationships*—Bateson defined feelings theoretically as an abstract idea or kind of proposition related to one's understanding of a context (unpleasant feelings arising from dis-ease in a context), while Rogers insisted that feelings understood more mundanely are at least as important as ideas or anything else and are essential to a whole person leading a balanced life, which he linked to understanding most fully the various contexts in which a person lives.

- *How to manage learning*—although both stressed the importance of structuring learning experiences, Bateson defined himself as more of a "teacher" with the intent to influence the learner in known directions and more concerned that learners be taught correct and important ideas, and Rogers was more willing to trust the learner as a "seeker" who can be helped to find what he or she needs and wants to know.

- *The use of language*—Bateson insisted on a technical language that allows for rigorous discussion, and Rogers was willing to use ordinary language and everyday metaphors in order to reach ordinary people.

- *The nature of the self*—Bateson insisted that the concept of self has become too clichéd to be useful theoretically, although it might have some temporary utility, and Rogers was willing to use self inductively as a self-reported but ultimately subjectively "real" concept. In effect, he heard the language of his clients as descriptions of their own phenomenology of the self.

They also agreed in interesting ways about other issues:

- Both were *passionate about the importance of education*, believing it to be crucial for the individual and for the society.

- Both recognized an *often-ignored level of learning* that transcends whatever content might be being taught or learned and that provides lasting lessons regarding human relationships and human character.

- Both believed that our *educational system has failed* in some important ways— although they disagreed about exactly what those are and perhaps even more about how they would repair or improve education.

- Both admitted that some of their own work was published prematurely, resulting in readers being misled and research and practice going astray.

After the opening statements of Rogers and Bateson, Farson introduces the interactional portion of the event by quoting a line that Bateson said on the way to the gymnasium. Asked how they will know whether they succeeded this evening, Bateson answered "if either Carl or I say something that we haven't said before, we'll know that it's a success" (34:06A). This is the gold standard of dialogue—that the parties speak and listen to each other well enough that something, as Rogers put it, is "sparked" and participants say something new. This encounter between the rigorously intellectual theorist and the action-oriented therapist provided an opportunity for Bateson to explain and clarify some issues in ways he doesn't do elsewhere.

First, Bateson clarified his use of *context* and provides a number of insightful examples in discussing this crucial term. He related context to Rogers's concept of significant learning, a term that Bateson hadn't used elsewhere, as far as we can determine. Significant learning, Bateson said, results from the context in which learning occurs and the relationship between the learner and the one structuring the learning. A context of a harsh and authoritarian environment, Bateson said, and Rogers agreed, could produce "little Hitlers," whereas a different kind of learning environment might produce dancers or artists or democratic citizens. We think Bateson was right when he suggested that this was their subject of discussion for the dialogue, and we wish that Rogers had engaged him more fully regarding this topic.

In this conversation, Bateson was revisiting issues he last discussed this directly, as far as we could determine, over 30 years previously, in a paper, "Social Planning and the Concept of Deutero-Learning," and reprinted in *Steps to an Ecology of Mind* (Bateson, 1972). Written during World War II, Bateson's paper responds to one by Margaret Mead in which she argues that when social scientists distinguish between ends and means, and then attempt to shape people toward ends they think desirable without awareness of or regard for the values implicit in the means, they are being manipulative and are promoting totalitarianism and negating democracy. Bateson's analysis, as one might expect, relies on context—that habits of learning acquired in an authoritarian context will be built into "habits of mind" and the learner's "whole philosophy of life" (p. 164). These habits, he says, are a "by-product of the learning process" (p. 164). Like Rogers's significant learning, as reinterpreted by Bateson, the lifelong lessons for character are those acquired accidentally, as by-products, from the meta-learning or deutero-learning (a term, incidentally, that he could have, but did not, mention to Rogers). He continues in this essay to elaborate and distinguish various classifications of learning contexts and how they relate to one another—as he put it to Rogers, the "technical business of the anatomy of contexts and how they interact, how they combine" (19:21A). Interestingly, he returned to explore this idea further two years after the dialogue in the 1977 address to which we referred earlier (Bateson, 1991, p. 197)

Bateson illustrated context in another insightful way. Perhaps knowing of Rogers's famous encounters with the behaviorist B. F. Skinner (see Kirschenbaum & Henderson, 1989), Bateson chose to explain context further through reference to the learning of pigeons whose behavior is shaped by operant conditioning. The behaviorist model is true, Bateson said, but only within its own very narrow limits or frame. The behaviorists ignore that the reinforcement schedule is only a part, and not the crucial part, of the learning context in which the pigeons are placed. The larger frame is that they are learning to peck as desired within a context defined by the loving behavior of the person who cares for them and who they adore. And the larger frame determines the context of the learning. We don't find this rather devastating critique of behaviorism elsewhere in Bateson's work.

In another example, he related contextual knowledge to the need to respond flexibly to new situations. Intellectual learning, far from being identified by a context marker that identifies it as of no use anywhere (as he in fact said at one point in the dialogue), allows for a kind of adaptability that will serve a person well in many situations without necessarily providing any immediately practical knowledge. This, of course, has long been the argument related to the value of liberal education.

In addition to describing and exemplifying the concept of context, Bateson also describes the meaning and limits of self in a way he hadn't quite done previously, perhaps because Rogers uses the term so often. Although Bateson wrote about self occasionally before the dialogue with Rogers, after their dialogue he made explicit that self is really no more than a "heuristic concept" of only temporary usefulness, "a ladder useful in climbing but perhaps to be thrown away or left behind at a later stage" (1991, p. 149). The discussions of the self in his 1977 address (1991) and in *Mind and Nature* (1979, pp. 145-155), both written shortly after the dialogue with Rogers, could be read as continuations of his conversation with Rogers.

In the dialogue with Rogers, Bateson was "sparked to say some new things," despite his discomfort, despite both he and Rogers not much enjoying the event, and despite his having "sheathed his claws," as Bateson wrote on June 11. Nevertheless, some very productive things happened. Bateson sharpened and tested his thinking about issues related to learning and context and provided several insightful examples of his concepts. Although, as Donaldson (1991, p. xvi) remarks, many of the problems of the world result from the human habit of turning differences into separation and separation into opposition, dialogue suggests an alternative in which differences can be explored without necessarily being reified or submerged. Although the Bateson-Rogers meeting was not the definitive model of dialogue (what conversation is?), Bateson and Rogers were successful communicators that hot evening in 1975. Far from "talking past each other" in a "fiasco" of misunderstanding, the two men—and especially Bateson—were quite clear in exploring important ideas in new ways (performing *extension* in our terminology) and in exploring their realistic differences (performing *distinction*). They did so not only when talking about the announced topic (learning) but also when discussing broader issues of human nature, research, and social practice. They may have remembered the event with disappointment, but scholars should revisit it with respect and interest.

References

Anderson, R., & Cissna, K. N. (1997). *The Martin Buber-Carl Rogers dialogue: A new transcript with commentary.* Albany: State University of New York Press.

Bateson, G. (1951). Information and codification: A philosophical approach. In J. Ruesch & G. Bateson, *Communication: The social matrix of psychiatry* (pp. 168-211). New York: Norton.

Bateson, G. (1972). *Steps to an ecology of mind*. New York: Ballantine.

Bateson, G. (1979). *Mind and nature: A necessary unity*. Toronto: Bantam Books.

Bateson, G. (1991). The birth of a matrix, or double bind and epistemology. In G. Bateson, *A sacred unity: Further steps to an ecology of mind* (pp. 191-213). New York: HarperCollins.

Bateson, G., Jackson, D. D., Haley, J., & Weakland, J. (1956). Toward a theory of schizophrenia. *Behavioral Science, 1,* 251-264.

Bateson, M. C. (1984). *With a daughter's eye: A memoir of Margaret Mead and Gregory Bateson*. New York: Washington Square Press.

Cissna, K. N., & Anderson, R. (1990). The contributions of Carl Rogers to a philosophical praxis of dialogue. *Western Journal of Speech Communication, 54,* 125-147.

Cissna, K. N., & Anderson, R. (2002). *Moments of meeting: Buber, Rogers, and the potential for public dialogue*. Albany: State University of New York Press.

Donaldson, R. E. (1991). Introduction. In G. Bateson, *A sacred unity: Further steps to an ecology of mind* (R. E. Donaldson, Ed.) (pp. ix-xix). New York: HarperCollins.

Gilbert, R. (1975, June). The meeting of the minds: A report on the Humanistic Theory Conference, April 4-6, in Tucson. *Association for Humanistic Psychology Newsletter*, pp. 1-3.

Harries-Jones, P. (1995). *A recursive vision: Ecological understanding and Gregory Bateson*. Toronto: University of Toronto Press.

Kirschenbaum, H. (1979). *On becoming Carl Rogers*. New York: Delacorte Press.

Kirschenbaum, H. (1995). Carl Rogers. In M. H. Suhd (Ed.), *Positive regard: Carl Rogers and other notables he influenced* (pp. 1-104). Palo Alto, CA: Science and Behavior Books.

Kirschenbaum, H., & Henderson, V. (1989). *Carl Rogers: Dialogues—Conversations with Martin Buber, Paul Tillich, B. F. Skinner, Gregory Bateson, Michael Polanyi, Rollo May, and others*. Boston: Houghton Mifflin.

Lipset, D. (1982). *Gregory Bateson: The legacy of a scientist*. Boston: Beacon Press.

May, R. (1977). Gregory Bateson and humanistic psychology. In J. Brockman (Ed.), *About Bateson: Essays on Gregory Bateson* (pp. 75-99). New York: Dutton.

Rogers, C. R. (1969). *Freedom to learn*. Columbus, OH: Merrill.

Rogers, C. R., & Russell, D. (2002). *Carl Rogers—The quiet revolutionary: An oral history*. Roseville, CA: Penmarin Books.

Snyder, M. (1989). The relationship enhancement model of couple therapy: An integration of Rogers and Bateson. *Person-Centered Review, 4,* 358-383.

Thorne, B. (1992). *Carl Rogers*. London: Sage.

Cybernetics And Human Knowing. Vol. 12, nos. 1-2, pp. 137-146

The Natural History Approach:
A Bateson Legacy

Wendy Leeds-Hurwitz[1]

Bateson's legacy includes many ideas, for he was a creative and original thinker. The one addressed in this article is the natural history approach, which has had substantial influence over many social interaction scholars. Bateson brought his assumptions about how to study the natural world into his studies of the social world, and his assumptions still guide much research today. This chapter describes the natural history approach and its connection to Bateson; shows the way in which this approach has moved through the communication literature; and discusses the ways in which this approach has influenced scholars writing today.

Bateson's legacy includes many ideas, for he was a creative and original thinker. The one I wish to address here, the natural history approach, has had substantial influence over my own research, as well as that of many other scholars who study social interaction. In what follows I will first, describe the natural history approach and its connection to Bateson; then, show the way in which the approach has moved through the communication literature, demonstrating the existence of an invisible college; and, finally, discuss the ways in which this approach has influenced my own work and that of other interaction scholars writing today.

Development of the Natural History Approach

Bateson grew up "in the middle of natural history and beetle collection" (Lipset, 1982, p. 44). With a father who was a famous biologist, it was typical for the children to go into the physical world and study the plants and animals they found there. Margaret Mead, at one point his wife, reiterated this: "Gregory had been reared as a biologist…He had a naturalist's training in attending to ongoing reality, instead of forcing nature in the laboratory to give limited answers to limited questions" (1972, p. 227). Mary Catherine Bateson, daughter of Bateson and Mead, further documents the way in which her father used the term *natural history* as she grew up: at different times they would "pursue natural history" (1984, p. 51), or they "did natural history" (p. 93; see also M. C. Bateson, 1994, p. 127), by which she means they would enter a natural setting and observe whatever they found there, much as Bateson had done as a child. Despite his early training, Bateson did not become a biologist, and so the application of natural history expanded beyond studying plants and animals, and grew to include studying people as well. This was an obvious connection, as M. C. Bateson points out, due to the state of anthropology in England at the time of his education

---

1. Communication Department, University of Wisconsin-Parkside, Kenosha, WI 53141-2000.
    Email: wendy.leeds-hurwitz@uwp.edu

there: "At Cambridge, anthropology was still very much a branch of natural history, however, with the emphasis on description" (1984, p. 161). In the case of anthropology, a natural history approach involved studying people in their natural environment, as if they were just one more part of the overall ecology, like animals and plants. Other anthropologists also occasionally used the phrase natural history to describe their work. For example, in 1959 Alfred Kroeber wrote, "we [anthropologists] tend strongly here toward the natural history approach" (p. 399). As M. C. Bateson goes on to explain:

> In anthropology, you usually cannot specify in advance what it will be important to pay attention to. This was particularly true in the twenties and thirties when anthropologists had few theoretical models and were often working in previously undescribed societies. One must be open to the data, to the possibility that very small clues will prove to be critical and that accident will provide pivotal insights. You go out, ready at least to do natural history, as the three Bateson brothers went out in Gregory's boyhood, with their butterfly nets and collecting boxes. You may take a few specific collector's ambitions but you will be attentive at the same time to whatever you see and ready to find something quite unexpected. (1984, p. 163)

Bateson thus brought his early attention to plants and animals in their natural habitat with him as his interests shifted from biology to anthropology; as he moved to the study of humans as living beings, he kept the sense of natural history as description of what he found in an ongoing system. As stated in a letter to Norbert Wiener in 1954, what interested him at that point was "the study of the natural history of human communication" (quoted in Lipset, 1982, p. 205; see also G. Bateson, 1972, p. 448). His interests included *system* and *pattern* (M. C. Bateson, 1984, pp. 189 & 229 respectively; see Bateson & Bateson, 1987, p. 177 on system; see G. Bateson, 1972, p. xvi, & p. 131 on pattern), the connection between *structure* and *process* (Bateson & Bateson, 1987, p. 37) and, above all, *relationships* (p. 157). These are concepts best studied through description of what is found in a context constructed by the participants rather than in an experiment constructed by the researcher.

Bateson brought his assumption that natural history was the obvious approach to take to human communication, as well as his interests in system, pattern, relationships, structure and process, to the multidisciplinary research project *The Natural History of an Interview*. NHI was begun at Stanford University's Center for Advanced Study in the Behavioral Sciences in 1955-1956 because the psychiatrist Frieda Fromm-Reichmann wanted to teach her students what she knew how to do particularly well but could not describe, how to use intuition to appropriately handle patients (Leeds-Hurwitz, 1987, 1988). In addition to Fromm-Reichmann, the initial group included another psychiatrist (Henry W. Brosin), two linguists (Charles F. Hockett and Norman A. McQuown), and two cultural anthropologists (Alfred L. Kroeber and David M. Schneider). The first analysis demonstrated that one element of her intuition was paralinguistic phenomena. The project then was expanded to include Ray L. Birdwhistell, who had already begun examining kinesic behavior, and Bateson, then exploring family interaction in households where psychiatric problems were known to exist, because he could provide film data. The group's analysis resulted in an initial transcription and interpretation of linguistic, paralinguistic, and kinesic communication.

Work at the home institutions of Brosin and Birdwhistell continued until they completed the final document in 1968. Henry Lee Smith, Jr., and George L. Trager were brought in as consultants, for their knowledge of linguistic and paralinguistic analysis. The final document was primarily the result of continuing work by Birdwhistell, Brosin, and McQuown and their colleagues (most notably Starkey Duncan, Jr., William S. Condon, Adam Kendon, and Albert Scheflen). Despite their efforts, in its final form NHI is an unwieldy document, unpublishable due to a combination of its length and the complexity of the transcription forming the body of the material. In 1971, McQuown submitted it to the University of Chicago for inclusion in its microfilm series, making it at least moderately available beyond those involved in its creation.

NHI was an exploratory project, designed to discover what could be learned about communication through microanalysis. The group recognized that communication involves much more than words alone, and, as Bateson (1971) suggested, they wanted "to see every detail of word, vocalization, and bodily movement as playing its part in determining the ongoing stream of words and bodily movements which is the interchange between the persons" (p. 9). Communication was thus understood by the NHI researchers to be patterned behavior (and therefore analyzable).

Despite remaining unpublished, NHI was the cornerstone of the research tradition described in this paper. Given the group's emphasis on the socially constructed nature of interaction, and disinterest in researcher controlled contexts, it is ironic that, for reasons of confidentiality, the data used for this detailed analysis was actually an interview conducted by Bateson rather than an interaction involving the patient and her psychiatrist. Even so, the group felt that this interview provided adequate material for study. Bateson (1971) explained the choice of natural history as a method: "We start from a particular interview on a particular day between two identified persons in the presence of a child, a camera and a cameraman. Our primary data are the multitudinous details of vocal and bodily action recorded on this film. We call our treatment of such data a 'natural history' because a minimum of theory guided the collection of the data" (p. 6).[2] Later in the same chapter Bateson emphasized the significance of examining the data in its context as a critical element of their approach: "The work of this book starts from concrete natural history—from the recorded interaction between Doris' speech and movement and the speech and movement of Gregory. This placing of every signal in the context of all other signals is an essential discipline of our work" (p. 19). He even referred to those involved with the project as "natural historians" (p. 15), although this adaptation of the phrase did not catch on.

---

2. Although the entire volume remains unpublished, Bateson's Chapter 1 has been published in English (Bateson, 1996), French (Bateson, 1981), and Spanish (Bateson, 1983). Since the publication in English is in a book edited by a student of McQuown's, Hartmut Mokros (1996); the publication in French is in a book edited by a student of Birdwhistell's, Yves Winkin (1981); and the publication in Spanish is in a book edited by McQuown (1983); the connections to the invisible college are visible here too.

Spread of the Natural History Approach

Others picked up Bateson's use of the phrase *natural history* to refer to the study of human communication behavior, but most of those who used it got it from him.[3] As a result, following the use of the term reveals an *invisible college*. An invisible college can be defined as a "communication network…that links groups of collaborators" (Crane, 1972, p. 35). Essentially, an invisible college implies that people who are not obviously working together in the same literal context should be understood to be working in the same metaphorical context, sharing ideas as they share research in process. Despite this, most invisible colleges rely upon literal connections existing at some point: one researcher was a student to another, several scholars worked at the same university at a past time although they work in different locations now, or they met at conferences.

Mead, who was Bateson's colleague as well as his wife, was one of the first to use his phrase: "the essence of the natural-history approach is first-hand observation of living creatures in their natural settings" (1951, n.p.). Birdwhistell, who worked with Bateson on the NHI project, quoted a comment he attributed to Bateson as guiding the assumptions they held in common: "Our new recognition of the complexity and patterning of human behavior has forced us to go back and go through the natural history phase of the study of man which earlier scholars skipped in their haste to get to laboratory experimentation" (1970a, p. 39). Erving Goffman, who was a student of Birdwhistell's as an undergraduate and later his colleague at the University of Pennsylvania, at one point characterized himself as a "social naturalist" (in Erwin, 2000, p. 86), and another as a "Hughsian urban ethnographer" (in Verhoeven, 2000, p. 214), and used the phrase "natural history" as one characterization of his research (Goffman, 1968, p. 119), although he also used many other descriptors. Everett Hughes was a sociologist at the University of Chicago and one of Goffman's (and Birdwhistell's) professors. He sent students out to do a form of natural history of the urban context around the university. Being a "Hughsian urban ethnographer" was thus essentially a synonym for being a "natural historian."

Kendon, who worked with Birdwhistell, provides probably the best summary of what the approach entailed:

> The natural history approach proposed detailed description of whatever could be observed in an interaction. Since what was sought for was an understanding of the natural orderliness of interaction, observations must be in terms of what is there to be observed, not in terms of pre-established category systems. To decide what will be measured and counted before this is done will prevent the very understanding that is sought. It was the adoption of this approach that led to the need for the use of specimens of interaction, acquired by the (then available) technique of sound-synchronized cinematographic recording. (1990, p. 20)

---

3. Liberman (1995) is one of the few exceptions to this. While he did meet Bateson on several occasions, he came up with the term as "my own metaphorical way to describe a ruthlessly objective, painstakingly particular item-by-item inspection of what meanings waxed and waned during a long series of dialogues I had with a senior Tibetan scholar" (personal communication, August 6, 2004).

The natural history approach quickly morphed into context analysis, and then again into structural analysis. The three are related in obvious ways: the term *natural history* refers to observation of any socially constructed but actual (as opposed to experimental) behavior; given the emphasis on also studying the context of that behavior, the term *context analysis* came to be used; and then, given the emphasis on structure and process, the term *structural analysis* became a final synonym. Scheflen (whose connection to Bateson was via Birdwhistell) explained the shift in terminology this way:

> Natural history methods are used today, *when appropriate*, in every science (including the physical sciences). It should not be surprising that specific types have been developed to study human interaction...In 1956 the Palo Alto group [the NHI researchers] formulated a natural history method specifically for the study of communication in the interview and Birdwhistell and Scheflen have further developed this method. This approach is called 'Context Analysis.' (1971, p. 397, his emphasis; see also 1973)

McQuown, who had worked with Bateson on the NHI project, also published a discussion of the natural history/context analysis approach (1971), in which he suggested "The natural history method in social research is...constantly being rediscovered" (p. 431). McQuown prefers the term natural history method in his own writing, but links this to "the method which Scheflen calls context analysis" (p. 433). Kendon (1979) points out "In the context analysis approach, then, it is assumed that the process of communication is a continuous one and that the behaviour of people in face-to-face interaction is functioning in systems of reciprocal relation" (p. 71).

At a later point, Kendon (1990) described the third variant, the structural approach: "The interest of the structural approach...is to display the structures into which human behavior is patterned and to consider how these structures function in the construction of interactional events" (p. 42). Structural analysis made sense as a term describing the analysis of interaction because, as Bateson put it: "'Structure' is always a somewhat flattened, abstracted version of 'truth'—but structure is all that we can know" (in Bateson & Bateson, 1987, p. 161). Structural analysis was the term of choice for Duncan (1985), a psychologist who worked with McQuown and whose work was designed to pursue McQuown's goal of developing "the foundation of a general theory of the structure of human communicative behavior" (p. ix; see also Duncan & Fiske, 1985). Kendon (1990) ties these three terms together by suggesting that the natural history approach is called the structural approach by Duncan "because it proposes to provide an account of how, in terms of behavior, occasions of interaction are organized" and context analysis by Scheflen "because of the emphasis on the importance of examining the behavior of people in interaction in the contexts in which they occur" (p. 15).[4] Scheflen (1973) further pointed out the link to structural

---

4. There are a few other uses of the term natural history. For example, Silverstein and Urban (1996) say "We have chosen the title *Natural Histories of Discourse* to focus attention on contextually contingent semiotic processes involved in achieving text—and culture" (p. 2). Silverstein was a colleague to McQuown at the University of Chicago.

linguistics, and explicitly credits Birdwhistell as being the one to first make that connection: "The methods of structural analysis derive from the operations of the structural linguists…Birdwhistell (1952) first applied these operations to the study of nonlanguage communicational behavior" (p. 376, note 9).

So what are the steps actually entailed by taking a natural history/context analysis/ structural approach? Here is Scheflen's summary of the steps necessary for context analysis:

> First, go to the site where the event being studied normally occurs.
> Second, show up on the occasions at which it would happen anyway.
> Third, view experienced participants who know each other.
> Fourth, take all possible measures to avoid changing the situations.
> And fifth, observe rather than participate directly in the event under study. (1973, pp. 313-314)

In other words, it maintains all of Bateson's original interests in the natural world brought to an examination of the social world: viewing humans as one part of an existing system, searching for patterns and relationships (between people and behaviors) in naturally occurring phenomena, and looking for relationships, especially those between structure and process. What Scheflen took so much for granted that he did not even list it here as a separate step (although it is discussed at length elsewhere in the same publication) was the task of obtaining an audiovisual record of a transaction, in order to later analyze in detail what occurred. He explicitly credits Bateson with understanding the need to obtain an audiovisual recording, citing Bateson and Mead's book, *Balinese Character* (1942), as the pioneering work in this area.

Application of the Natural History Approach

Whether called natural history, context analysis, or the structural approach, Bateson's assumptions about how to study human communication underlie my work and that of many other social interaction scholars. My own connection to Bateson was through Birdwhistell, so I am part of the invisible college documented above. My first attempt to describe the critical characteristics of social interaction was published as Leeds-Hurwitz (1989). There the concepts of communication as behavior that is patterned, learned, context-bound, multi-channel, and multi-functional are emphasized. Bateson was obviously one of the major influences on me as I prepared this book. Some of the assumptions described below are so thoroughly taken for granted at this point that they are hard to make explicit, but I will try.

Direct observation of actual behavior.
Studying actual behavior means using direct observation as the primary method (rather than interviews, questionnaires, experiments, etc.). This implies studying real people in their natural settings. Although rarely described as such, it essentially is an ethological approach in that it involves going to the behavior you wish to understand

and experiencing it in its natural state. Kendon (1982) follows the obvious connections to ethology, especially to Blurton-Jones's work and his assumption of the necessity "for a 'natural history hypothesis generating phase' of inquiry" (p. 476). One current application for this in communication research is the emphasis on studying bona fide groups—that is, groups having their own reasons for existence both prior to and after the researcher attends to them (Putnam & Stohl, 1990). In terms of the study of social interaction, the major implication is that ethnography becomes a more obvious choice of research method than most others, and interviews, often the method of choice for interpersonal scholars, are specifically downgraded in terms of value and use. The issue is that people do not always accurately describe what they do, only what they think they do, or what they think they should do, or what they think the researcher wants to hear. (This is a point Birdwhistell stressed in courses at the University of Pennsylvania, although he did not often write about it.) In my own research, this has been an ongoing theme, beginning with Leeds-Hurwitz (1989).

Study behavior in context.
Studying behavior in context means understanding that communication behaviors, whether verbal or nonverbal, do not have permanent meanings attached to them, but only contingent meanings. As Birdwhistell (1970b) put it, meaning "requires a statement of context" (p. 269); see also Kendon's (1982) statement, "the interactive functioning of any item of behavior in interaction depends upon its context of occurrence" (p. 442). The implication is that the same behavior/word/movement in different contexts may convey different meanings to participants, so moving the behavior out of its natural context merely for the convenience of the researcher is inappropriate. It also implies that much of meaning will come from what Gumperz (1992) calls "contextualization cues" (related to the 'context of situation,' put forth earlier by Malinowski and Firth, as described in Robins, 1971). In other words, meaning is found in the usage of the behavior/word/ movement by specific participants at a particular time, not permanently attached to it. The amount of context necessary to understand any given behavior is assumed to be different each time—there is no one set guideline for how to tell when you have included a large enough circle of information. The goal is to understand the wider context well enough to be able to interpret the behavior/word/movement in the same way that participants do. Again, this has been an ongoing theme in my research (e.g., Leeds-Hurwitz, 1993).

Discover the invisible structure underlying the more visible process.
All we can observe is interaction, and we can only see one interaction at a time. An interaction is an example of process, which is always visible. The guidelines underlying the choices made at the level of process are what can be called structure, but structure remains invisible. We know of its existence only because of the regularities we find in interaction. This means finding logical sets of behaviors to study, and paying attention to the regularities found to exist in these sets. This is why researchers study conversational openings or closings, or service encounters, or civil

inattention—the goal is to find a type of communication behavior, and then examine many different examples in an effort to begin to understand how that type works. Kendon (1982) discusses this aspect of interaction when he finds "the units into which the behavior of the participants in interaction is organized, at any level of organization, to have a characteristic or customary structure" (p. 443). As Kendon continues, "meaning is thus born in the social process" (p. 447). In my research, this is part of what has led me to value semiotic theory as a tool to understanding how people create meaning for themselves and others (Leeds-Hurwitz, 1993).

Look for patterns and relationships.
The goal of studying human communication behavior is to determine the patterns underlying the behavior. This means a lot of examples must be studied superficially, but at least some must be studied in detail. This implies long-term observation to meet the goals of the former, and using videotapes or audiotapes and transcription to meet the goals of the latter. Videotapes, audiotapes, and transcriptions are all tools in the effort to freeze interaction so we are able to observe the same stretch of behavior repeatedly. Because there is so much going on—words, movements, spacing, touch, etc. – researchers have a difficult time consciously observing everything at once when it occurs at normal speed. Of course, participants do all this during interaction, but participation is easier than observation and analysis, because much of the effort of participation remains unconscious. Once we have located a logical set of behavior, we try to understand the connection between that set and others. If there is an opening to an interaction, there is likely to also be a closing. If there are guidelines for service encounters, there are likely to also be some governing civil inattention, and some way to tell which is appropriate when. As Kendon (1982) puts it, "when people interact they come to participate in a system of behavioral relations that can be abstracted and considered as an object of study in its own right" (p. 442). What we do today when we study interaction is to attempt "a formulation of pattern" (p. 479). This has led me to the study of social constructionism generally (Leeds-Hurwitz, 1995), and the social construction of rituals as complex events specifically (Leeds-Hurwitz, 2002).

Conclusion

This list could go on, including other topics such as learning and metacommunication that also were of great interest to Bateson (Rawlins, 1987), but I think the statements provided above are the most basic assumptions guiding how scholars study social interaction today. We observe actual behavior in its context, we look for connections between process and structure, and we attempt to discover the patterns and relationships governing interaction. So many people take these assumptions for granted today that they do not even label their work as being part of the tradition described here under any of the available terms: natural history, context analysis, or the structural approach. But this is from where these ideas derive. As Kendon (1982) argues, Bateson influenced "the *kinds of questions* that came to be asked about interaction, the *kinds of phenomena* that came to be looked at, and the *strategy of investigation*" (p. 447). In this way, Bateson brought his assumptions about how to study the natural world into his studies of the social world, and his assumptions still guide much research today. This is one important part of Bateson's legacy.

References

Bateson, G. (1971). Chapter 1: Communication. In N. A. McQuown (Ed.), *The natural history of an interview* (pp. 1-40). Microfilm Collection of Manuscripts on Cultural Anthropology, 15th Series. Chicago: University of Chicago, Joseph Regenstein Library, Department of Photoduplication.

Bateson, G. (1972). *Steps to an ecology of mind*. New York: Ballantine Books.

Bateson, G. (1981). Communication. In Y. Winkin (Ed.), *La nouvelle communication* (pp. 116-144). Paris: Éditions du Seuil.

Bateson, G. (1983). Communication. In N.A. McQuown (Ed.), *El microanalisis de entrevistas: Los metodos de la historia natural aplicados a la investigacion de la sociedad, de la cultura y de la personalidad* (pp. 69-95). Mexico City: Universidad Nacional Autonoma de Mèxico.

Bateson, G. (1996). Communication. In H.B. Mokros (Ed.), *Interaction and Identity* (pp. 45-70). *Information and Behavior, Vol. 5*. New Brunswick, NJ: Transaction Publishers.

Bateson, G., & Bateson, M.C. (1987). *Angels fear: Toward an epistemology of the sacred*. New York: Macmillan.

Bateson, G., & Mead, M. (1942). *Balinese character*. New York: New York Academy of Sciences.

Bateson, M.C. (1984). *With a daughter's eye: A memoir of Margaret Mead and Gregory Bateson*. New York: William Morrow and Company.

Bateson, M. C. (1994). *Peripheral visions: Learning along the way*. New York: Harper Collins Publishers.

Birdwhistell, R. L. (1970a). *Kinesics and context: Essays in body motion communication*. Philadelphia: University of Pennsylvania Press.

Birdwhistell, R. L. (1970b). Some meta-communicational thoughts about communicational studies. In J. Akin, A. Goldberg, G. Myers, & J. Stewart (Eds.), *Language behavior: A book of readings in communication* (pp. 265-270). The Hague: Mouton.

Crane, D. (1972). *Invisible colleges: The networks of scientific communication*. Chicago: University of Chicago Press.

Duncan, S., Jr. (1985). Introduction. In S. Duncan, Jr., & D.W. Fiske, with R. Denny, B.G. Kanki & H.B. Mokros, *Interaction structure and strategy* (pp. ix-xx). Cambridge: Cambridge University Press and Paris: Éditions de la Maison des Sciences de l'Homme.

Duncan, S., Jr., & Fiske, D.W. (1985). Approaches to structural research. In S. Duncan, Jr., & D.W. Fiske, with R. Denny, B.G. Kanki & H.B. Mokros, *Interaction structure and strategy* (pp. 65-88). Cambridge: Cambridge University Press and Paris: É ditions de la Maison des Sciences de l'Homme.

Erwin, R. (2000). The nature of Goffman. In G. A. Fine & G. W. H. Smith (Eds.), *Erving Goffman* (vol. 1, pp. 84-96). London: Sage. (Originally published in 1992)

Goffman, E. (1968). *Asylums: Essays on the social situation of mental patients and other inmates*. Harmondsworth: Penguin. (Originally published in 1961)

Gumperz, J. J. (1992). Contextualization and understanding. In A. Duranti & C. Goodwin, (Eds.), *Rethinking context: Language as an interactive phenomenon* (pp. 229-252). Cambridge: Cambridge University Press.

Kendon, A. (1979). Some methodological and theoretical aspects of the use of film in the study of social interaction. In G. P. Ginsberg (Ed.), *Emerging strategies in social psychological research* (pp. 67-91). New York: Wiley.

Kendon, A. (1982). The organization of behavior in face-to-face interaction: Observations on the development of a methodology. In K. Scherer & P. Ekman (Eds.), *Handbook of methods in nonverbal behavior research* (pp. 440-505). Cambridge: Cambridge University Press.

Kendon, A. (1990). *Conducting interaction: Patterns of behavior in focused encounters*. Cambridge, England: Cambridge University Press.

Kroeber, A. L. (1959). The history of the personality of anthropology. *American Anthropologist, 61*, 398-404.

Leeds-Hurwitz, W. (1987). The social history of *The Natural History of an Interview*: A multidisciplinary investigation of social communication. *Research on Language and Social Interaction, 20*, 1-51.

Leeds-Hurwitz, W. (1988). La quête des structures: Gregory Bateson et l'*Histoire naturelle d'un entretien*. In Y. Winkin (Ed.), *Gregory Bateson: Premier état d'un héritage* (pp. 67-77). Paris: Éditions du Seuil.

Leeds-Hurwitz, W. (1989). *Communication in everyday life: A social interpretation*. Norwood, NJ: Ablex.

Leeds-Hurwitz, W. (1993). *Semiotics and communication: Signs, codes, cultures*. Hillsdale, NJ: Erlbaum.

Leeds-Hurwitz, W. (Ed.). (1995). *Social approaches to communication*. New York: Guilford Press.

Leeds-Hurwitz, W. (2002). *Wedding as text: Communicating cultural identity through ritual*. Mahwah, NJ: Erlbaum.

Liberman, K. (1995). The natural history of some intercultural communication. *Research on Language and Social Interaction, 28*, 117-146.

Lipset, D. (1982). *Gregory Bateson: The legacy of a scientist*. Englewood Cliffs, NJ: Prentice-Hall.

McQuown, N. A. (1971). Natural history method: A frontier method. In A.R. Mahrer & L. Pearson (Eds.), *Creative developments in psychotherapy* (pp. 430-438). Cleveland, OH: Case Western Reserve University Press.

McQuown, N. A. (1983). *El microanalisis de entrevistas*. Mexico City: Instituto de Investigacioned Antropologicas, Universidad Nacional Autonoma de Mèxico

Mead, M. (1951). What makes the Soviet character? *Natural History Magazine*. Retrieved on July 15, 2004 from http://www.naturalhistorymag.com/editors_pick/1951_09_pick.html

Mead, M. (1972). *Blackberry winter: My earlier years*. New York: Simon and Schuster.

Mokros, H. B. (1996). *Interaction and identity: Information and behavior* (Vol. 5). New Brunswick, NJ: Transaction.

Putnam, L. L., & Stohl, C. (1990). Bona fide groups: A reconceptualization of groups in context. *Communication Studies, 41*, 248-265.

Rawlins, W. K. (1987). Gregory Bateson and the composition of human communication. *Research on Language in Social Interaction, 20*, 53-77.

Robins, R. H. (1971). Malinowski, Firth, and the "context of situation." In E. Ardener (Ed.), *Social anthropology and language* (pp. 33-46). London: Tavistock.

Scheflen, A. E. (1971). Natural history method in psychotherapy: Communicational research. In A.R. Mahrer & L. Pearson (Eds.), *Creative developments in psychotherapy* (pp. 393-422). Cleveland, OH: Case Western Reserve University Press. (Originally published in 1966)

Scheflen, A. E. (1973). *Communicational structure: Analysis of a psychotherapy transaction*. Bloomington: Indiana University Press.

Silverstein, M., & Urban, G. (1996). The natural history of discourse. In M. Silverstein & G. Urban (Eds.), *Natural histories of discourse* (pp. 1-17). Chicago: University of Chicago Press.

Verhoeven, J. C. (2000). An interview with Erving Goffman, 1980. In G. A. Fine & G. W. H. Smith (Eds.), *Erving Goffman* (vol. 1, pp. 213-236). London: Sage. (Originally published in 1993)

Winkin, Y. (Ed.), (1981). *La nouvelle communication*. Paris: Éditions du Seuil.

Cybernetics And Human Knowing. Vol. 12, nos. 1-2, pp. 147-158

Gregory Bateson and the Promise of Transdisciplinarity

Alfonso Montuori[1]

Gregory Bateson was a thinker beyond disciplines, contributing not only to specific disciplines ranging from Communication to Family Therapy to Ecology, but also helping us to think about the nature of inquiry, thought and disciplinary organization. In this paper I argue Bateson was a transdisciplinary thinker, and illustrate how his work can lead us to a new approach to inquiry. I conclude by outlining the 5 central features of transdisciplinarity: inquiry-driven rather than exclusively discipline-driven; meta-paradigmatic rather than intra-paradigmatic; informed by thinking that is complex, creative, contextualizing, and connective; inquiry as a creative process combining rigor and imagination.

Introduction

When I tell people that several of Gregory Bateson's works are being re-issued in the book series I started at Hampton Press, I inevitably get some puzzled looks. The puzzlement is principally because Gregory Bateson just does not seem like the kind of author who would or should ever be out of print. But the puzzlement is also almost inevitably followed by an attempt to situate Bateson. This is usually along the lines of "Bateson, the anthropologist/psychiatrist/family therapist/cyberneticist/dolphin guy, right?" Fair enough. Where *did* Bateson belong? It's not an easy question to answer.

The lack of an apparent intellectual home for Bateson is not unconnected to the fact that he was temporarily out of print. First of all, what category would one put a Bateson book in? Anthropology? Science? Philosophy? New Age? (In the United States, *Mind and Nature* was in fact published in the Bantam New Age imprint.) What discipline supports Bateson? Who reads his work? What research agenda was he associated with? Psychology? Family therapy? Evolutionary theory? Organizational learning? Communication? His work has certainly been influential in all of those areas.

Browsing through the Table of Contents of *Steps to an Ecology of Mind* (Bateson, 2000), we find essays devoted to the double bind theory of schizophrenia, evolution, communication (including the cetacean variety), national character, epistemology, learning, ecology, education, cultural anthropology. Why would such a book, with essays on such widely disparate subjects, appeal to anyone? What is, dare I ask, the pattern that connects these topics?

---

1. California Institute of Integral Studies, 1453 Mission St., San Francisco, CA 94103 USA.
   Email: amontuori@ciis.edu

A second problem with Bateson is that he is often categorized as a "difficult" thinker. Two factors compound this difficulty. Bateson's style is sometimes difficult ("not immediately transparent," in Ernst Von Glasersfeld elegant formulation on the back cover of the Hampton re-issue of *Mind and Nature*). It is not dry traditional social science and definitely not a breezy essay style. The other central problem is that despite Bateson's intra-disciplinary contributions, such as his work on the understanding of schizophrenia, most of the time he is working at a meta-level, an epistemological level, engaged in thinking about thinking, inquiring about inquiry, historically topics that, partly because of their self-reflective nature, point in a direction opposite to "immediate transparency."

Despite the heterogeneity and difficulty of his writings, Bateson's work has been widely influential and continues to be cited in many different disciplines. In Europe, particularly in Mediterranean countries, where one can still be considered "a thinker" without having to declare a disciplinary affiliation, there is a small but impressive series of books about Bateson's *oeuvre*. In fact, in Italy, where books and conferences on Bateson abound, *Steps to an Ecology of Mind* is even available as an audio-book. One can only guess at the effect on the human nervous system of listening to Bateson's words while negotiating Italian traffic.

In this essay I want to explore some of Bateson's key insights into inquiry, and use them to sketch out the outline of an approach to transdisciplinary inquiry, drawing from principles outlined in Bateson's work and drawing from Edgar Morin's explicit efforts to "reform thought" and develop the philosophical foundations of a transdisciplinary perspective. Transdisciplinary inquiry is not merely the additive use of knowledge from several disciplines to confront a problem, which is how I characterize interdisciplinary efforts. As I outline it here, transdisciplinarity is an attitude towards inquiry, informed by certain epistemological presuppositions, and an effort to frame inquiry as a creative process that recognizes as central the subjectivity of the inquirer and challenges the underlying organization of knowledge.

Homeless: Some Personal Context

The Batesonian predicament of intellectual homelessness is very familiar to me. From management to psychology to sociology to international relations to evolutionary theory, all the disciplines I have been loosely affiliated with are fascinating to me. It took me a while to realize that I was ultimately not particularly wedded to a specific discipline, and that ultimately there was nothing wrong with that. I have always been fascinated by certain topics, like creativity, or the relationship between culture and identity, or the role of uncertainty and ambiguity in human affairs. But in the case of all my interests, I felt they could not be contained by a particular discipline, even as those individual disciplines and sub-disciplines shed light on my subject in different ways.

During the late 70s and early 80s, while I was pretending to go to high school and college, I spent several years working as a professional musician, leading my own band in London. When I later came across the voluminous research on creativity, I realized there was very little research on creativity in musical groups, or any kind of groups, for that matter (Montuori & Purser, 1995). The dominant literature on creativity was in the field of psychology, with a smattering in other disciplines such as philosophy and sociology. Psychological research on creativity focused almost entirely on the individual, not the group, or the relationship between creativity and interaction. And while playing in a band required individual creativity, a huge interactive portion of the process was being left out of the discussion. The research simply did not reflect the full extent of the experience of performing musicians.

My inquiry was therefore not defined by the discipline of psychology's research agenda into creativity, but by my own interest, by my own experience of the creative process in the context of a musical group, and by the apparent lack I found in the literature. This lack eventually forced me to cross over into several disciplines to draw together what little we know about creativity and collaboration (Montuori & Purser, 1999). It was apparent that social and/or group creativity existed in a kind of no-man's land, between psychology, sociology, and anthropology, and that one key reason why it had not been addressed was that it simply did not fit into any particular discipline's research agenda. Creativity "belonged" to psychology. Groups and social factors belonged more to social psychology (a branch of psychology that did not address creativity, which had historically been considered to be more in the personality/cognitive domain). Management, with its pragmatic orientation, straddled the fence, with some interesting research on Research and Development groups, but little sustained research. At the same time, I did become intimately familiar with what was, and remains, the dominant literature on creativity, more specifically the psychology of creativity.

It also became apparent that the fundamental way of thinking about issues in much of social science was governed by the twin principles of *reduction and disjunction*, isolating variables and separating them from their environment. Reduction and disjunction were two key organizing principles shaping much of psychology's choice to focus on the individual, at the expense of "societal factors," for instance. Creativity was reduced to the discipline's fundamental unit of analysis, and anything outside of that unit of analysis was considered epiphenomenal. My early interest in systems thinking was triggered by its focus on context and relationship, so lacking in much of the work I was seeing in academia, and indeed in most of what we called "thinking," whether about family or politics, sports or entertainment.

As I spent more and more time in academia, I became aware of how decontextualized most of the knowledge was. And, as Bateson stated:

> Without context, words and actions have no meaning at all. This is true not only of human communication in words but also of all communication whatsoever, of all mental process, of all mind, including that which tells the sea anemone how to grow and the amoeba what he should do next. (Bateson, 2002, p.14)

In the case of creativity, the focus on the individual's creative process decontextualized creativity by isolating that process from anything happening outside the individual, from the larger process that is involved in making an idea into a product, whether a painting or a new widget. This almost inevitably involves social interactions, dialogue, debate, economics, and so on. The creative process was also decontextualized because there were no connections made to perspectives and approaches from other disciplines—the study of creativity was, in other words, decontextualized from the larger network of knowledge generated in other disciplines. When Ron Purser and I put together the first volume of our *Social Creativity* series (Montuori & Purser, 1999), we brought together psychologists, systems theorists, anthropologists, philosophers, and others, and asked them to explore the phenomenon of social creativity, or the social dimensions of the creative process. They all approached creativity from radically different perspectives, drawing on disparate literatures, with little or no overlap in sources. The result was fascinating because it showed a plurality of different paradigms and models with which to approach the social dimensions of creativity, and how those different approaches shed light on different aspects of the creative process. It also showed that the mainstream view in psychology, namely that the social is ultimately epiphenomenal in the creative process, closely parallels the "folk" understanding of creativity, with its focus on the "lone genius" (Montuori & Purser, 1995).

There are some extremely deep philosophical assumptions underlying the dominant cultural views on creativity in the US, closely paralleling psychology's position that the individual could somehow be isolated from the social (Montuori & Purser, 1999). Can one really say that the social world is epiphenomenal, as some psychologists have argued? That creativity happens "inside" an individual, and that social factors do not really play a role? All sorts of questions arise—not least of which is how can a painter or musician or scientists participate in a domain—actually even *be* a painter, scientist, musician—without a social world that provides a context, that provides the raw materials, the questions, the role models, the disciplines, the instruments, the approaches, the traditions to follow and defy, and so on? Assuming for a moment that this methodological individualism is indeed a legitimate philosophical position, whether one agrees with it or not is almost less problematic than the fact that in psychology's discourse of creativity those assumptions are almost always taken for granted. Indeed, when questioned, one leading psychologist I spoke to replied "I don't do metaphysics." This is all good and well, but of course the dismissal of (implicitly "fluffy") metaphysics in favor of a "hard" scientific posture seeks to obscure the fact that there's no escaping metaphysics, since we all have underlying principles and theories that in-form, that shape and guide our work. The more interesting question is the extent to which we are aware of them. But in a certain attitude towards science and inquiry, these metaphysical assumptions are not taken *as* assumptions, but as "the way things are." There is little or no awareness of their enormous implications, or of the nature of other approaches with perhaps contradictory assumptions. The underlying paradigm, if you will, is buried and invisible.

Towards Transdisciplinary Inquiry

Let me step back now and attempt to articulate what I believe connects my own experience with Bateson's work. First of all, of course, there is the problem of disciplinary fragmentation. As human beings have developed more and more knowledge, there has been a concomitant division of labor. Disciplinary fragmentation is the result of increasing specialization. This is fundamentally an issue of *organization*. Industrial organization used division of labor and specialization, to increase, articulate, and facilitate production, and the production of knowledge has, for all intents and purposes, followed the same organizational model.

The early philosophers ranged far and wide, covering fields from biology to ethics, from politics to physics. With increasing production of knowledge, facilitated by the printing press, communication, a greater educated class, and increasing cultural exchanges, it became progressively harder to know everything under the sun. If individuals could not keep abreast of all knowledge, they could specialize in one or more areas. The broad category of philosophy was slowly broken down, and new fields emerged, and eventually becoming disciplines with their own university departments. These departments differentiated and ultimately *separated* one field from the next, and were also subject to internal differentiation and separation. In psychology one might have experimental, clinical, social, personality, cognitive, and so on. Eventually, the likelihood of members of these sub-disciplines talking to each other became more and more remote, and indeed it became likely that their relationship would be oppositional at best. There was a form of evolutionary drift, whereby even the sub-disciplines increasingly became their own worlds, with fundamental assumptions radically differing, and a tendency, as Bruce Wilshire (1990) has so carefully described, to create strong borders and safeguard the (sub-) disciplinary "purity" against the "pollution" of perspectives from other disciplines.

The key principles of reduction and disjunction meant that inquiry went increasingly deeper into smaller and smaller subsections of knowledge, and disjunction meant separation—in other words, every smaller sub-section of knowledge was separated out into its own world, and became an "identity," an "A" which could not be "B." The creation of sub-disciplines, therefore, could be said to have created sub-cultures with their own identities and their own "turf" to protect. The organization of knowledge-producing institutions is paralleled by the organization of thought. Bateson writes that

> While so much that universities teach today is new and up-to-date, the presuppositions or premises of thought upon which all our teaching is based are ancient, and, I assert, obsolete. (Bateson, 2002, p. 203)

Reductive and disjunctive thought is, as Bateson, Morin and others have shown, central to most inquiry, and arose out of Descartes' sustained effort to understand how best to think. In his *Discourse on Method*, Descartes (1954) explored the basic laws of thinking, and fashioned them into a methodology for inquiry. Below are two key points Descartes made under the telling heading of *Rules for the direction of the mind*, published originally in 1701:

RULE V
The method consists entirely in the orderly arrangement of the objects upon which we must turn our mental vision in order to discover some truth. And we shall be observing this method exactly if we reduce complex and obscure propositions step by step to simpler ones, and then, by retracing our steps, try to rise from the intuition of all of the simplest ones to knowledge of all the rest. (p. 157)

RULE XIII
If we are to understand a problem perfectly, we must free it from any superfluous conceptions, reduce it to the simplest terms, and by process of enumeration, split it up into the smallest possible parts. (p.179)

The problem with this in many ways extremely successful approach is that it can become extremely limiting if taken to extremes. Simplicity is all very well, and indeed admirable, but if through reduction and disjunction we take our subject out of its context, out of the complex network of relationship, the ecology that sustains it, and then focus on one small part of the subject, we have a situation where simplicity has been achieved at the expense of complexity. In its effort to reduce to simplest terms, isolate variables, and remove exogenous factors, simplicity then mutilates, and indeed obscures complexity. Bateson wrote that

> there are many catastrophic dangers which have grown out of the Occidental errors of epistemology. I believe that this massive aggregation of threats to man and his ecological systems arises out of errors in our habits of thought at a deep and partly unconscious level. (Bateson, 2002, p. 487)

The errors of thought, of which decontextualization is a central one, have become institutionalized in our North-American organization of knowledge. It is perhaps easier to recognize these errors of thought when they reveal themselves in physical structures, in the architecture and organization of the university. They are generally harder to find as phenomena that pertain to the very way we think—because that requires thinking about thinking, a process that seems not to come naturally.

There are clear parallels between the disciplinary organization of the university and the organization of thought. This problematic organization of knowledge is something that was central to Bateson's work. Bateson wrote that:

> At present, there is no existing science whose special interest is the combining of pieces of information. But I shall argue that the evolutionary process must depend upon such double

increments of information. Every evolutionary step is an addition of information to an already existing system. Because this is so, the combinations, harmonies, and discords between successive pieces and layers of information will present many problems of survival and determine many directions of change. (Bateson, 2002, p. 19)

There is no science linking what has been increasingly fragmented. We notice this most particularly when exploring the *application* of knowledge. Knowledge *in context*. I am presently working on a textbook on creativity and innovation in organizations. Most of the work on creativity has focused on the individual level, largely addressing how to think creatively. But if we looked at the reality of creativity and innovation from idea to product, the experience of being an individual with a bright idea in an organization, we see that having an idea is simply not enough. We must also be able to work with others, to influence others, to assess the viability of our idea, know our market, and so on. Anybody who has worked in an organization realizes the gap between having a great idea and seeing that idea enacted in the organization. In other words, the reality of bringing a new idea into the world in an organizational context goes far beyond the generation of an idea, a process studied by psychologists.

The different fragments of knowledge about creativity and the creative process lie scattered across sub-disciplines, often with little awareness of each other, and the practitioner is expected to somehow integrate this knowledge, in the miraculous event that he should somehow find it, buried as most of it is in esoteric journals. The task of integration into the lived experience of the practitioner is hardly ever seriously addressed. Simplicity may be honored, but at the expense of complexity—not some esoteric theoretical complexity, but the complexity that arises out of the lived experience of actually trying to get something done in an organization, for instance. Context and connection are missing. It is so much easier, in a way, to point the reader to some of the literature on the psychology of creativity, preferably some creativity "tools" like lateral thinking, and let the individual sink or swim with this "technology" in hand, than to explore the real complexities of what Frank Barron (1995), the noted creativity researcher and colleague of Bateson's at Santa Cruz, called the ecology of creativity.

To address the creativity of an individual and an organization, the "tools" approach is profoundly decontextualized—here's your hammer, start banging away, you're bound to hit *something*. An alternative, contextual, ecological approach is what I believe can be aimed for with a transdisciplinary approach. Such an approach recognizes the lived experience and subjectivity of the inquirer, the person reading the book who then hopes to put some of this material into practice. The lived experience occurs in a context, in a network of relationships, in an ecology. One way of addressing the complexity required of such an approach, is through the development of a transdisciplinary approach.

Cornerstones of Transdisciplinarity

Transdisciplinary inquiry attempts to address some of the key problems that Bateson has brought to our attention. I will focus on 5 areas that I believe are central, and distinguish transdisciplinary inquiry from inter-disciplinary and disciplinary approaches. In summary, I will argue that transdisciplinary is:

- inquiry-driven rather than exclusively discipline-driven
- meta-paradigmatic rather than exclusively intra-paradigmatic
- informed by a kind of thinking that is creative, contextualizing, and connective (Morin's "complex thought")
- inquiry as a creative process that combines rigor and imagination

(1) Transdisciplinarity is "inquiry-driven." Disciplinary inquiry is generally "discipline-driven." By discipline-driven I mean that traditionally one is socialized into a specific discipline that focuses on a specific set of issues, a disciplinary agenda, and the disciplinary "boundaries" that establish what topics belong, and do not belong, and even what questions may and may not be asked in the research agenda. In a university context, during the socialization of most academics, this agenda can sometimes more specifically be one's advisor's research agenda. Transdisciplinary inquiry is driven by the inquirer's agenda, by a question that emerges through a dialogue between the inquirer's experience and passion, the subject of inquiry, and the bodies of knowledge available. Inquiry-driven does not mean eschewing the contribution of disciplinary knowledge. On the contrary, it engages disciplinary knowledge and adds to it pertinent knowledge from a plurality of other disciplines, through the development of a plurality of perspectives on the same topic, and through a constant interaction with the inquirer's context and his or her own lived experience, values, and beliefs.

(2) If we are to bring a plurality of perspectives from a variety of disciplinary perspectives to bear on our topic, how do we organize and think about this knowledge? The traditional approach to inquiry has, as we saw, been reductive and disjunctive, with ever increasing separation and differentiation, but with little or no effort to connect and contextualize. Interdisciplinarity typically joins two previously separated disciplines to address a problem, but rarely questions disciplinary organization. The process is additive. So along with the question of how do we organize knowledge, we also have to ask, what are the principles behind that organization, and what are the underlying principles in the various disciplines that are being brought together? Interdisciplinarity does not address these fundamental issues. It generally accepts the present system of disciplines, and the fundamental principles of knowledge-organization.

When we draw on different disciplines, these disciplines, sub-disciplines and approaches often reflect very different paradigmatic assumptions. In disciplinary approaches, the underlying assumptions remain fundamentally unquestioned, and the same is true for interdisciplinary approaches.

Transdisciplinarity should, I believe, be a *meta-paradigmatic* approach. By this I mean that transdisciplinary inquirers should be able to understand not only the content of various disciplinary approaches to issues, but their underlying assumptions or paradigms, and how those paradigms shape the inquiry. This process would also, of course, put into question the inquirer's own paradigmatic assumptions, and offer an opportunity to question and explore one's own assumptions. It is in the exchange with different perspectives that our own perspectives become most clearly elucidated and articulated.

As we become aware of the underlying assumptions of various perspectives on the same issue—as in the case of creativity—we can see that there is a pattern of oppositional identity that connects them. Psychologists studying creativity have largely been ontological atomists, and sociologists and anthropologists ontological holists. Tracing the history of these positions we can see how they have arisen and how the positions have identified themselves in opposition to each other (Fay, 1979). Indeed, once we begin to study the underlying philosophical assumptions of most forms of academic inquiry, we can begin to recognize this process of oppositional identity formation in any number of different areas, from idealism/realism in political theory to objectivism/constructivism in epistemology to atomism/holism in ontology.

This oppositional identity is mutually constitutive—it is a circular process whereby A acts on B which acts on A. In the work of Fay (1996), Morin (1984, 1992, 1994), and Bateson (2002), we can see how the history of ideas is full of schismogenic processes, where positions polarize as they define each other in opposition to each other. At the same time, Bateson (2002, p. 19) wants to "bring to people's attention a number of cases in which two or more information sources come together to give information of a sort different from what was in either source separately." In other words, Bateson is arguing for the creativity that emerges out of the interaction of multiple perspectives. The creative process has been defined as seeing "a single idea in two habitually incompatible frames of reference." The existence of a multiplicity of perspectives, at times mutually opposed, can therefore be transformed into an opportunity for creativity, *if* we accept the possibility of multiple ways of knowing, that there is more than one perspective that has something to offer, and no one perspective has the monopoly, *and* recognize the possibility that the perspectives can co-exist and also be brought together to develop an creative integrations.

(3) Transdisciplinarity should therefore be self-reflective (Steier, 1990) and encourage a kind of creative thinking that contextualizes and connects, distinguishes rather than separates. Bateson's affiliation with cybernetics and systems thinking reflects his desire to find an articulation of this "new thinking."

Striking parallels exist in the findings of psychologists studying higher forms of cognitive development (so-called post-formal thought), research findings on creative thought, and the work of systems thinkers, particularly Edgar Morin's articulation of "complex thought" (Montuori, Combs, & Richards, 2003). One of the original dreams of systems approaches was to develop a framework to integrate all the sciences, of course. With the second-order cybernetics of Von Foerster (Morin, 1992) and the "epistemological turn" of which Bateson was one of the key figures, the focus shifted from observed systems to observing systems, and a recognition of the importance of the observer and the nature of thinking.

In *Mind and Nature*, Bateson articulates some essential premises "if the schoolboy is ever to learn to think" (Bateson, 2002, p. 19), and this challenge of learning to think contextually and creatively, lies at the heart of transdisciplinary work, I believe. Today, the work of Edgar Morin (Morin, 2005) is perhaps the most original and profound articulation of such a new way of thinking, which he calls "complex thought."

(4) Disciplinary and Interdisciplinary inquiry generally leave the inquirer's subjectivity out of the inquiry process, and indeed have historically gone to great lengths to purify the inquiry of any "subjectivity" (Steier, 1990). In Transdisciplinary inquiry, since we start off with a way of thinking about inquiry that stresses passion, creativity, context and connection, the inquirer's subjectivity is an inextricable part of the inquiry's context and indeed not just deeply connected to, but constitutive of the inquirer's construction and interpretation of the context. The inquirer's own paradigmatic assumptions are surfaced and enter into a dialogue with a plurality of other assumptions from other perspectives, from other ways the subject has been addressed. Since the work is inquiry-driven and not only discipline-driven, the inquirer's motivations are explored, assessed, and contextualized. One might ask oneself, why am I doing this? Not necessarily because it's my advisor's research agenda, for example. What do I bring to this subject, with my personal history, my academic trajectory? What are my biases, beliefs, blind spots? Every inquiry therefore becomes an opportunity for self-inquiry—indeed, self-inquiry becomes a necessary part of the research process.

Another key question that arises with the introduction of the inquirer into the inquiry has to do with our fundamental assumptions about the nature of human nature. What is our understanding of human capacities? If every inquiry is, indeed, an opportunity for self-inquiry, what can we hope to achieve? What is the human capacity for transformation? A Freudian view of human nature, and of human change possibilities, is quite different from that offered by the work of humanistic psychologists such as Maslow, or even transpersonal psychologists (Montuori, Combs, & Richards, 2003). Once again, inquiry becomes an opportunity for self-contextualizing, self-inquiry, and also self-creation.

Finally, given the explicit focus on the inquirer and his/her subjectivity, context, motivations, etc., transdisciplinarity demands an ongoing process of self-and-other-inquiry, inasmuch as the assumption is not that we are "discovering" "facts" about a world "out there," but rather that there is a an ongoing inter-subjective co-evolutionary process of construction. Learning is not the acquisition of "things," but an ongoing process of self-eco-re-organization (Montuori, 2003).

5) Bateson stressed the importance of striking a balance between rigor and imagination. Whereas academia has focused on the context of justification (the development of a defensible "position"), it leaves the creative process leading up to the development of that position (the context of discovery) out of the picture. It is only

in the biographies and autobiographies of scientists and other creative individuals that we get to see their creative process, with all its complexities, wrong turns, anxieties, imaginative twists, conflicts and collaborations. In the academic context, we largely get presentations, articles, and book, that stress the rock-solid defensibility of the position being presented. When not balanced by imagination, the quest for rigor leads to rigidity. I believe it is essential to re-introduce this creative dimension, this dimension of imagination into inquiry. Without this dimension, our very understanding of the nature and process of inquiry is deeply mutilated and anemic. And this is certainly not something that can be addressed by a course in "lateral thinking" (Montuori, 1998). The larger challenge is to envision inquiry as a process that navigates the twin requirements of rigor and imagination, in a way that the two contribute to each other and to inquiry, rather than schismogenically fly away from each other.

The Journey Home

I have briefly outlined some key aspects of what I believe to be a transdisciplinary approach, to some extent making explicit some of the characteristics that I see in Bateson's work, and drawing also extensively on the work of Edgar Morin. A transdisciplinary approach is, at this point, an aspiration whose characteristics need to be more fully fleshed out. Bateson's work pointed to a great need in our culture, and to a realm of possibilities for new forms of inquiry.

And where did Bateson belong, then? I believe Bateson was a perpetual traveler, taking a meta- point of view on and across the nature of inquiry, and pointing in the direction of a different world, a world of creative, transdisciplinary inquiry that we can aspire to as a way of reconnecting fragmented and decontextualized knowledge. Indeed, it is arguably the knowledge and inquiry that Bateson critiqued that is truly homeless, deprived as it is of context and knower.

References

Barron, F. (1995). *No rootless flower: Towards an ecology of creativity*. Cresskill, NJ: Hampton Press.

Bateson, G. (2000). *Steps to an ecology of mind*. Chicago: University of Chicago Press

Bateson, G. (2002). *Mind and nature: A necessary unity*. Cresskill, NJ: Hampton Press.

Descartes, R. (1954). *Philosophical writings*. London: Open University Press.

Fay, B. (1996). *Contemporary philosophy of social science*. New York: Blackwell Publishers.

Montuori, A. (1998). Creative inquiry: From instrumental knowing to love of knowledge. In J. Petrankar (Ed.), *Light of knowledge*. Oakland, CA: Dharma Press.

Montuori, A. (2003). The complexity of improvisation and the improvisation of complexity. Social science, art, and creativity. *Human Relations, 56* (2), 237-255.

Montuori, A., Combs, A., & Richards, R. (2003). Creativity, consciousness, and the direction for human development. In D. Loye, (Ed.), *The great adventure: Toward a fully human theory of evolution*. Albany, NY: SUNY Press.

Montuori, A. & Purser, R. (1995). Deconstructing the lone genius myth: Towards a contextual view of creativity. *Journal of Humanistic Psychology, 35* (3), 69-112.

Montuori, A. & Purser, R. (1999). *Social creativity* (Vol. 1). Cresskill, NJ: Hampton Press.

Morin, E. (1984). *Science avec conscience* [Science with conscience]. Paris: Fayard.

Morin, E. (1992). *Method: Towards a study of humankind. The nature of nature*. New York: Peter Lang.

Morin, E. (1994). La complexité humaine. [Human complexity]. Paris: Flammarion.

Morin, E. (2005). *On complexity*. Cresskill, NJ: Hampton Press.

158 Alfonso Montuori

Steier, F. (Ed.) (1991). *Research and reflexivity.* Newbury Park, CA: Sage.
Wilshire, B. (1990). *The moral collapse of the university: Professionalism, purity, and alienation.* New York: SUNY
   Press.

Cybernetics And Human Knowing. Vol. 12, nos. 1-2, pp. 159-167

Virtual Logic—The One and the Many

Louis H. Kauffman[1]

I. Introduction

Georg Cantor, the mathematician who discovered transfinite set theory, said:

"A set is a unity that can be seen as a multiplicity."

More specifically, he said (Cantor, 1941, p. 85): "By an 'aggregate' (*Menge*) we are to understand any collection into a whole (*Zusammenfassung zu einem Ganzen*) M of definite and separate objects *m* of our intuition or our thought."

This definition lives next door to a deep philosophical problem: If one begins with a unity, how can multiplicity arise? How can many come from one? If one begins with multiplicity, how can unity arise? How can one come from many?

It would seem that we must begin in multiplicity. Any explanation of unity must begin in multiplicity. It is possible to structure such an explanation so that it points beyond itself to a unity that it can never reach.

There is a curious duality between indications that point to the void (i.e. they point to the absence of indication) and indications that point to infinity. In both cases we ask language to do more than it is capable of doing. Nothing without distinction can be fully represented in language because anything we say is too much. Nothing with infinitely many distinctions can be represented in finite language because anything we say is too little. Yet language can reach toward nothing, and language can reach toward infinity. In the reaching of language we see an essential identity of nothing and everything. It is an identity in a domain that can only be shown and not described.

We begin by discussing sets and how sets that are obtained from nothing but the act of collection can give rise to arbitrary multiplicity. Numbers emanate from nothing under the magic wand of set collection. The key to this emanation of multiplicity from void is the formation of singleton sets {**x**} and the distinction between the singleton set {**x**} and its member **x**.

The set theoretic method for producing multiplicity from unity involves a very strange construction indeed. What is the singleton {**x**}? *If a set is a unity that can be seen to be a multiplicity, what is the nature of a set with one element?*

These considerations lead to a dialogue about multiplicity, sets and physical reality. In modeling physical reality we are tempted to identify the singleton and its member. In mathematics we find ourselves constrained by logic and the need for multiplicities to keep the singleton and its member distinct. This creates a tension between physical and mathematical realities that finds its expression in many realms.

---

1. Math Department., University of Illinois–Chicago, Chicago, IL. Email: kauffman@uic.edu

Infinities of possibility collapse into finite actualities at the cusp of observation. This situation is very much in accord with our experience of quantum mechanics.

II. On Sets

A set **S** is a collection of objects.

These objects are said to be the members of the set **S**.

Sets are said to be equal if and only if they have the same members.

The simplest set is the empty set, denoted by empty brackets as { }.

Theorem. An empty set exists.

Proof. Consider the collection of all sets that have no members. Call this collection **Mu**. Suppose there is no empty set. Then there are no sets that have no members. Hence **Mu** has no members. Therefore **Mu** is empty. This is a contradiction! Therefore there must be an empty set. **QED**

Remark. This proof has a curious flavor. If we begin in a world with no empty sets, then **Mu**, is empty and the world suddenly has an empty set, but one moment later **Mu** has a member, namely itself! But a moment after that **Mu** loses this member because **Mu** is now not empty! **Mu** oscillates between emptiness and non-emptiness if we begin in a world without an empty set.

In the darkness of a world without emptiness, the sentence
"The set of all empty sets"
Appears, and with it,
Emptiness appears out of the darkness.
Once this emptiness has appeared and been seen to be void,
It is no longer void, and
We descend into the darkness of no emptiness once more.
But the sentence remains
And flashes its emptiness yet again,
Only to be immediately extinguished by the darkness.
An eternal flicker of emptiness in the dark.
This is the appearance of Mind.

Theorem: The empty set is unique.

Proof. Suppose that sets S and T are both empty. Then S and T have exactly the same members, namely none! Hence S and T are equal. QED

From the empty set, we can build an infinity of different sets via the

Principle of Collection: Any sets that already exist can be selected as members of a new set that is created from them. We refer to this new set as ***obtained by collection.***

Note that the empty set, { }, is obtained by collecting nothing, and that the set consisting of the empty set, {{ }}, is obtained by collecting the empty set. This primordial singleton, {{ }}, is distinct from the empty set, since it has a member.

We apply the principle of collection to the void and obtain infinite multiplicity:

0={ }
1={0} = {{ }}
2={0,1} = {{ },{{ }}}
3={0,1,2} = {{ },{{ }}, {{ },{{ }}}}
...
n+1 = {0,1,2,...,n}
...

Multiplicities arise from the concept of a set and the principle of collection. In the above construction, each new set (**n+1**) is obtained by collecting all of the previously created sets. The sets are all distinct from one another, by the principle of membership. Note how it works.

0 has no member (0 is the empty set).
1 has member 0, and hence 0 and 1 are not equal.
2 has distinct members 0 and 1, and hence is distinct from 0 and from 1.
3 has distinct members 0,1 and 2 and hence is distinct from
0, 1 and 2.
The process continues and produces representatives for all finite
non-negative numbers.

In this way, set theory shows a way to produce multiplicity from the unity of the void.

We can also make a series of distinct sets, each with one element:

[0]= { }
[1] = {{ }}
[2] = {{{ }}}
[3] = {{{{ }}}}
[4] = {{{{{ }}}}}
...

We can imagine the limiting set

W = {{{{{{{...}}}}}}}

with an infinite descending chain of membership.

In this limit, we obtain a singleton set that is a member of itself, for

W= {{{{{{{...}}}}}}}} = { W }.

From this point of view we have to take a limit in order to arrive at a singleton that is equal to itself.

III. The Strange Case of the Singleton Set

The key conceptual operation in set theory is the act or process of collection. The act is indicated by the placement of braces { } around the objects that are being collected. Thus **{1,3,5,7}** denotes the set that collects the first four odd numbers.

Already there is a strangeness. Suppose we have a single element such as "**1.**" We form the singleton collection consisting of **1**. This singleton is **{1}**.

There is a definite distinction between **1** and the singleton **{1}**.
What is the nature of this distinction?
There is a lamp on my desk, **L**.
There is the set whose member is the lamp on my desk, **{L}**.
L is on my desk.
Is **{L}** on my desk?
Does **{L}** have a location?

If singletons are on my desk, the world of "things" on my desk is infinite. Here are some of them:

$$L$$
$$\{L\}$$
$$\{\{L\}\}$$
$$\{\{\{L\}\}\}$$
$$...$$
$$\{L,\{L\}\}$$
$$\{L, \{L\}, \{L,\{L\}\}\}$$
$$\{L,\{L\}, \{L,\{L\}\}, \{L, \{L\}, \{L,\{L\}\}\}\}$$
$$...$$
$$\{L,\{L\},\{\{L\}\},\{\{\{L\}\}\},\{\{\{\{L\}\}\}\},...\}$$
$$...$$
$$...$$

What a crowded desk this is getting to be! And yet, every object that I have listed above is located in exactly the same place as my lamp. My lamp is superimposed with an infinity of lamp-collections, and when I observe them they all collapse to the "one lamp" that lights the desk.

What sort of a unity is a singleton set?

What is the unity of {**L**}?

If something is a unity, then there should be a point of view in which that thing is indivisible. If you take it apart it should turn into something else.

The singleton {**L**} is a fusion of **L** with the act of collection. It is like Scrooge McDuck's lucky dime. That dime is just an old dime, but it is the fusion of that dime with Scrooge that creates the confidence maintaining the old duck's wealth and power. *It is the fusion that is the unity*. You cannot separate Scrooge and the dime, and maintain the luck. It is all of a piece. And yet this fusion has only one dime.

Just so, the singleton set. The braces indicate the fusion of **L** with the act of collection. **L** by itself is not a collection. {**L**} is the unitary collection of **L**.

What if the world consisted in irreducible (atomic) entities **a,b,c,d,...,z**? We could declare that each irreducible entity is its own singleton. Then

{a} =a, {b}=b, ..., {z}=z.

What about other collections?

Well {**a,b**} is fine. You can now get a multiplicity by collections of subsets of {**a,b,c,...,z**} but no fancy stuff. *When singletons are equal to their contents,*

$$\{A\} = A,$$

the infinity of sets formed from each individual collapses to the individual.

$$\{a,\{a\}\} = \{a,a\} = \{a\} = a$$

The entire halo surrounding **a** is collapsed to **a** itself. Now there is no bootstrapping to infinity. A finite collection will only generate a finite collection. It will generate $2^{\{N\}}$ sets from **N** individuals. From a perceptual physical point of view it makes sense to collapse the singletons of individuals so that

{**I**} = **I** for each individual **I**.

We have arrived at what, at first sight, seems a magnificent idea! Find the irreducible atoms of the world. Realize that these atoms are inherently self-referential cybernetic entities. Endow them with set-theoretic self-reference in the form of the collapse of their singletons. Let the world be generated by these entities! Will there be objections?

Yes, there will be objections. The major objection is that no one has ever seen such a "world atom." Such entities have not been seen in science and they have not been seen in mathematics. When the entities that compose your world are not truly fundamental, then it is not easy to call them self-referential in the sense of collapsed singletons.

But, what about mathematics? Surely there are atomic entities in mathematics?

Why is it that mathematicians do not commonly identify an individual (like a point **P**) and its singleton set **{P}**? The point in geometry can be a complex structure. The point in geometry can itself be a set. For example, if **P** is a point in the two dimensional plane, then we commonly model **P** with coordinates, and so **P** is an ordered pair

P = (x,y)

where **x** and **y** are real numbers.

What is an ordered pair?
Ordered pairs **(a,b)** are intended to have the property that **(a,b) = (c,d)** if and only if **a=c** and **b=d**. Furthermore, one wants a set theoretic definition of an ordered pair. *One wants a set-theoretic definition of every mathematical entity.*

An ordered pair **(x,y)** is by definition the following set

(x,y) = {{x}, {x,y}}.

The definition is due to Norbert Weiner and to Kasimir Kuratowski. (See Kelley, 1960, p. 78.) *The importance of the definition is that the concept of ordered pair can be expressed fully in set theory.*

Spaces made of coordinate points, such as the plane, can be expressed using only set theory. This definition of ordered pair works very well, acting to discriminate the roles of **x** and **y** in the pair.

With this definition of ordered pair, we can see why mathematicians do not want to identify singletons with their members. Consider that we now have defined

(x,x) = {{x},{x,x}} = {{x},{x}} = {{x}}.

This singleton tells us that we are dealing with the point **(x,x)** in the plane. Even if it is difficult to assign a meaning to **{x}**, we have a geometric interpretation for **{{x}}**.

If singletons are identified with their members, then the diagonal points **(x,x)**, **(x,x,x)**, **(x,x,x,x)**,...will all be identified with **x** itself. This would collapse the world of Cartesian geometry.

So you see, the logicians win, and mathematicians and geometers concede that singleton sets should be distinct from their members.

IV. David Lewis on Singletons

In his book *Parts and Wholes* the philosopher David Lewis (1991) has the following things to say about singletons:

After a time, the unfortunate student is told that some classes—the singletons—have only a single member. Here is just cause for student protest, if ever there was one.... he has just one single thing, the element, and he has another single thing, the singleton, and nothing he was told gives him the slightest guidance about what one thing has to do with the other.(p. 29)

I don't say that classes are in space and time. I don't say that they aren't. I say we're in the sad fix that we haven't a clue whether they are or whether they aren't.(p. 33)

Singletons, and therefore all classes are profoundly mysterious. Mysteries are an onerous burden. Should we therefore dump the burden by dumping all classes? If classes do not exist, we needn't puzzle over their mysterious nature. If we renounce classes, we are set free. (p. 57, Section 2.8)

No; for set theory pervades modern mathematics. some special branches and some special styles of mathematics can perhaps do without., but most of mathematics is into set theory up to its ears. If there are no classes, then there are no Dedekind cuts, there are no homeomorphisms, there are no complemented lattices, there are no probability distributions,... For all these things are standardly defined as one or another sort of class. If there are no classes, then our mathematics textbooks are works of fiction, full of false "theorems." Renouncing classes means rejecting mathematics. That will not do. Mathematics is an established, going concern. Philosophy is as shaky as can be. To reject mathematics for philosophical reasons would be absurd. If we philosophers are sorely puzzled by the classes that constitute mathematical reality, that's our problem. We shouldn't expect mathematics to go away to make our life easier. Even if we reject mathematics gently—explaining how it can be a most useful fiction, "good without being true"—we still reject it, and that's still absurd. Even if we hold onto some mutilated fragments of mathematics that can be reconstructed without classes, if we reject the bulk of mathematics, that's still absurd

  That's not an argument, I know. Rather, I'm moved to laughter at the thought of how *presumptuous* it would be to reject mathematics for philosophical reasons. How *you* like the job of telling mathematicians that they must change their ways, and abjure countless errors, now that *philosophy* has discovered that there are no classes? Can you tell them with a straight face, to follow philosophical argument wherever it may lead? If they challenge your credentials, will you boast of philosophy's other great discoveries: that motion is impossible, that a Being that which no greater can be conceived cannot be conceived not to exist, that it is unthinkable that anything exists outside the mind, that time is unreal, that no theory has ever been made at all probable by evidence (but on the other hand that an empirically ideal theory cannot possibly be false), that it is a wide-open scientific question whether anyone has ever believed anything, and so on and on, *ad nauseam*?

  Not me! And so I have to say, gritting my teeth, that somehow, I know not how, we do understand what it means to speak of singletons. And somehow we know that ordinary things have singletons, and singletons have singletons, and fusions of singletons sometimes have singletons. We know even that singletons comprise the predominant part of Reality.(pp. 58-59)

V. Notes on Physical Reality

The very short notes that follow are meant to examine the difference between worlds where singletons are distinct from their members and worlds where this is not so. I suggest that this is very much like the difference between the world of our concepts and the physical world. It is in the conceptual world that the difference between the singleton and its member occurs. Without this difference we are in the "purely physical" world.

  The parallel is very suggestive, particularly in regard to the quantum mechanical relation of observers and physical realities. In that quantum world, there is an essential collapse in the deterministic mathematics of the model whenever an observation occurs. This is a collapse from possibility to actuality. It is very much like the collapse of conceptual worlds that occurs as we release the distinction between a singleton and its member.

It is not the purpose of this essay to create the details of this analogy. We present it here as a seed idea.

1. The act of collapsing singletons as in $\{P\} = P$, returns one to the ground of perception where meaning and measurement coincide.

2. The empty set { } is distinct from the physical.

3. $\{\{\{\{...\}\}\}\} = J$ with $J = \{J\}$ is obtained both from the void and from the physical, by tunnelling from different sides. From the void we take a limit to infinity:

$\{\}$
$\{\{\}\}$
$\{\{\{\}\}\}$
$\{\{\{\{\}\}\}\}$
$\{\{\{\{\{\}\}\}\}\}$
...
$\{\{\{\{\{\{\{\{\{\{\{\{...\}\}\}\}\}\}\}\}\}\}\}\} = J$
$\{J\} = J$

From the physical, we start with the collapse of the singleton
$P = \{P\}$. There is no need for limits or for the concept of infinity (in the physical realm).

4. If $\{P\}$ and P are distinct then the object P is surrounded by, indeed replaced by, an infinite sea of possibilities. This sea of possibilities collapses via $P=\{P\}$ when we observe the object. The pattern of this collapse is a precursor to the collapse of the wave function in quantum mechanics. In quantum mechanics the wave function is a catalogue of all possibilities for the given physical situation. Observation collapses the wave function to an actuality.

5. We define an *observational physical reality*, to be a domain where such a collapse must occur in the event of an observation.

VI. Epilogue

This column has been concerned with the question of the emergence of multiplicity from unity, and we have seen how this idea appears in set theory, where infinite multiplicities emerge from emptiness. The keystone of this notion is the formation of the empty set { }, and the continued use of singleton sets such as {{ }} to produce multiplicities. In fact the singleton **1** = {{ }} shows the strangeness of set theory's construction of **ONE**. For {{ }} represents **ONE** in set theory, and yet {{ }} requires two steps from the void, which is surely the original **ONE**. Each singleton {**P**} is itself a unity, and yet seems to decompose into its member, and the act of collection that produced it.

Clouds of possibility, generated by the acts of set formation, surround any physical object. This is a fruitful place for the exploration of foundations of physical theory, mathematics and cybernetics.

References

Cantor, G. (1941). *Contributions to the founding of the theory of transfinite numbers.* Chicago: Open Court Publishing Company. (Cantor's original papers appeared in *Mathematicshes Annalen* in 1895 and 1897).
Kelley, J.L. (1960). *Introduction to Modern Algebra.* New York: Van Nostrand.
Lewis, D. (1991). *Parts and Wholes.* Oxford: Basil Blackwell Ltd.

Cybernetics And Human Knowing. Vol. 12, nos. 1-2, pp. 168-174

ASC
American Society for Cybernetics
a society for the art and
science of human understanding

Gregory Bateson, Heterarchies, and the Topology of Recursion

Peter Harries-Jones[1]

There is a generalized history circulating on the Internet and in academic papers that Gregory Bateson was so wedded to first-order cybernetics that he did not fully appreciate the significance of Spencer Brown and the recursive logic that Spencer Brown introduced. It therefore fell upon Francisco Varela and Humberto Maturana to take up the logical aspects of recursive forms in their conceptualization of autopoiesis, and make the big leap forward. Today, Maturana and Varela are often cited as the originators of the recursive view. In a sense this is correct. Varela did take up the mathematics of recursive forms over many years and Bateson did not. But the belief that they won the debate with Bateson over recursion (Dell, 1985; Capra, 1996) is suspect. This column will take the position that at minimum, the actual situation is far more complex, moreover there are good reasons for Bateson's hesitancy in embracing the mathematics of recursion.

The ASC Meeting, Toronto.

The many fascinations of G. Spencer Brown's *Laws of Form,* his mathematics of recursion, are still apparent 35 years after initial publication. The most recent annual meeting of the American Society for Cybernetics held in Toronto in August heard Lou Kauffman review both evidence for, and the grounds for refutation, in a session that lasted two hours and could have easily gone on for another two. Spencer Brown's longevity is undoubtedly due to his claims, and the timing of them. They were monumental. *Laws of Form* "modestly" claimed that the proofs of Bertrand Russell's Theory of Types, a special rule disallowing vicious paradoxes to occur in Boolean algebra, were unnecessary. Another calculus, his own, could permit self-referential paradoxes that had been prohibited and discarded in the Theory of Types. Further,

---

1. Dept. of Anthropology, York University, Ontario. Email: peterhj@yorku.ca

Spencer Brown's Calculus of Indications, permitting recursions, would provide a more perfect match between logic, arithmetic and praxis among electrical engineers. His timing was perfect. Questions about electrical circuits that re-entered themselves were perplexities for engineers with Ph.D's in 1973. Ten years later the first personal computers were already on sale. Computer programmers dealt with interactive loops as a matter of course. The questions of how many loops within loops could be permitted within a computer programme without it crashing, and how to configure re-entry had moved from being theoretical, logical issues of algebra and mathematics to being a simple issue of technique.

Kauffman, in his presentation to the ASC, reiterated the major objections to the calculus of indications. It remains too close to classical set theory; unlike, for example, fuzzy set theory. It can be applied only in certain instances, when there is a clear cut case of "either/or" (i.e., a perfect distinction between the *either* and the *or* exists). Undoubtedly this is possible in a wide range of phenomena, yet, Kauffman noted, there are countless examples, where a difference does not make a distinction—in the language of Spencer Brown, difference does not cleave a space. In such instances his calculus of marked and unmarked states would not apply. Simple examples of these would be perceptual cues with respect to the foreground and background of a gestalt. A more complex example would be the Mobius strip where the distinction lies in the form, but the form of the distinction does not cleave a space; it is not, in that respect, distinct.

Most examples where distinctions are apparent and do cleave space occur with thing-like objects. By contrast, difference does not necessarily make a distinction in social relations. Social relations of dominance and submission permit clear differences in relationships, but such relationships often derive from interactions that are complementary to each other. Significantly, examples of complementarity in relational differences can provide excellent examples of patterns of feedback. It was upon this observation that Bateson and his colleagues in Palo Alto built their systemic family therapy. As therapy, they inserted Russell's Theory of Types in order to get their client/patients to draw appropriate distinctions about complementarity, distinctions that would otherwise not be discernible in their interactive patterns of feedback.

Bateson approached recursiveness through Russell's ladder of types. This, he recognized in letters to his critics, had its slippery edges, though he also pointed out that his hierarchy was not the typical hierarchy of either mathematics, nor of any organisation of control, nor of power hierarchies (Harries-Jones, 1995). He made one major modification to the notion of hierarchy: Bateson's hierarchy of types focussed upon relations that exist between levels of a hierarchy. So while Russell's logical typing imposed a higher, more inclusive meta-level, on a lower level, Bateson's "meta-context" gives rise to a *logic of in-between*. It also embraces meaning. The recursive logic of in-between requires oscillation between two dimensions, context and meta-context, and the meaning of an event emerges from this oscillation. This version provides better psychological correspondence to psychological circularities than either the simple descriptive correspondences of wholes and parts in mathematical set theory or the strict re-ordering which Russell's logical types of class and its members proposes (Neuman, 2004).

Recursion: Digital, Analogue or Both?

Bateson was primarily interested in social, animal, interspecies and ecological relations patterned in analogical rather than digital codes. He held to the position that for meaning to arise, whether it be evolutionary meaning, cognitive meaning or social meaning, both digital and analogical codes had to be present; but while both codes were evidently required, the one could not be reduced to another. As is evident from the AUM transcripts (posted on the Internet)[1] Spencer Brown's purported discovery of the mathematics of recursive forms appeared to be viable only in situations coded digitally. Therefore, the mathematics and the logic thereof had limited benefits for Bateson. On the other hand, he was keenly interested in any intellectual advance affecting formal aspects of circularity or recursiveness and the Spencer Brown calculus seemed to yield understanding of an aspect of feedback processes which he (Bateson) had not yet undertaken.   To quote him:

> To continue my sketch of [my] epistemology...the next point is recursiveness. Here there seem to be two species of recursiveness, of somewhat different nature, of which the first goes back to Norbert Wiener and is well known, the "feedback" that is perhaps the best-known feature of the whole cybernetic syndrome....The second type of recursiveness has been proposed by Varela and Maturana. These mathematicians discuss the case in which some property of a whole is fed back into the system, producing a somewhat different type of recursiveness, for which Varela has worked out the formalisms. We live in a universe in which causal trains endure, survive through time, only if they are recursive. They "survive"—i.e., literally live upon themselves—and some survive longer than others. If our explanations or our understanding of the universe is in some sense to match that universe, or model it, and if the universe is recursive, then our explanations and our logics must also be fundamentally recursive. (Brockman, 2004)

Spencer Brown gave inspiration to those who could perhaps reveal how a property of the whole could feedback into its parts. Varela went on to elaborate the Calculus of Indications, by showing how the mark of re-entry could be taken as a third arithmetic value, so that conditions of self-reference could be generated through a three valued logic. Subsequently dissatisfied with this approach, Varela went on to examine all expressions possible in Spencer Brown's calculus in terms of the way in which one form was included within another. In other words, Varela created a mathematics, a lattice, in which whole to part transitions are possible.[2]

Nevertheless, a lattice in the mathematical form of trees and networks to represent actual connections and relations among elements in a system is a highly truncated (pun intended) way to exhibit the ebb and flow of feedback in natural relations and of recursive forms in general. I myself discovered this as early as 1966 when I was

1.   The AUM (American University of Masters) Conference in 1973 was an important introduction of Spencer Brown's ideas to North America. [John Brockman recalls his initial meeting with Bateson at that conference in an article on the Internet written in honour of the Bateson centennial.]

among a group of anthropologists making the first attempts in the discipline to render connections and relations in human relations through nodes and paths in directed graphs. The limitations of treating actual social relations in this manner (which would take an article in itself to describe), are formidable. Further problems lie in the lack of a means in digraph analysis through which the key problem of *meaning* underlying self and other in a social relationship can be addressed.[1]

The primary organization of living systems relies upon sensing differences and responding to these differences in terms of their own "self-organization." In a recent article, McNeil asks the question of whether iterations of self-reference in computer algorithms actually demonstrate "self-ness." Or does the attribution of self-reference simply hide an otherness of technical machinations that are hidden in re-enterable programming procedures? If the latter is the case then the whole notion of self in self-organization is at stake in all computer simulations. Any model of self-organization must clearly distinguish its own context of self from other in generating order. This requires an ability to specify self or other in meaningful contexts of repetition, reverberation, re-volution and rotation, all aspects of feedback, through other topologies (McNeil, 2004).

Finding a Suitable Topology for Heterarchy

The more Bateson moved into ecological orders of his "ecology of mind" the less a single tree-like hierarchy seemed to be appropriate to depict the many recursions of an ecological order. For many years he had the idea of depicting circularity in terms of oscillations in *heterarchical ordering,* an idea of multi-level order first developed by his friend, the well known cyberneticist, Warren McCulloch. McCulloch suggested in his classic paper on the topology of human nervous nets (McCulloch, 1965, pp. 40-45) that the topology of nervous nets exhibit multiple hierarchies occurring among the synapses of the nervous system which are, in turn connected through recursive reverberation. This renders the relation between any nervous input and any outcome from nervous activity highly non-linear and—in terms of any linear expression— highly indeterminate. McCulloch admitted that he could not proceed much beyond this suggestion because the mathematics of his time could not deal with so profound a non-linear phenomenon. McCulloch's problem, a lack of a non-linear mathematics

---

2. Varela's lattice exhibits a complementarity between the system plus its environment, as a unity with given properties, the internal constitution of a system where environment is considered merely as a background source of perturbations. The complementarity built into Varela's mathematics permits a flip from one complementary state to another as the observer moves through levels of a hierarchy (Goguen & Varela, 1979, quoted in Mingers, 1995, p. 59). One could well say that Goguen and Varela have attempted to depict Bateson's view of the natural world (holism) as complementary to a normal science view of reductionism.

1. In effect, the construction of a loop-free pointed graph of reachable elements substitutes density patterns for interactive looping or feedback among people, but this mathematical representation of reachability records only one dimension of actual patterns of communication, which are inevitably reciprocal and which are, in Bateson mode, generated through periods of actual interaction. No matter how sophisticated an algorithm of multiple values I had worked out, a one-dimensional mapping cannot replace a dialogical phenomenon. No linear mapping would be thick enough to accomplish this.

was solved with the rise of a computer technology. Yet problems associat[ing] heterarchy with meaning, still remained.

Feedback has circularity as its central process, though as Bateson pointed out, circularity did not mean a precise circle in which events repeat themselves in the same circular path. All living forms reproduce and in doing so re-enter the domain of their forebears. These are recursive events, but in the case of species reproduction at species level, the flow and ebb of species formation over evolutionary time means that species never step into the precise spot in the same stream twice-over. The arrow of time intervenes. A truly circular path would preclude emergence of new forms. Thus Bateson indicated that a characteristic form or topology that captures the recursiveness of both biological form and human cultural and historical experience, is that of a spiral, a circularity that rotates in time. *Spiral* was always a metaphor, rather than an operational framework in Bateson's epistemology because he was unable to find a topological order of spirals that embrace meaning. On one occasion, as Brockman mentions, he gave a subjective appraisal of how a torus might suffice:

> A smoke ring is, literally and etymologically, introverted. It is endlessly turning upon itself, a torus, a doughnut, spinning on the axis of the circular cylinder that is the doughnut. And this turning upon its own in-turned axis is what gives separable existence to the smoke ring. It is, after all, made of nothing but air marked with a little smoke. It is of the same substance as its "environment." But it has duration and location and a certain degree of separation by virtue of its in-turned motion. In a sense, the smoke ring stands as a very primitive, oversimplified paradigm for all recursive systems that contain the beginnings of self-reference, or, shall we say, selfhood.
>
> But if you ask me, "Do you feel like a smoke ring all the time?" of course my answer is no. Only at very brief moments, in flashes of awareness, am I that realistic. (Bateson quoted in Brockman, 2004.).

McNeil states is that there has yet to be a definitive study by topologists of the topology of meaning. For all their vocabulary of closed surfaces, and the way that their vocabulary of connectedness, closeness, and relative invariance is rich in significance for a whole range of disciplines, topologists are loath to give any examples that can be taken up outside the world of other topology. Even if the question of meaning is taken up, its study continues to be attached to another type of topology, that of the sphere. Spheres fit closely with the western tradition of rationality, that is to say, they have an orientable surface (i.e., they set apart an inside and an outside); they have inherent symmetry; and they are simply, rather than complexly, connected. In a sphere, that is to say, the only kind of shortest line that can be drawn between two points is an arc of a circle. The ultimate topological incapacity of a sphere, McNeil argues, is that it has no condition permitting a second-order circularity, and which in the form of a second-order circularity is a minimal condition for some sort of dialectics of meaning to occur. However, a torus is complexly connected, and does permit second order circularities. Since the topology of a torus is one of an orthagonal coupling between annular and meridial circularities, the topological form of a torus permits not only possibilities for a dialectic of meaning but also for a heterarchical order to appear in a life-like topology that no tree-and-network algorithm could possibly emulate.

Torus topology remains uninvestigated in these dimensions but Bateson's prudence in avoiding a whole- hearted embrace of *Laws of Form* seems therefore, to have been justified, although he was unable to find a topological form that would enable him to pursue his ideas. And while he supported both Varela's pursuit of mathematical approaches to recursion and that of Maturana, he seemed to become worried by the stringent structuralism that appears in Maturana's writing which seemed to push problems of meaning to the periphery.

Perhaps I am pushing my own inferences too far, but some passages in *Angel's Fear*, Bateson's posthumous publication, seem to be a gentle rebuttal of Maturana's position. Maturana worked systematically through the proposition of whole, rather than part, as causal mechanism. In doing so he held that structure-determined systems are perfect in the sense that they never make mistakes; they always behave according to their structure. It is only because a system behaves according to the autonomous dictates of its own structure that it can be out of phase with its environment and make what we call *mistakes* in the first place (Dell, 1985, p. 11).

Bateson had no difficulties with Maturana's discussion of process but his appraisal of structure is somewhat different. The structure we devise of any system is incomplete and conspicuously full of holes. That incompleteness which enters into the organism's relations that we are trying to describe, the structure of relations gained from outside observation, also appears in every aspect of the organism's own structural information (i.e., its interrelated aggregate of messages in the media in which it participates). This is why, unlike the physical world, both error and pathology are possible: the map always differs from the territory. Yet structure is all that we can know, the reality of that which is (Bateson & Bateson, 1987, pp. 151-166).

Is that map a doughnut? And the structure? *Ceci n'est pas une pipe.*

REFERENCES

American University of Masters. 1973. [Transcripts of the AUM Conference Session Three, Tuesday Morning, March 20, 1973. Online. Retrieved January 15, 2005 from http://www.lawsofform.org/aum/

Bateson, G. & Bateson, M. C. (1987). *Angels fear: Towards an epistemology of the sacred.* New York: Macmillan Publishing Company.

Brockman, J. (2004). Gregory Bateson: The centennial. Retrieved January 15, 2005 from http://www.edge.org/3rd_culture/bateson04_index.html/

Capra, F. (1996). *The web of life.* New York: Anchor Doubleday.

Dell, P. F. 1985. Understanding Bateson and Maturana: Toward a biological foundation for the social sciences. *Journal of Marital and Family Therapy, 11* (1), 1-21,139-141.

Goguen, J., & Varela, F. (1979). Systems and distinctions: Duality and complementarity. *International Journal of General Systems, 5,* 31-43.

Harries-Jones, P. (1995). *A recursive vision: Gregory Bateson and ecological understanding.* Toronto: Toronto University Press.

Harries-Jones, P. (2004). Editorial: In celebration of Gregory Bateson's centennial. *S.E.E.D Journal* 4(1), March 2004. [Retrieved January 15, 2005 from http://www.library.utoronto.ca/see/pages/SEED%20journal%20library.html]

McCulloch, W. (1956). A Heterarchy of Values Determined by the Topology of Nervous Nets. In *Embodiments of mind* (pp. 40-45). Cambridge: The M.I T. Press.

McNeil, D. H. (2004). What's going on with the topology of recursion *S.E.E.D Journal* 4(1). March 2004, p.2-37. [Retrieved January 15, 2005 from http://www.library.utoronto.ca/see/pages/SEED%20journal%20library.html]

Mingers, J. (1995). *Self-producing systems: Implications and applications of autopoiesis.* New York: Plenum Press.

Neuman, Y. (2004). *Mirrors mirrored: Is that all there is?* S.E.E.D Journal 4:(1). March 2004, p.58-69 [Retrieved, January 15, 2005 from http://www.library.utoronto.ca/see/pages/SEED%20journal%20library.html]
Spencer Brown, G. (1969). *Laws of form.* London: George Allen and Unwin.

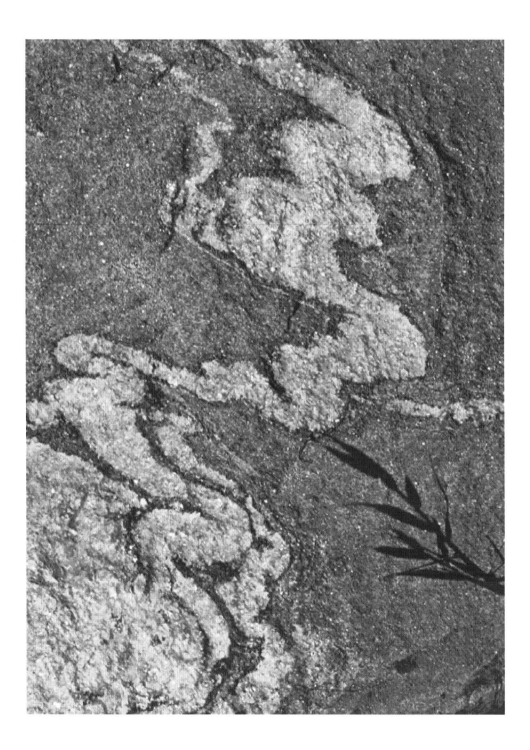

Cybernetics And Human Knowing. Vol. 12, nos. 1-2, pp. 175-178

International Encyclopaedia of Systems and Cybernetics, second edition[1]
Edited by Charles François

Ranulph Glanville[2]

The first edition of Charles François' Master Work, "International Encyclopaedia of Systems and Cybernetics," was published in 1997. I reviewed it in this Journal in 1999 (Glanville, 1999). The first edition was itself an extension of an earlier publication with 475 entries, *Diccionario de Teoria de Sistemas y Cybernética.*

The essence of my review of the first edition was to express thanks for that enormous and remarkable work: a true labour of love and a vital element in the development of cybernetics and systems. It is an astonishing achievement of one man working doggedly and diligently with affection and respect for his work area, studying texts in many languages and from many different cultures: a task that perhaps only François could undertake. I wrote my review in the context of an exploration of the notion and origin of the encyclopaedia and how that forms a view of knowledge that is built into it.

Now there is a new, second edition which I have been invited to review. And the inevitable question is what can I review (what is there to write about)?

New?

Let me start by talking about what's new.

Firstly, we now have two volumes. These volumes are slightly thinner than the single volume of the first edition, and the type is spaced more generously giving a more pleasant and much easier to read appearance. This is enhanced by the choice of paper: a polished and bleached paper rather than the possibly more ecologically correct original. (Further indications of the scale of the Encyclopaedia are the 61 pages of bibliography, including an almanac of journals; and 13 pages of index people referred to, listed in three columns per page!) We too easily ignore the importance of the physical appearance—the presence—of a book. The first edition was, in retrospect, difficult to read because of the density of the type and the paper quality. This failing has been corrected.

Secondly, there is a rounding and enriching in the entries. I'm just as much an individual user as any other, and I think this is a moment for me to talk from an explicitly personal point of view. It's hard to consider the whole Encyclopaedia, so

1. 741pp, published in 2004 by K.G. Saur, Munich; price €350.00
2. CybernEthics Research, Southsea, UK. E-mail: ranulph@glanville.co.uk

(for my sample) I have dipped into areas that I'm most interested in (and, paradoxically, probably least need the Encyclopaedia for!) to sample the improvements in this second edition.

There is, for instance, an extensive entry on *Deconstruction* in the new edition, missing in the first edition. What is interesting about this entry is that it specifically shows the extensive similarities between *deconstruction* and *second order cybernetics* (which are pretty much contemporaneous), a link often claimed by cyberneticians but generally ignored.

The entry on *Objectivity* has also been expanded to integrate the constructivist and second-order cybernetic perspectives. This emphasises the link with the Encyclopaedia's entry on *Ontological skepticism*, giving a historical continuity while not reducing the radical content of these points of view.

Equally, the entry on the *Observer* is improved by implicitly linking the role of the observer to that of the controller and by strengthening the connection with criteria of validation and selection that even classical observers use. However, the (immediately preceding) entry on *Observational language* remains unchanged: an already strong entry which (as with the entry on *Deconstruction*) makes links between cybernetic thought and French philosophy during the last half of the Twentieth Century (in this case, Foucault).

The entry on the *Black Box*, which might perhaps be considered as a basic cybernetic method (there is a separate entry on *Black Box method*) has been expanded, too, to reflect *second-order cybernetic* understandings of *observing*. Thus, the actuality of the purported contents of the Black Box are allowed to be unknown and unknowable. This reflects the transition of our understanding of the Black Box from being the mechanistic device that was used by, for example, B.F. Skinner, to a means for making descriptions. Without this transition, several earlier cybernetic luminaries would have remained deeply unhappy with the notion. In particular, I remember the reaction of Sir Geoffrey Vickers to the early Black Box notion. He would have been much happier with the revised entry in this edition.

Thirdly, I should mention the introduction. In the second edition of the encyclopaedia, there is a new introduction to the (original) introduction in which François talks about his intentions in developing the Encyclopaedia. This provides a lovely example of how this work can sustain individual learning: even the editor is learning! As to the original introduction: just read it! It is, amongst other things, a valuable characterisation of cybernetics and systems.

Improvement?

Is this new edition an improvement? The answer must be an emphatic yes. The first edition was magnificent, but there were gaps and, occasionally, imbalances and omissions of representation that resulted from too narrow a view. Understand, this is not intended as an attack of any form on François: Probably nobody else could have managed the initial task so well.[3] But what the first edition gave us, as added value, was a catalyst: a catalyst to enrich. Many people wrote in with suggestions for areas that they felt were either missing or inadequately discussed, and in the seven years between editions François has evaluated and then incorporated these suggestions. This both enriches the material covered (requiring, an mentioned, two volumes and an increase of 75% from 423 to 741 pages, albeit some of this results from the improved layout), and reflects the cybernetic origins of the work, for now it is explicitly a product of learning, albeit an unusual, collaborative type of learning.

It has also acquired an editorial board. This is an important step by François that ensures the continuation of the Encyclopaedia. (François recently celebrated his 80th birthday, marked by the publication of a festschrift edited by his friends and colleagues Ernesto Grün and Eduardo del Caño (2003). While he shows no evidence of slowing down, succession is an important and long term concern, ignored at peril.) The editorial board and the moves to install a new editor inform us that the Encyclopaedia is here to stay and will provide a continuing opportunity for group learning among cyberneticians and systems scientists. My personal communication with the editor confirms these points.

Buying?

Should you buy the Encyclopaedia? And who would you be, who might buy it?

At €350, this is probably not within the budget of most individuals, which is a shame. For this is a wonderful research tool. But certainly it is, I believe, indispensable for all organisations—universities, companies, governments, research outfits—that work with cybernetics and systems, not only for what it says, but also for what it opens up: the enormous range of sources (many from the non-English speaking world); and the variety of interpretations that are acknowledged. In a sense many entries are written as mini-theses in which the strand of ideas and the debate between these ideas is used to provide a rich overview and, sometimes, a well argued (and surprising) resolution.

It is to be hoped that one day (soon) this work will appear on the web. This medium is already implicit in the Encyclopaedia where bold text is used to show related entries that the reader may link to (hyperlinks in print) and where a classification system partitions entries in an alternative way to alphabetic sequence. A web version might make it easier for individuals to afford the Encyclopaedia. It would certainly make the already implicit process of moving across references easier, although there is something rather satisfying about leafing through pages and flicking back and forwards, comparing. And it would make the role of the Encyclopaedia as a collaborative effort in constant expansion ever easier and more responsive. If the editors of the *Oxford Dictionary of the English Language* have decided this is the way forward, it would be a pity if the Encyclopaedia of the subject that has a large

---

3. I should emphasise that, during the Encyclopaedia project, François has frequently spoken of it at conferences and has always invited help in building it. So the first edition is not quite such a solo effort, and the change in collaboration I point to in the second edition is not as dramatic, as I paint it.

responsibility for the development of the means that make this possible were not to follow the same path—the path it had itself made possible!

And what else might be added? To my mind, the one single big omission is people. Of course, some will argue that an Encyclopaedia is not a place for people but for the contents of its subject. However, cybernetics (in particular) is interested in the included observer: to be true to its subject, then, the Encyclopaedia should include material on the authors cited, as well as material from those authors. I think I would find even greater use for the Encyclopaedia if it contained material such as is found on the ISSS site in the luminaries section.

Meanwhile, we continue to owe Charles François an enormous debt of gratitude for what he has inaugurated and achieved, and special thinks for caring enough about this as an endeavour in cybernetics and systems to make sure of a succession. Not all those who have made important and significant contributions have cared to place the future of the subject above their own need for adulation.

References

Glanville, R. (1999). A (Cybernetic) Musing: Encyclopaedias and the Form of Knowing. A Celebration of Charles François' 'International Encyclopaedia of Systems and Cybernetics: a Sort of Self-Referential Work of Reference.' *Cybernetics and Human Knowing, 6*(1)
Grün, E., and Caño, E. del, (Eds.). (2003). *Ensayos sobre Sistémica y Cybernética*. Buenos Aires: Editorial Dunken

ISA - International Sociological Association
RESEARCH COMMITTEE 51 ON SOCIOCYBERNETICS
Honorary Presidents: Walter Buckley, USA; Felix Geyer, The Netherlands

World Congress
Programme Coordinator:
Karl-Heinz Simon
University of Kassel - CESR,
Germany
Fax: +49 561 804 7266
simon@usf.uni-kassel.de

President:

Bernd R. Hornung
University of Marburg,
Germany
Fax: +49 6421-286-6572
hornung@med.uni-marburg.de

Secretary:

Richard E. Lee
Fernand Braudel Center
SUNY-Binghamton, USA
Fax: +1 607-777-4315
rlee@binghamton.edu

XVIth World Congress of Sociology
THE QUALITY OF SOCIAL EXISTENCE IN A GLOBALISING WORLD
Durban, South Africa, July 23-29, 2006

1st Call for Papers

CONGRESS THEME:

Within the overall theme of the XVIth World Congress of Sociology—the great quadrennial event of international sociology where more than 50 Research Committees and several Working Groups and Ad Hoc Groups will organize a total of well over 700 sessions in different fields of sociology—RC 51 will organize up to 16 sessions on **Sociocybernetics.**

SESSION TOPICS:

At this point the following topics for sessions were proposed and accepted. At an appropriate time a reorganization may be necessary depending on the papers which will actually be proposed.

Session 1
Joint Session RC51 and RC16 Sociological Theory
Sociology and Systems Theory
Organizers: Jeffrey Alexander, Yale University, USA, jeffrey.alexander@yale.edu and Raf Vanderstraeten, University of Bielefeld, Germany, raf.vanderstraeten@uni-bielefeld.de
Session 2
Joint Session RC51 and RC33 Logic and Methodology
Organizers: Cor van Dijkum, Utrecht University, The Netherlands, C.vanDijkum@fss.uu.nl and Hans van der Zouwen, Free University Amsterdam, The Netherlands, J.van.der.Zouwen@fsw.vu.nl
Session 3
French Language Session on
Rétroactions déstabilisatrices en géopolitique - Destabilizing Feedbacks in Geopolitics
Organizer: Marie-Noëlle Sarget, École des Hautes Études en Sciences Sociales, Paris, France, sarget@atacama.ehess.fr

Session 4

Spanish Language Session on

Capital social y redes sociales: El "pegamento" del desarrollo social—Social Capital and Social Networks: The "Glue" of Social Development and Welfare

Organizers: Chaime Marcuello-Servós, Universidad de Zaragoza, Spain, chaime@unizar.es, Dario Menanteau-Horta, University of Minnesota, USA, dmenante@umn.edu and Juan D. Gomez Quintero, Universidad de Zaragoza, Spain

Session 5

Portuguese Language Session on

Igualdade e desigualdade: Género, economica e cidadania—Uma aborgadcm sociocibcrnética

Equality and Inequality: Gender, Economy and Citizenship—A Sociocybernetic Approach

Organizer: Manuel Lisboa, Universidade Nova de Lisboa, Portugal, m.lisboa@fcsh.unl.pt

Session 6

Causes and Consequences of Innovation: Systemic Approaches

Organizers: Matjaz Mulej, University of Maribor, Slovenia, mulej@uni-mb.si and Eva Buchinger, ARC Systems Research, Austria, eva.buchinger@arcs.ac.at

Session 7

The System of Mass Media and Social Transformation

Organizers: Juan Miguel Aguado, Universidad de Murcia, Spain, jmaguado@um.es, and Vessela Misheva, Uppsala University, Sweden, Vessela.Misheva@soc.uu.se

Session 8

Communication and Ethics or Sociocybernetics and Cyberethics

Organizers: Arne Collen, Saybrook Graduate School, USA, acollen@saybrook.edu and Vessela Misheva, Uppsala University, Sweden, Vessela.Misheva@soc.uu.se

Session 9

Precursors of Sociocybernetics: Systemic Thinking in the History of the Social Sciences

Organizer: Pavel O. Luksha, Russia, bowin@mail.ru

Session 10

Emergence in Social Systems and Sociocybernetic Theory

Organizer: Bernd R. Hornung, Marburg University, Germany, hornung@med.uni-marburg.de

Session 11

The Concept of Self-reference in Theories of Information Society

Organizer: Czeslaw Mesjasz, Cracow University of Economics, Poland, mesjaszc@ae.krakow.pl

Session 12

Analyzing and Estimating Feedback Relationships in Empirical and Simulation Studies

Organizers: Han Oud, Radboud University Nijmegen, The Netherlands, j.oud@pwo.ru.nl, and Cor van Dijkum, Utrecht University, The Netherlands, C.vanDijkum@fss.uu.nl

Session 13

Complex Societal Problems and Issues

Organizer: Dorien J. DeTombe, International, Euro & Dutch Research Group Complex Societal Problems & Issues, The Netherlands, DeTombe@lri.jur.uva.nl

Session 14

Sociocybernetics of Emotions

Organizers: Christian von Scheve, University of Hamburg and ZiF University of Bielefeld, Germany, xscheve@informatik.uni-hamburg.de, and Bernd R. Hornung, Marburg University, Germany, hornung@med.uni-marburg.de

Session 15

Music in the Context of African Society

Organizer: Mario Vieira de Carvalho, Universidade Nova de Lisboa, Portugal, mvc@mail.telepac.pt

Session 16

Participatory Sustainable Development in Rural Areas and the Contribution of Systems Theory

Organizer: Philippos Nicolopoulos, University of Crete and University of Indianapolis - Athens Campus, Greece, nikolop@groovy.gr

MORE INFORMATION:

For more details please consult the web at http://www.ucm.es/info/isa/congress2006/rc/rc51_durban.htm A short description of the contents and objectives of each session is available on the website.Moreover, several pre-congress tutorials will possibly be organized. Please regularly consult our website

CONDITIONS OF PARTICIPATION:

For presenting a paper, membership both of RC 51 and of ISA is mandatory. Both memberships can be obtained through the website of the ISA. The membership form for RC 51 is also available at our website: http://www.unizar.es/sociocyberneticsnewmembers.html.

ABSTRACTS AND THE REVIEW PROCESS:

Abstracts for papers should be 500 to 1000 words detailed abstracts for the review process and the definite assignment to a particular session. At a later point in time 250 words regular abstracts are needed for publication on the Internet by ISA. All abstracts should be sent to the RC 51 World Congress Programme Coordinator. On the basis of the abstracts the papers will be assigned either to the session requested by the author or to an appropriate session selected by the Programme Coordinator in consultation with the respective session organizer. In either case the session organizer will make a preliminary decision on acceptance of the paper for the particular session. Abstracts should preferably deal with one of the session subjects mentioned above, although papers dealing with other issues of sociocybernetics can also be accepted.

DEADLINES:

October 31, 2005:	500-1000 word detailed abstracts, indicating preferred session if possible.
December 15, 2005:	Notification of acceptance.
January 15, 2006:	250 word regular abstracts.
January 31, 2006 (ISA):	Programme of sessions available, submission to the ISA.
March 31, 2006 (ISA):	Pre-registration. The names of participants not registered by this date will not appear in the Programme Book and their abstracts will not be published.
March 31, 2006 (ISA):	Electronic submission of accepted abstracts to Sociological Abstracts at: http://www.csa.com/socioabs/submit.html Only abstracts from pre-registered authors will be accepted by the system.
June 15, 2005 (RC):	Definite confirmation of participation and dates of arrival and departure to the RC 51 World Congress Programme Coordinator.
June 30, 2005 (ISA):	Submission of full papers by e-mail to the Congress Secretariat in Durban and to the RC 51 World Congress Programme Coordinator. Final programme available and submitted to the ISA.

CONTACTS AND INFORMATION:

For any further questions and information you may consult the RC 51 website at:
                    http://www.ucm.es/info/isa/congress2006/rc/rc51_durban.htm
or the ISA Durban website at:
                    http://www.ucm.es/info/isa/congress2006/index.htm
These may already answer many of your questions, or you may also directly contact the RC 51 World
Congress Programme Coordinator or any of the members of the RC51 International Scientific
Committee.

RC51 INTERNATIONAL SCIENTIFIC COMMITTEE:

Felix Geyer, RC51 Honorary President (Chair)   geyer@xs4all.nl
Bernd R. Hornung, RC51 President   hornung@med.uni-marburg.de
Vessela Misheva, RC51 Vice-President   Vessela.Misheva@soc.uu.se
Richard E. Lee, RC51 Secretary   rlee@binghamton.edu
Karl-Heinz Simon, RC51 Programme Coordinator   simon@usf.uni-kassel.de
Soeren Brier   sbr@kvl.dk
Arne Collen   acollen@saybrook.edu
Chaime Marcuello   chaime@posta.unizar.es
Bernard Scott   B.C.E.scott@cranfield.ac.uk
Cor Van Dijkum   c.vandijkum@fss.uu.nl